AF557771

SYSTEM AND WORKING OF JOURNALISM

SYSTEM AND WORKING OF JOURNALISM

Seema Sharma

2006

SBS Publishers & Distributors Pvt. Ltd.
New Delhi

ISBN : 81-903098-3-8

Indian Price - Rs 745

First Published in India in 2006
Reprint 2006

Published by:
SBS PUBLISHERS & DISTRIBUTORS PVT. LTD.
2/9, Ground Floor, Ansari Road, Darya Ganj,
New Delhi - 110002, INDIA
Tel: 23289119, 41563911
Email: mail@sbspublishers.com

CONTENTS

Preface *ix*

1. **Evolution of Journalism** **1**
Continuous Alteration • Importance of Journalism • Journalism and e-Media • Audience's Part • The Feedback • The Communication • Centres of Communication

2. **Journalists' Role** **31**
Duty and Worth • The Analysis • Information and Approach • Disputing Matters • Leading Strategy

3. **Rapid Growth** **43**
Society at Work • Factors Responsible • The Assets • Influence in General • Changed Face • Functional Dimensions • The Administration • The Power

4. **Basic Concepts** **97**
Defamatory Issue • Global Trends • Part of the Committee • Grand Analysis

5. **Fundamental Elements** 145

Various Offshoots • Conveyance of Reality • Communication Needs • Importance of Language • A Firm Base • Basic Rights • Various Types • Two-way Communication • Direct Connection • The Interrelationship • Various Stages • Cumulative Communication • Ways of Communication • Many Types of Communication • European Method • Various Patterns • Sign of Authority

6. **Motives and Purposes** 169

Elements of Necessity • Calm and Alignment • The Interrelationship • Inter Communication • Importance of Society • Global Picture • Behavioural Norms

7. **System at Work** 183

Basic Needs • Way of Working • Daily Working • The Pamphlets • Different Sides • Basic Norms • Various Codes • Etiquettes of Journalism • The Interconnectedness • Functional Dimensions

8. **Practical Aspects** 215

Career in Reporting • Use of Sense • Functional Side • Trends in Career • Functional Aspects • Role of Education

9. **News Perception** 235

The Requirements • Concise News • News Traits • Sudden News • Newspaper's Importance • Quality of News

10. **News Presentation** 253
Presenting News • Social Issues • Computer's Role • Technological Aspects • Various Kinds • Importance of Photography • Drafting of a News

11. **Editorial Job** 317
Ability of an Editor • Individual Matters • Need of Interest • Regular Connection • Knowing Public • Role of Editorial • Tough Job • News Editors • Role of Sub-editor

12. **News Making** 345
The Growth • Things of Importance • The Expression

Bibliography 363

Index 369

PREFACE

The weakest nation is that which has no or the least institutions of press. The press is the backbone of a nation. Its weakening results directly in multi-faceted chaos. Metaphorically, society gets strangled in case the press is curbed or suppressed.

Another interesting analogy is that of a mirror. Just as a mirror reflects with cent per cent accuracy what it is exposed to, similarly, the press does. It mirrors society and all that concerns it and thus called the Fourth Estate.

That is why journalism is deemed to be an honourable and serious profession with huge power. A journalist is not a layman; he or she possesses many a quality. Straightforwardness, unprejudiced outlook, faculty for comprehending and analysing the facts and power of reasoning and a nose for news, may be mentioned to name a few.

Despite all this, a journalist is a man. Profession apart, he or she is a member of society. He, too, eats, drinks, sleeps, laughs, weeps, feels and so on. He is not something ultra-mundane. He has his roots in this very earth. Owing to all these characteristics, a few shadows of biases and obsessions are bound to distract his attention. However, these need not be emphasised beyond proper limit.

The working of journalism is of a coherent and joint nature. It is not an individual's game. In search of fame and fortune, some people pine for getting entry into this magnificent arena but for lack of stamina, they soon are lost and then seen nowhere.

The book in your hands is, no doubt, a treatise on the subject. Prepared especially for those concerned and the professionals, it should prove equally beneficial for general readers, as well.

Readers' guiding suggestions are welcome.

— **Author**

1

Evolution of Journalism

In India, Press has been closely associated with the freedom struggle. In the 19th century, the press fought for the freedom of information and the right to criticise. But in the early 20th century, the freedom struggle took a new turn and it was no longer petition-making. And thus, restrictions were imposed on it. The Hindu-Muslim disunity led to the division of the Indian Press into two categories-nationalist press and the Anglo-Indian Press. In all the national movement events-Jallainwala Bagh massacre, non-cooperation movement, Cripps mission, Quit India Movement the press was a direct participant. The nationalist press underwent the same kind of suffering as the freedom fighters.

Continuous Alteration

Newspapers in India have undergone revolutionary changes. The number of publications has increased seven times and circulation by ten times as compared to that of 1950. In 1985 there were 3,000 publications, with a total circulation of over 26 million. Earlier, just 6 publications, namely The Time of India, Indian Express, Malayalam Manorama and Anand Bazaar Patrika (dailies) and Malaya Manorama Mangalam and Kumudam (weeklies) have a combined circulation of five million, while 150 other publications have a total circulation of 25 million.

The press is widely acknowledged as a watch-dog in a democratic country. Today the press is not merely informing, illuminating, investigating and exposing but even warning and biting, particularly when acting in the public's interest.

Effects of the Press : Newspaper readers, though numerically small in India, largely constitute the intelligentsia. The press has a 'multiplier effect' its message spreads far and wide. The impact of the press can be determined only in the perspectives of current development and pace of change in the country. The power of the press is mainly seen as responsible for the major political developments in India during the 1990s. The capacity of Indian press to generate a healthy debate on public issues has been partially realised. But with increasing literacy it holds out infinite possibilities in the future.

Impact of Radio : Radio is serving as an effective medium not only to inform and educate people, but also to provide healthy entertainment. It can justifiably be called the medium for the masses. Radio has the inherent advantage to overcome three major hurdles to meaningful communication such as-mass illiteracy, lack of efficient means to reach the remote places and poverty which prevents access to mass media.

Impact of Films : In India, with its cultural and linguistic diversities and the problems of illiteracy the film is the most powerful medium of mass-communication. It gives not merely information, but creates a demand for change and modernisation. It has earned universal acclaim and is a versatile means of communication.

Impact of Television : Television is considered one of the greatest inventions of man. It is a multi-media system predominated by the visual medium. It has the power to instil desired attitudes among the masses.

Effects of TV : TV can transport the viewers to the actual scene of action to see things as they happen. Take the example of the Kargil war or the rescue of the people from under the debris due to earthquake in Gujarat on 26 Jan., 2001. But many have also come to hold TV responsible for inciting violence, corrupting the young and creating a make belief world of illusion.

Video, Cable T.V. and Satellite : Video burst on the Indian scene sometime in the mid 80s. It holds out infinite promises of entertainment and information. Its safe and easy facility for stop, go, forward, reverse viewing is invaluable for teaching and learning. But with the advent of the cable TV and satellite TV the demand for video has reduced although not lost totally. And it was due to satellite TV only that one was able to experience all the horrors of Gulf war sitting in any corner of India. Cable TV has emerged as an important medium for advertisements as well.

Impact of Mass media : Areas of Danger—Mass Media has an intense impact on the Indian society. It is claimed that this proliferation of information and the swiftness of its distribution would certainly improve the human conditions. However, with positive values it has also created areas of danger.

Manipulation : Clever uses of electronic devices can alter the meaning of recorded visual and audio material, making it appear to be what it really isn't.

Privacy : The whole question of co-relating the right to privacy with public interest has become a vexed problem for policy planners and social scientists alike.

Security : Protection of secret government information, private transactions, and institutional records in computer systems has become a matter of concern.

Democratic Process : Democracy functions best when voters are widely informed on all problems and issues. But if given power to select the information they desire with the aid of new technologies and by choosing to see and hear only what interests them most, will they be able to vote intelligently.

Isolation : Although the communication revolution has the power to draw the global community closer together, it also isolates individuals and small groups. Both adults and children sit for hours, aware only of what appears on small screens often they seem visually drugged.

Importance of Journalism

The Print Media, like others, have power, and this power must be exercised with a sense of responsibility. The printed word, as a carrier of knowledge, information and news stories was in vogue in China, Korea and Japan, a thousand years ago. In India, printing came first to Goa in 1556 and penetrated into Calcutta and inland provinces through the coastal towns.

One of the chief characteristics of print media is that they offer extensive news coverage and in-depth treatment of themes. They provide a large variety of coverage, through different kinds of writings, than any other media in India. Understandably good newspapers are described as Readers, University. The main weakness of the print media is that they can be read only by the literates. Secondly 93% of the newspapers are concentrated in Urban areas. Thirdly, the increasing rise in the price of newspapers and magazines prevent a large number of our people from purchasing them.

The Development : The two notable developments are shift towards commercialisation and introduction of new printing technologies.

Commercialisation : The national newspapers, during the British period, functioned basically with a missionary zeal and acted as the voice of the freedom fighters and stimulated the monument through advocacy journalism. But after independence, the missionary zeal of the newspapers evaporated. It soon became a publishing industry. And the theory of delinking of the press from business houses engaged in other industries was not accepted by the newspaper magnates.

New Printing Technologies : The introduction of modern printing technologies has brought about a new climate of working in the print media organisations. Printing today has become a graphic art. The newspapers are elegantly printed, bearing creative typographical and layout designs.

Small Newspapers : A large number of our newspapers belong to the category of small or medium papers with status no better than that of a cottage industry. They can not tap adequate advertising support to become financially strong. The cooperative type of management has not gained ground. The bottom line of the Indian newspaper industry remains weak. And it is well known that some of the newspapers have been censured by the press council for having succumbed to temptations of different kinds, which is a serious problem.

Professional Discipline : Professional discipline is necessary for all media. The western press has evolved codes of ethics to ensure discipline. The first press commission had empowered the Press Council of India to evolve such a code. There is a code only on the coverages of communal riots. The Press Council finds it difficult to enact an enforceable formal code and thus just lays down certain guidelines in its decisions taken from time to time.

Journalism and e-Media

Radio and T.V. are called the electronic media and are today the supreme media of mass communication. In the 1930s, the television made its bow in the west. Its true development took place after the 2nd world war. In India, the new glamour medium came in 1959.

Characteristics of Radio : Radio is a sightless or a viewless medium. It is also called blind medium as the performer doesn't see his audience and the listeners can not see the performer. The main characteristics of radio are:

A Medium of Sound : It is an auditory medium, a medium of the ear. The three elements of a radio broadcast are the spoken work, music and sound effects. They are all sounds carried on the air waves to the listener. All these sounds must be pleasant and expressive for the ears of the listener.

A Medium of the Voice : Radio is the medium of the voice. The producer mixes his voice with music and sound effects. A radio listener has a highly developed ear and so the broadcaster shouldn't sound fake or untruthful. A truthful vocal expression will come only if the whole person's mind, soul, psyche and imagination and his body are all in the tune with one another.

A Link between Speaker and Listeners : Microphone is the only instrument through which a radio broadcaster speaks to his listeners. It is a hi-fi instrument that catches the softest sigh, the tiniest rustle of the paper. It exposes all vocal lies, and tell all, the truth from a lie.

An Intimate Medium : A broadcaster must imagine as if the listeners are sitting by his side and to the listeners, it should sound as if the broadcaster is speaking from within the sound box or the-transistor. The best subjects for radio broadcasts are those which intimately concern the listeners. The words and the manner of their expression must be intimate as the condition in which broadcasts are received are very informal.

A Mass Medium : Radio is a medium of mass communication. Its broadcasts reach hundreds of thousands in one go. The task of the performer is to find out the lowest common denominator to communicate well with the largest number of listeners. It is a much cheaper medium of mass communication. Thus, it is very relevant to developing countries like India.

Simple Language : Large number of people are illiterate or semi-literate in India and other developing countries. So, the language of the radio broadcasts must be simple and should be closer to the spoken language that the common people use.

A Mobile Medium : Radio is a mobile medium, and so it is a most convenient medium for anybody. It doesn't respect units of time, place and action as prescribed by Aristotle.

A Cheap and Quick Medium : It is a medium of the 'here and now' as it can report the events almost instantly. Radio is a much cheaper and quicker medium than TV for production of programmes; thus, it can produce a wide variety of programmes.

No Shared Experience : Radio listeners are sitting alone or with one or two members of the family, and not like the stage where spectators are sitting in a crowd. Thus the psychology of reception for a radio broadcast is much more informal. The radio listener will not accept any untruth in a radio performance nor does he see any glamour personality to be impressed.

Characteristics of Television : Television is an audio-visual medium and its broadcast is uniquely telegenic. TV has both sound and sight.

An Audio-visual Medium : A TV broadcast is conceived and produced and received in audio-visual terms. Thus, it directly affects two senses simultaneously, those of hearing and seeing. It is more effective than radio broadcast as radio is a unisense medium, affecting only one sense.

Features of Other Media : TV has borrowed certain features from the other media of communication like the stage, the film and the radio. TV has integrated all these into a whole that makes TV a uniquely new medium, different from all other medium.

Wide Reach and High Credibility : TV is a supreme medium of mass communication. And with the help of satellite technology, today, it can reach all the concerns of the globe. TV has turned world into a global village. Thus, it has widened the mental horizons of man and has become the supreme educator of man.

TV is a credible, a believable medium. Seeing is believing. Things shown on TV become effectively truer than those that one reads in the print medium or listens to the radio.

A Glamourous Medium : One can watch on TV the glittering personalities and events, international conferences, sports, festivals, travel shows etc. The facility of watching almost round the clock enhances the glamour appeal still more. Because of its glamour, TV has been called the magic box. The tele-addiction has become the greatest addiction of our times. And thus, the reading habits are declining as people now get their news and information more from TV and earlier also.

A Medium of the Close-up : It is an ideal medium for expressing reaction and interaction between people for presenting an interview and a discussion etc. If something has happened or somebody has said something, the camera would slow the reaction of several people, one-by-one, in a close-up.

A Living Room Medium : TV is a medium of and for the family. TV brings theatre and cinema auditorium to the living-room and brings together the family increasingly. Earlier, people used to get dressed up specially to witness a stage drama or a film. It is the reverse process now. The film or the theatre comes in your drawing room under home conditions.

A Democratic Medium : It is available to all people. It deals with the problems of all sections of the society. It democratises information and informal education and also democratizes literature, by discussing it in broadcasts, or by telecasting it in a dramatic version. But it can not afford to be highly artistic like stage, as things might go over the heads of the common viewer.

A Medium of Immediacy : It captures the events even as they are happening, much before the newspaper comes out with information on events next morning. TV is a supreme reporter. TV operates in fixed time units. And the time unit must be respected.

Advertiser's Influence : TV is the great salesman of modern times. The businessman sells his products and services through TV. Advertisements can reach millions of people at the same time.

Characteristics of Films : Cinema is a highly mechanical medium. It uses many mechanical devices like Cameras, Microphones, Dubbing machine, Editing machine etc. Film is a product of interaction between machines and artistic and technical people.

A Mass Medium : It is a medium of mass communication. Millions can watch the movie in a country and can be watched by a very large number of people in several other countries also. Today, a film can also be transferred from the celluloid to the video cassette and the cassette can be played at home also.

Mechanically Reproducible : Film can be preserved and can be seen again and again. It can be useful for research on a relevant subject.

A Collaborative Medium : So many people collaborate to make the film and to reach out the film to the people. No other medium depends so much on so many people. It is the director's medium. All artists and technical people have to work in a team spirit but the director is the boss. And every body must carry out his directions.

An Art Medium : In the beginning, it was considered as a medium of cheap entertainment but now it has come to be considered as art form. Intellectuals and serious thinkers have associated themselves with cinema.

Government's Role : Harsh rules and high taxes imposed by government give an impression that cinema is treated as an undesirable activity. Thus, the licensing rules for cinema must be relaxed. The setting up of some organisations for promoting cinema goes to the credit of the government.

A Medium for Development : Film is an effective medium for development. Development means the growth of the individual and the society in all aspects, which include political, social, economic and cultural aspects. Film can also promote national and emotional integration.

A Medium that Demands People's Concentration : The conditions under which a film is screened and is received by the cine-goers in a cinema house demand concentration of different sections of society, sitting together in the same hall and constituting the audience. All these people tend to be unified Concentration is centred on the screen and the audience almost appears as a unified mass.

A Realistic but Expensive Medium : The film can be effective in hitting the consciousness, sometimes conscience of the audience with the camera. Film is a realistic medium.

Camera and microphone can never be kind to any exaggeration. But it is an expensive medium. Although, film making is expensive but it is a cheap medium of entertainment. Because of the high cost our films tend to be cheap commercial cinema. By providing cheap entertainment, the producers think that, they can recover the cost and earn profits.

Audience's Part

Information technology has advanced too much in the recent years that it is now possible for people, while sitting in the drawing rooms, to witness the events taking place in any part of the world or even in space. National boundaries hold no barrier for mass communication.

Meaning of Mass : The word mass is used to refer to common people, especially the lower classes. In general usage, the word mass refers to people in a large number. If it is said that masses are ignorant, we mean that a very large proportion of the population is ignorant. Similarly, if we say mass destruction, it means destruction on a very large scale. The most important feature of mass is its very large size in terms of the number of individuals and second is that masses are geographically distributed.

Emergence of the Theory of Mass Society : Society is a large and complex society with modernisation the complexity of the society further increases. Such a society which is very large in size but where members are isolated and relationships are contractual is called a mass society.

However, the concept of mass society is not to be equated with that of massive society. It is more than the massive society. There are many traditional societies-that are very large in numbers but are not necessarily mass societies. It will be useful to understand the concept of mass society using a set of contrasts with other kinds of units in social life, like groups, crowd and public. In a small group, all members know each other. The members of a group interact with each other for a purpose.

The crowd is a spontaneous collection of individuals. It is temporary and never reappears with the same composition. Members of crowd share the same mood but there exists no order in the crowd. Crowd is physically present at a particular place. Unlike crowd, public is widely dispersed. Its size may be small or large. Public may be quite heterogeneous and members may not be aware of each other. Political parties treat us as public.

The Media Audience : The commonly used meaning of the term Media audience is the aggregate of persons forming readers, listeners, viewers of different media. That is, audience is a group of individuals with a common pattern of media consumption. There are four different ways of looking at media audiences. They are:

Media Reach : The owners and producers of mass media conceive the total population whom their communications can reach. It may be different for different means of communication.

Media Access : Mass media may be available but the capacity or willingness to use the media may not be there. A large section of the population doesn't have the radio or TV sets. But access may not overlap ownership. Group watching of television at a TV shop is a common sight. Many families don't buy newspapers but they may read at some other place.

Media Exposure : Everyone who has access to radio or television doesn't necessarily use them. In a family that subscribes to a newspaper, everyone doesn't read it. So only those individuals who actually expose themselves to the media are the media audiences.

Media Effects : Another way to think about audiences is in terms of individuals who have been exposed to mass communication products and have undergone a change in their knowledge, opinions, attitude or behaviour. A person may not recall anything of the information received after listening or watching a news programme. But the same person, after watching an advertisement, may immediately rush to buy that product.

Quality of Audience : The most interesting feature of a mass communication audience is its dual nature. Media audience is a collectivity formed in response to media content. Audiences, are both the cause as well as the response to the mass communication process.

Audience Types : The types of audiences can be distinguished on their demographic characteristic and mental make-up.

Elite Audience : They are composed of the people who are decision-makers and trend-setters in the society. They are economically well to do and are highly educated. Their number is small but their influence is strong.

General Audience : They are very large and highly diverse groups that represent the broad cross-section of the society. Majority of the people belong to this category.

Specialised Audiences : These are composed of individuals who possess similar characteristics. They are relatively small in number.

Nature of Experience : Audience is the single most important element in any conception of mass communication. If we observe the media audience relationship, we find that the audiences actually exercise their choice as to which medium is to be used and also which content they would like to be exposed to. But the question is why does an audience choose a particular medium or a specific content of the media? Wilbur Schramm proposed a formula for this.

$$\frac{\text{Promise of Reward}}{\text{Efforts required}} = \text{Probability of selection}$$

Rewards may be immediate or delayed but the focus is on the satisfaction of the audience needs. The effort required for attending to mass communication may be considered in terms of availability of the media.

The Feedback

The producers of mass communication keep a hand on the pulse of their audiences in order to make their products more and more acceptable. AFS are the mechanisms through which information regarding audience reactions is taken back to the owners, controllers and producers of the media.

Marked-based Feedback : Mass Communication receive the following information through the M-BF System:

(1) Audience Access to the media

(2) Audience Exposure to the media

These informations are received by three methods:

(i) Audience Decision Making

(ii) Direct Feedback

(iii) Media Review

ADM : Audience decision to subscribe to newspapers or magazine is a direct feedback about the popularity of the publication. Sales at box-office is a good feedback about the popularity of a film.

DFb : Newspapers and magazines have columns reserved for letters to the editor sent by the readers. Similar is the case with radio and television. It is rendered recently that the needs for direct feedback from the audiences is increasing.

MR : Media gives the greatest importance to the feedback received through the reviews. There are regularly reviews of films, audio and video cassettes published in newspapers and magazines. The role of media reviews is two fold: (1) The owners, producers, controllers of radio and television programmes take the comments very seriously (2) The reviews provide information to the audience.

Research Based Feedback : The market based feedback and the reviews are more or less passive systems feedback information gets generated without the producers making effort for it. Research based feedback systems are created to provide systematic information about audience responses to a particular mass communication products of services. Many media organization have their own audience research system.

The Communication

A message may be communicated through words, pictures, gestures, signs and symbols or even through silence. But if it is not understood properly by the audience concerned, it is an exercise in futility. The message to be effective must have certain attributes.

Clarity, Coherence and Consciousness : The message which is clear, lucid and concise is generally understandable. Coherence is another attribute of a good message it should be a narration of a story.

Simple Language : The path to good and effective communication is plainness, simplicity, orderlines and sincerity. There is a need for the communicators to take all precautions to ensure that messages are not misunderstood.

Credibility of the Source : "Who" is another important factor in communication? The credibility of a speaker in respect of a particular topic matters a lot.

Persuasion : The contents and appeals should have the power to influence the receiver's attitudes, Communicators today are acquainted with the package of techniques which can endow that thrust to the message.

Enchancing Impact : Even ordinary messages can be turned into interesting ones. They can become very convincing and credible if presented graphically and supported by statistics.

Pathetic Stories : One can narrate a pathetic story to evoke an effective human response. Human misery can be vividly illustrated by a small documentary.

Statistics in Support of Correctness : The use of statistics in an economic survey can lend support to the correctness of conclusions drawn from the survey.

Emotional Appeals : Emotional appeals, if used properly at an appropriate time, can stir imagination. Appeals and self-esteem or social status have made people buy costly goods which normally they wouldn't.

Perception Filter : Any message is called a stimulus, and a strong emotion-laden message is termed as a strong stimulus. However, before any stimulus or message can transfer knowledge, create an image or change an attitude or a behaviour. Perception is the process whereby an individual receives stimulus through the various senses and interprets them.

Hot and Cold Messages : Marshall McTuhan differentiates between hot and cold messages. By the former, he means the message with highly understandable specific contents. Such messages are good for disseminating specific information, e.g. announcement of a new product in the market.

Cold messages are on the other hand more appropriate if the objective is to have people intervalise and retain the information. In such messages, there is more involvement of the people.

Creative AD Message : A print copy is described as "Salesmanship in print". Creativity in the ad format is required towards this end. The message must be concise, precise and eye-catching.

Radio and Copy : Radio copies, messages and jingles are very vigorous although they are oriented only to the ears of the listeners. Radio copywriting is an imaginative and professional job.

T.V. Commercial : This medium draws more ads than any other individual medium does as it is a combination of all the virtues, strengths and beauty that audio-visual technology can import. TV commercial must ensure that viewers grasp the entire story the first time they watch it.

Journalism in this Country : In general sense by press we mean "printing press" but in journalistic and mass communication terminology by "press" we mean print media-newspapers, journals, magazines, periodicals, leaflets, books etc. A newspaper means "any printed periodical work containing public news or comment on public news."

Origin of Press in India : The writings on the walls and on stones dating back to several centuries before Christ were the first signs of the origin of the press in India. The newsletters, later, were regularly issued during the Mughal period. It is the dissemination of these newsletters which perhaps inspired James Augustus Hicky to start his newspaper Bengal Gazette in 1780. The first printing press was established in Bombay in 1674, 2nd in Madras in 1772 and 3rd in Calcutta in 1779. Micky's newspaper Calcutta General Advertiser or Bengal Gazette was born on 29 January, 1780. Some other weeklies and monthly newspapers started in 19th cent in Bengal were Dig Darshan, Samachar Dai-pan, Friend of India and The Statesman.

Nationalism and the Indian Press : The growth of the press in India was facilitated by the nationalist movement for freedom. Press frequently took up the cudgels with the authorities and transmitted the messages of freedom to the masses of India.

Vernacular Press Act : Lord Lytton, worried over the increasing impact of the writing in the press enforced the Vernacular Press Act on March 1st, 1878, for controlling the Press. He also instituted the post of "Press Commissioner for India."

When the World War I broke out in 1914, British Government released nationalist leaders from jail with a view to soliciting their support in the conduct of war. But several newspapers took divergent steps and as a result 180 (approx.) newspapers were asked to pay security deposits and assure support to the government in 1914-15.

During the World War II the press initially supported the stand of the British government in India. But soon a conflict arose on reporting the war news in the newspapers. It was around this time that All India Newspapers Editors Conference came into being.

Post Independence Press : After Independence in 1947, a new era began in India in which the role of the press changed slowly. It had to shoulder new responsibilities now. A thorough inquiry into the structure and functioning of our press was made by the Press Commission during 1952-54. Among the many recommendations of the commission, one was for the appointment of a Press Registrar and setting up of a Press Council.

The 2nd Press Commission in 1982 recommended the delinking of the press from its connections with other industries. One of its major recommendations was to set up a National Development Commission.

Now we have a large and well developed press. These is use of latest technologies and management by the press in India now and it has a bright future ahead.

Radio, Television and Cinema : In U.S.A. the beginning of Radio was made somewhere in 1909. But regular and systematic broadcasting began only in 1920.

In India, amateurs were the first to start broadcasting. The Radio Club of Bombay, broadcast its first programme in June, 1923. In November, 1923 the Calcutta Radio and on 31st July, 1924 the Madras Radio club started broadcasting. But it soon closed down. However the Madras corporation restarted the broadcast service in 1930.

Organised broadcasting in India was started by the Indian Broadcasting company in 1927 but was closed down in March 1930. However, the government took over the Bombay and Calcutta station in April, 1930 and the Indian Broadcasting Service was formed. But due to the world wide depression, the IBS was closed down on October 10, 1931. However, later it was decided to start a radio station in Delhi and it actually went on air on January 7, 1936.

All India Radio : The BBC loaned the services of Lionel Fielden who became the Controller of Broadcasting. He got together a group of devoted young people. And he soon started short wave service in 1938, to cover the entire country. A new broadcasting house was built on Parliament Street, New Delhi. In the midnight of August 14-15, 1947, Nehru broadcast his famous speech "Tryst with Destiny".

After Partition 6 Radio Stations Cameup : Bombay, Calcutta, Delhi, Tiruchi, Lucknow and Madras. When the princely states became a part of India, five more station Hyderabad, Aurangabad, Baroda, Mysore, and Trivandrum, were taken over by AIR.

Chanda Committee : In 1964 a committee on

Broadcasting and Information Media was set up under the Chairmanship ofA.K. Chanda. It recommended in his report of 1966 separation of radio and television with two independent corporations. Although not accepted by the government then, later the separation ultimately came about in 1976, and TV set-up was called Doordarshan. Another recommendation was that of set-up of a commercial service, which was started from Vividh Bharati in 1967.

Verghese Committee : In 1977, Janta government appointed a working group under B.G. Verghese, to suggest an autonomous set up for AIR and Doordarshan. It recommended the creation of Akash Bharati in 1978 and thus a bill was introduced in 1979 in this regard. But, with the fall of Janata government the bill lapsed.

Origin and Development of TV in India : TV came to India On September 15, 1959. It was feared that TV might alienate us from our cultural roots. The first rural programme "Krishi Darshan" was started from Delhi on the Republic Day, January 26,1967. On 3rd December, 1971, the first English news bulletin was introduced.

In 1975, the Satellite Instructional Television Equipment was conducted. The one-year SITE exercise proved to India itself that it was ready for the satellite television. Educational programmes were broadcast direct from a satellite to the TV sets for the first time.

National Broadcast Trust : On April 6, Doordarshan was separated from All India Radio or Akashvani. But both AIR and Doordarshan continued to be under the Information and Broadcasting Ministry.

The Verghese Committee recommended the National Broadcast Trust, to look after both AIR and Doordarshan. The trust would be responsible to the Parliament through its budget, annual reports, auditor's reports etc., by AIR and Doordarshan.

Joshi Committee : Joshi committee set up under the chairmanship of P.C. Joshi on Software for TV in its report of 1985 criticised Doordarshan for concentrating mostly on the North for its programme content. It also recommended the setting up of a National Doordarshan Council and the decentralisation of Doordarshan. However the committee didn't ask for an autonomous corporation for Doordarshan. But it asked the organization to find its roots in the rich Indian heritage and develop a strong Indian personality.

Effectiveness of Doordarshan : Our TV offers a wide variety of programmes. These programmes are generally divided into general audience and special audience broadcasts. First category includes programmes of general interest like news, films, current affairs etc. Second category include broadcasts for particular sections of the population.

Our TV has made some contribution no doubt but there is much left to be desired. Although it has provided entertainment to the viewers, it has served the farmers by informing them of new methods and techniques of agriculture, it has made people aware of what is happening beyond India but it has not been impartial and fearless in reporting political developments. It has not been an effective medium for social change and development.

Origin and Development of Films in India : Indian cinema is almost a century old. It remains a cheap medium of entertainment for the masses. The films in India are made in several languages and regions. The first important step in the motion picture industry was the invention of kinetoscope by Edison. The first film to be ever shown in India was screened at Watson's Hotel, Bombay.

In 1902, J.F. Madan in Calcutta launched his "bioscope" showings in a tent. By 1905, it was possible to have a film of 30-40 minutes duration. The first attempt to make a film with a dramatic story and treatment was made by Torney, who made Pundalik released in 1912. Dada Saheb Phalke made Raja Harish Chandra in 1913.

From 1913 to 1931 was the era of the silent cinema in India. About 1300 films were made during this period. In 1930, came the first attempt to make an Indian talkie programme and the first talkie film which came in 1931 was Alam Ara.

The first attempt to produce a film in colour was made in 1932 by Madan Theatres. The film was Bilwa Mangal. And then started the trend of coloured films.

Folk Media : Traditional Folk Media is a term used to denote 'people's performances'. It describes folk dance, rural drama, and musical variety of the village people. This term speaks of those performing arts which are cultural symbols of people. Traditional folk media have been consciously persuaded to come out of their shell to give a personal touch to the otherwise impersonal mass media programmes. Traditional Folk Media are personal forms of communication, of entertainment.

Strength of Folk Media : Since these arts are woven into the social and cultural fabric of the rural society, their role in educating the non-school population assumes significance. They have lived and grown with the rural people and so the rural masses, without any inhibition, get involved in their game and emerge more relaxed and better informed.

There are many advantages of traditional folk media for the purpose of informing and educating the rural illiterate. They are rich in variety and readily available and economically viable. They command the confidence of the rural masses as they are LIVE. And above all they are in a 'face to face situation' between the communicator and the receiver of the message.

In India, traditional folk media have been reckoned as

successful mass-motivators. They inspire the masses during the times of stress and strain. These forms of art are a part of the way of life of a community and provide acceptable means of bridging development issues into the community on its own terms. Mass media have extended the area of coverage of a folk performance, while traditional folk media with their aspiring colour and costume, dance and music, have enriched the content of the mass media channels.

Role of Traditional Folk Media : There is a tremendous wealth and variety in traditional folk media of India. Conventionally, the traditional folk performances have been theme-carriers, usually carrying themes of morality. The rural drama, with its stock characters, has also carried across modern messages, without, in any way hurting the community's traditional culture. During the past few years they have slowly acquired a functional dimension without losing their cultural roots.

Soon after achieving freedom the National Government started a full-fledged Song and Drama Division in 1954, with the objective of, training and utilising the service of traditional folk performers to inform the rural masses about the planning and development programmes of the country.

Flexibility is the most important factor which determines the viability of a folk medium for rural communication. Flexibility of a folk medium might reveal itself either in its form or theme or in both.

Various Categories : Depending on the nature and extent of flexibility, the traditional folk media reveal themselves in three categories-rigid, semi-rigid and non-rigid.

Rigid Media : It is those that reject the new message summarily. These are ritualistic or intensely religious in form and theme. Their content is hard-core and are unchangeable e.g., African and Indian ritual dances.

Semi-rigid : They are those that provide limited scope for the new message. Even while dealing with a classical theme, the medium would have in-built characters or situations which hold out flexibility.

Non-rigid : They are those that absorb new messages without any reservation to reflect them effectively in the field.

Increasing the Efficiency of Communication Strategy: For increasing the efficiency of communication strategy in order to obtain the intended results there are 4 methods.

Multi-media Approach : The multi-media approach holds glamour for the field, covers different aspects of the message and interacts with different sections of people simultaneously. It demands careful planning and faultless coordination. Folk media performances in-built into the multi-media package, would surely establish a two-way communication channel. The programme would also pave the way for smooth functioning of an extension service. The multi-media approach demands fool-proof planning and involves more expenditure.

The Package Plan : It is an integrated time-bound work programme which eliminates time-lags between communication, extension and service and brings to fruition the efforts of the communicator.

Utilising Rural Structure and Village Functionaries : Mass media channels of sound and sight do bring awareness to the people of a developed theme, and traditional folk media succeed in reinforcing it with information and education by a personal approach. However, motivation for action could be energised by change-agents who are inter-personal communicators and one should look for such change-agents in the rural situation itself. The service of the traditional folk artists will draw good results with village-based functionaries.

Objective Evaluation of the Strategy : A need for scientific research on the role of folk media in communication is essential. With the feedback collected it should be possible for the communicator to identify attitudes 'that need to be changed in order to create the necessary social and psychological climate' in the field for people to receive the needed message. The programme package should then be suitably altered to incorporate the required messages.

Evaluation studies may tend to become quantitative rather than qualitative in terms of achievement. They may prove to be general assessments of the impact of all types of media and not of folk media in particular. It is therefore, time that specific studies were developed in folk media 'in an effort to acquire some reliable measurements for further guidance'.

Centres of Communication

News agencies form a major part of the print media, without which many newspapers would find it difficult to function.

What is a News Agency? : A news agency is an organization which collects or gathers news and supplies it to different newspapers, magazines, radio stations and television stations. News gathered/reported by reporters/ correspondents is sent to newspapers via electronic teleprinters or computers and these newspapers, in turn, pay a monthly subscription to use news agencies for the news they receive. The news agency works round the clock.

How is it Different from a Newspaper?: News agency works in a completely different fashion from a newspaper-

(1) The news agency doesn't publish any newspaper of its own. All the reports are transmitted to the

newspapers and radio and television stations. And then it is upto the newspaper to use the news item sent by one news agency or that sent by another. In fact, at times a newspaper may even prepare an item quoting some paragraphs from one agency and some from another agency.

(2) Every news agency report has to be attributed to a source, unlike a newspaper story, i.e., every news item has to be quoted from someone.

(3) There will be no comments, editorializing or interpretation in a news agency report and it will be purely a factual report.

(4) For the news agencies, it is a deadline every minute. Since a newspaper goes to the press after midnight, a reporter knows that he has plenty of time to file his report. But a news agency reporter must file his report immediately.

(5) Accuracy and speed being very essential for a news agency, it becomes important that a news agency report should be crisp, precise, and to-the-point.

(6) Since there is no time for a news agency reporter to confirm or re-confirm facts, it is important that there is an eye on accuracy. The newspaper reporter has a whole day to correct any mistake but a news agency will not get another chance.

(7) A news agency is not serving the city in which it works, but the whole nation and beyond. Therefore, its news will not be purely from a local perspective, whereas, newspaper devotes lots of space to local stories, reporting the events in great detail.

(8) A news agency generally avoids publicity of commercial units. A newspaper on the other hand may not mind publishing an individual.

(9) A news agency always gives its news without any comment or personal opinion. This is unlike a newspaper which may be permitted not only to give a news item without a source, but also to put in reasonable comments.

Ownership Pattern : Both the main agencies-Press Trust of India (PTI) and United News of India (UNI) are owned by groups of newspapers who have bought shares to run them.

These newspapers have established Boards of Directors, each headed by a chairman to make the policies of the respective news agencies. There is a constant professional competition between the two agencies. But these boards do not interfere in the day-to-day working of the agencies.

Financial Structure : Various newspapers and the electronic media, apart from government departments and private entrepreneurs, buy the news from the agencies. The newspapers and other subscribers pay a monthly subscription fee, plus rental charges for the computer, teleprinter, apart from the installation charges paid when the subscription was first taken. Government don't own these agencies but is the largest subscriber.

The Organizational Structure : The agency is run by a General Manager-cum-Chief Editor, who is assisted by Deputy General Managers. The Editorial Desk is under the charge of a News Editor and reporting section is under the Chief of Bureau. The reporting staff is divided into-two sections-the reporters who deal with the day-to-day reporting are under a chief reporter and correspondents who deal with Ministerial and Legislative reporting are under the Chief of Bureau. Thus, the Chief Reporter is answerable to the Chief of Bureau.

The news agencies are the first to get wind of a news

break. The agencies have offices in all the state capitals, many world capitals and at the United Nations.

The Growth : When India attained its independence on 15 August, 1947, some vestiges of the British remained behind. The news agencies operating in the country at that time were either foreign agencies with offices in India or British-owned Indian agencies. The foreign agencies operating in India then, which are still reporting from India, include Reuter, the United Press International, the Agence France Presse etc.

However, with the help of the government, some major newspapers joined together to form a trust, and then came the Press Trust of India in 1949. It took over the business of the Associated Press of India.

Although both PTI and UNI are professional rivals, the UNI owes its birth to PTI. UNI was formed in 1961 and registered under the Societies Act. The PTI had headquarters in Bombay, while UNI had its head office in Delhi.

In 1948, a Hindi news agency had come into being, called the Hindustan Samachar. In 1966, came up another Hindi news agency called the Samachar Bharati. The Asia News International (ANI) came up in the eighties.

The National Emergency of 1975 imposed Press Censorship in the entire country. A censor office was established in the Press Information Bureau. From time to time, the government issued certain directives about what to report and what not to report. The government, in a surprise action, decided to merge the news agencies into a single unit so that it would be easier to control. On February 16, 1976 orders were received by the agencies that all of them had ceased to exist and a new news agency called Samachar had been created and that UNI and the two Hindi agencies would be sent down. The topmost posts were given to the staff of the PTI. The Hindi Agencies not doing well financially, welcomed this merger. However, UNI staff felt let down. But the situation was accepted and the agency continued to work as one. But after the defeat of Mrs. Gandhi in 1977 elections, large sections of the staff of Samachar, mostly belonging to the former UTI, demonstrated with the Janta Party government. And in April 1978, the government announced that Samachar would cease to exist from September 1978 and the former four news agencies would be brought to life again.

Services Provided by News Agencies : As the agencies grew in size in terms of subscribers, both the agencies felt the need to diversify. Now, both the news agencies are providing several other services, some of them aimed at specialised business interests.

Services Provided by PTI : News Scan, Comscan, Features (sent as mailer service weekly in English and Hindi on various subjects), Economic Service, Science Service, Stockscan, Photo service, PTI, TV, NITEL, some of the other additional services of UNI are-Stock Exchange Service, Financial Service, UNICON, UNEN, Agriculture Service, Feature Service, Backgrounder Service, UNICAN, Photo service, Unidarshan (TV), Videotex, UNI Graphics.

Role of News Agencies in Non-aligned Countries : In the late seventies, the non-aligned countries, at one of their summits, discussed how the international news agencies and visual media, were damaging the understanding amongst people by misrepresenting facts. And so it was commonly adopted by all, that the non-aligned countries should have their own news agency. It was also agreed that before such an agency could be set up, one national news agency would coordinate on behalf of each member country to present and disseminate news on behalf of a non-aligned newspool. In India, this task is being performed on by the PTI on behalf of the government.

Foreign News Agencies : Indian newspapers get news transmitted by AP or D P through UNI, and that transmitted by AFP, Reuters, or UPI through PTI. Similarly, while they do have their own bureaus here, they depend mostly on the Indian agency they subscribe to and then add their own background before transmitting any news abroad. However, some news agencies have now sought permission to operate directly. Some of the foreign news agencies operating in India are-Reuter-British news agency founded in 1851 by Paul Julius Von Reuter; Associated Press (AP) established in New York in 1848; Agence France Presse (AFP) established in Paris in 1944; United Press International (UPI) founded in U.S.A. in 1907.

Syndicated Columnist : A syndicated columnist is a senior journalist whose much sought opinions, views and analyses are distributed by feature agencies. The feature agencies undertake to sell such articles to one or more newspapers. A feature agency depend solely on freelance writers. The feature agencies working in India are Indian News & Feature Alliance, which is the oldest and the best, Indian Press Agency, Gemini Features, Compass Features,

2

Journalists' Role

Walter Lippmann made a painful distinction over fifty years ago between "news" and truth. "The function of news is to signalize an event; the function of truth is to bring to light the hidden facts, to set them into relation with each other and make a picture of reality on which men can act."

Because news-reporting and truth-seeking have different ultimate purposes, Lippmann postulated that "news" could be expected to coincide with truth in only a few limited areas such as the scores of baseball games or elections where the results are definite and measurable. Lippman concluded pessimistically that if the public required a more truthful presentation-interpretation-of the world they lived in, they would have to depend on institutions other than the press.

That is not the first, nor will it be the last, time that the press has been lambasted, and not just for falling short in the pursuit of truth. Though an occasional editor, in the manner of Pilate, might with justification ask "What is truth?" the fact remains that the press, in general has been somewhat remiss in other fields as well as, for example, in the matter of social responsibility.

"Social responsibility" is an omnibus term that covers a wide range of activities. One of the most trenchant critics of the press, Prof. N.S. Ramaswamy, Director of the Indian Institute of Management, Bangalore, has asserted that "a survey of the various professions, including the mass media, would reveal that their social relevance is not high."

Duty and Worth

Responsibility and relevance are two different concepts, but are deeply intertwined. According to Prof. Ramaswamy, "social relevance" of a society can be deemed to be high, as indeed that of any profession, "when its economic; social and political ideologies and instruments are oriented to meet the essential needs of the masses." One would presume that when the profession becomes socially relevant in a conscious and organized manner, it fulfils its responsibility.

Everybody would agree that the communications media are important instruments to involve the masses towards achieving national aspirations. Next, perhaps, to politics, the mass media is the most potent instrument of a society for economic and social transformation. And yet, claims Prof. Ramaswamy, "the way professions and institutions are now structured, organized and compensated, has resulted in low social relevance." Why is this so?

Let us examine a few facts about our mass media. For a country of 640 million, the total circulation of all our dailies was only 9.38 million in 1976, according to the report of the Registrar of Newspapers for 1977-78, which is about the circulation of just one Japanese paper. And the total newsprint consumed in India is less than what a number of daily newspapers in England and the United States singly consume.

And what do Indian newspapers publish? In an extension

lecture delivered at Bangalore University, Mr. H.Y. Sharada Prasad, Director of the Indian Institute of Mass Communication reported that while he was editor of Yojana the Planning Commission's journal, he attempted a rather impressionistic survey of the development coverage of the Press and found, no doubt to his surprise, that the space devoted to development came to the "magnificent" figure of six per cent of total editorial space and that included editorial comments and reports of parliamentary debates, besides news items and features on agriculture, animal husbandry, irrigation, industry (rural and urban), power, transport, education, health, family planning, women's and children's welfare and other aspects of social change. That was 15 years ago.

Have things changed since then? The Department of Communication land Journalism of Osmania University undertook a content analysis of eight major English newspapers in four regions in June August 1978 and the finding was that on the average, the eight newspapers devoted only 9.05 per cent of space to "social issues" which, again, included health, education, employment, crime, law and order, corruption (excluding the political variety), poverty and welfare, caste, religion, marriage and dowry, language, prohibition, housing, strikes and agitations.

Prof. Ramaswamy himself quotes another study of two national dailies during May 1975 of percentage distribution of space given to various items of news (based on a random sample of seven days, representing each day of the week).

What does that tell about our press and its predilections? That, as a rule, it does not care very much for developmental activities and the need for social relevance? That it does not understand the importance of its own role in social development? That its values are distorted and its conscience dormant, or worse, that it has no conscience worth the name?

The Analysis

A few observations and conclusions become immediately possible from the findings noted above. One is that Indian papers are predominantly urban-centred and what is worse, urban-oriented. Another is that they are obsessed with politics, whether Indian or foreign. A third is that developmental journalism still remains unattractive to a large number of editors journalists. Yet one other possible conclusion is that editors are indifferent to the welfare of masses because of the vast gulf separating them.

But why are newspapers obsessed with politics? One reason is that their editors and owners, until 30 years ago, took a leading part in the struggle for independence and cannot tear' themselves away from the peculiar fascination that the struggle for power has cast on them in the intervening decades. No matter how indifferent they claim to be to the goings-on in state capitals and in Delhi, these men have a natural affinity to the politicians that they cannot easily shed.

Another reason, one may presume, lies in the fact that a second generation of newsmen, trained in the humanities, social sciences and other sciences have yet to get hold of the levers of editorial power. The older generation still-to a large extent-hold the key to the gate. It is this generation that still dictates what should go into each edition and what should not. This brings us to that new vogue word in communication vocabulary-the "gatekeeper problem."

Gatekeepers, as we all know, are the ones who regulate the traffic in and out of any sanctora. And one thing that is certain about gatekeepers is that they are certain about themselves. And while certitude is no test of certainty, as that wise American judge oliver Wendell Holmes rightly remarked, the certitude of our newspaper gatekeepers-the news editors-is such that there is apparently no appeal beyond them. What they say is news becomes news.

Information and Approach

In science, accepted theories are overturned by accession of new knowledge. Science grows by its disprovability. In a profession like the law, again, precedent is often discarded when a powerful legal mind turns its searchlight on dim recesses of right and wrong. In journalism, especially in India, with its paucity of communication studies, the professionals are wrapped up in their own self-opinion and are not asking hard questions on what the people really want, and what aspects of knowledge will enhance their capacity for judgment. It is the gatekeeper's obsession with politics in India and his desire to favour or fight certain political parties, groups and personalities, that have made him neglect the compulsions and implications of social forces.

But what is the answer of the "gatekeeper"? Whether he has a basis in fact in insisting that he is giving to the reader what he wants or not, obviously the rising circulation of dailies and weeklies has its own tale to tell. It is a vicious circle, the "gatekeeper" gives to his urban reader what he things the reader wants; and having been conditioned to get a certain type of news and a certain type of newspaper, the reader merely asks for more of the same. The one merely augment the argument of the other. Once the reader is accustomed to a particular fixture he, too, ceases to demand change. So politics continues to be the staple of most newspapers and weeklies. And editors, conscious that their jobs depend on rising circulation, increasingly get timid and tend to look over their shoulders' at circulation managers and advertisement executives. The circle is complete.

For a brief-all too brief-period, in early 1979, the Indian Express bravely tried to get off the beaten path but quickly reverted to journalistic normalcy. The "gatekeepers" were to have the last laugh and the last word. Were the "gatekeepers" moved by knowledge, reason or public opinion in opting for the known rather than experimenting with the unknown? Importantly, is public opinion necessarily a safe guide? It is a well-known axiom that there is always a conflict between the popular and the salutary, between priya and hita and obviously, at least in the case of the Indian Express, the priya won over the hita, the popular over the salutary. Not everybody has the courage of an Abraham Lincoln who, finding that on a difficult decision he was outvoted in his cabinet seven to one, firmly declared: "One for and seven against; the ayes have it, the ayes have it." Most editors in India prefer to play safe. Non-conformism becomes a habit when editors have nothing to lose. A Sadanand would have dared the government of his day-as indeed he did-and faced closure of his paper, in the pursuit of principles. Today's editor evidently is made of less stern stuff. Not in today's India is a Tilak to be found, a Tilak who wrote that his object in running the Kesari was to made the rulers know about the aspirations and the agonies of the ruled and to make the ruled feel more fearless. The object put forth by Tilak remains relevant even today. Only, we do not have a Tilak.

It would, however, be unrealistic to expect that in any conflict between the popular and the salutary, the latter should necessarily win. There is always a hiatus between the ideal and the possible and while one should aim at the ideal, it is unrealistic to believe that it can ever be attained, except in an authoritarian society where the needs of the regime more than the profit motive reign supreme. The experiment was carried out in India during the Emergency, with what results we know now.

The aim of the Indira Gandhi government during the Emergency was laudable enough: it was to make Indian newspapers more responsive to the needs of development. But there is this about all laudable aims: they have to be the result of self-regulation on the part of newspapers, not of government fiat. And this is where the question of government role in the functioning of the newspapers comes in. What should be the government's role vis-a-vis the press? The obvious answer is nothing. To leave it alone. That is too simplistic an answer for in India the press depends on the government for purchase of news print. It cannot do so on its own.

Smaller newspapers also depend largely on the government for advertisements and this source of income can be turned off or on at the discretion of those in power. This leaves editors of small newspapers little leverage to fight the Establishment.

Even the import of printing and composing machinery has to be processed by the Chief Controller of Imports and Exports, though it is the Registrar of Newspapers who advises the Chief Controller on the essentiality of printing, composing and allied machinery required by newspapers or associated presses.

In the circumstances, the government in effect already plays a role in the efficient functioning of newspapers in the land. The fact that Publisher A, B or C has the will and the necessary finance to start a newspaper and run it is largely irrelevant. He will at all stages be dependent on government goodwill to run his institution, as became abundantly clear during the Emergency.

But even if individuals were free to start and manage news papers on their own without looking backward at what officialdom may think, there will always have to be cross fertilization of ideas between editors and officials. Together they have a responsibility towards the larger public in keeping it reasonably and accurately informed. Officials have the duty to keep newspapers informed of what is going on newspapers have the further duty to assess the information, process it for accuracy and validity and then publish it. One cannot do without the other.

Disputing Matters

The confrontation arises when officials become chary and newspapers become suspicious. This can be as dangerous, in the end as when newspapers go to bed with officialdom. Both are situations that are best avoided, the first by mutual respect and under standing between the parties concerned and the other by a healthy appreciation of the newspapers' duties towards their readers.

Much can be said in favour of an adversary relationship between officialdom and newspapers and given a such a choice relationship is probably to be desired, if only to keep officialdom on its toes; and newspapers on the alert. For, as Mahatma Gandhi said, the sole aim of journalism should be service. As he put it:

> The sole aim of journalism should be service. The press is a great power, but just as an unchained torrent of water submerges whole countryside and devastates crops, even so an uncontrolled pen serves but to destroy. If the control is from without, it proves more poisonous than want of control. It can be profitable only when exercised from within. If this line of reasoning is correct, how many of journals in the world withstand the test? But who would stop those that are useless? And who should be the judge? The useful and useless must, like good and evil generally go together and man must make his choice.

Gandhi correctly raised the question of who should be the judge, as well as prescribed the answer: man-meaning the reader. But is the reader always the best judge? If it were left solely to the reader to dictate what should be published, our newspapers and magazines would, in all probability, contain a lot more information of celebrities and politicians than even the "gatekeepers" are willing to permit in their pages. For all we know, our "gatekeepers" are serving a much more useful function than some of their critics are willing to admit.

In fact some of the advice given to news editors by well-meaning critics deserves examination. In his Elihu Root lecture delivered under the auspices of the US Council on Foreign Relations, James Reston, the distinguished Journalist referred to the US State Department where, he said, the Foreign Service officers had a fable. The grasshopper, worried about getting through the winter, sought advice from the cockroach, who seemed to thrive on cold weather. The cockroach was sympathetic. One the night of the first frost, he suggested, find a warm spot of a radiator in a bakeryturn your self Into a cockroach, and stay there happily until spring. "But how," asked the grasshopper, "do I make myself into a-cockroach?" "Look," the cockroach replied, "I'm merely giving you policy guidance."

Leading Strategy

Most critics of the press would give much the some kind of policy guidance to the news editors. Transform yourself into something quite different from what you are; stop giving the customer just anything they want: any amusement, any violence, anything that sells from bras to Zenith radio-and give them instead information they need to know to be good citizens in a democracy. There are two flaws to this way of thinking. One, as Reston amiably put it, it is not much use advising grasshoppers to be cockroaches, or newspapers to be monographs on foreign affairs, (since) the problem is to see whether, human nature being what it is, the people who sell newspapers can change to meet-all these new responsibilities without losing the patronage of the people who buy and advertise in newspapers. Obviously, newspaper publishers cannot serve the national interest by going broke.

The other flaw in thinking is to underestimate the absorption capacity of the ordinary—even illiterate-citizen. Newspapers did not have to tell the Hindi belt citizen that the Emergency was bad for him: he knew it without having it explained to him in lengthy features, informed news stories of profound editorials. When the "miracle seeds" first became available through the Government of India, it was the Punjabi farmer who rushed to buy it and experiment with it-successfully. There was no exhortation from newspapers who continued their allegedly wayward ways printing speech by politicians. The point is not that newspapers should not have done some exhortations on their own but that farmers went their way despite the lack of exhortation, which speaks something for the alleged power of the press and the credibility of its critics.

This is not to say that progress will and can be maintained without the cooperation of the press. There are entire areas of knowledge that are denied to the average reader by a press which is more concerned with profits than with promotion of meaningful information. But a survey of the press would show that many newspapers aren't soley devoted to pornography, violence or human aberrations but are trying to do as good a job as circumstances would permit them. Their editors are not always machines turned on by their paymasters but often men of conscience, if sometimes ill-directed.

A further point can be argued. And this is that power lies not in the media but in the idea. The idea gains validity by its own truth, not by the number of people subscribing to it. There were no printing presses in the time of the Apostle Paul nor even in Sankara's time and yet so powerful were their ideas that they spread far and wide. Too often those critics who castigate the press for all its sins of omission and commission forget that the Buddha's ideas travelled over land and sea without the coordinated assistance of All India

Radio and the Indian press. In the circumstances it is not what the mass of Indian newspapers say of do not say that really matters as what even one newspaper prints and wins respect by its proven credibility. A newspaper's sense of purpose and integrity, rather than its circulation, would determine its influence, though the two need not be-and are not-mutually exclusive. A newspaper that does not take itself seriously is not taken seriously by others. By that same token, a newspaper that does take itself seriously is taken seriously by others as well, no matter how small-circulation-wise-it is. Or else why would the Government of India have pounced on A.D. Gorwala's Opinion during the Emergency?

There will always be two opinions as to what exactly a newspaper should do, or a government should do by way of compelling newspapers to be socially responsive. Critics are treading dangerous, mine-strewn grounds here. As knowledgeable an individual as B.Y. Sharada Prasad-he has been news editor of the Indian Express, editor of Yojana press adviser to Mrs. Indira Gandhi be fore and during the Emergency and is now Director of the Indian Institute of Mass Communication-has cautioned against too much governmental interference with mass media:

> "I am afraid" he said in his Extension lecture at Bangalore University, "We have been a little thoughtless in seeking to bend the traditional media to development purposes. It is true that the traditional media have always carried a message-most often a religious message-but whether all such are forms could carry an official message without losing their distinctive character is open to question. A person with extensive knowledge of Indonesia was tolling us recently that the highly publicized not-the dilemmas of Government in dealing with the communal situation and the problem of maintenance of order

> and security in a country which had just been partitioned amidst brutal carnage. It was the first instance of an administration pleading national interest over press freedom and it was not to be the last in independent India.

The "I-Know-What's-Good-For-The-Country" syndrome, it may be said, is not peculiar to the politician or the high official. The editor suffers from it, too, except that the politician in power can, suppress a paper while an editor, at best, can only work at overthrowing a minister, not suppressing his right to have an opinion. This must be clearly understood. A minister out of job is not out of voice but a paper decommissioned is a paper dead. And no matter how vicious an editor may be, in the end he will get his comeuppance from his readers. Gandhi is right: the ultimate judge is man.

It is amazing how fast even liberal politicians, once they come to power, can change. It was Thomas Jefferson who said that if he were to choose between a government without the press and the press without government, he would choose the latter. What he would have done if he had to contend with a New York Times, a Washington Post, Time or News week which did not exist in his day, we do not know. But we do know that once he became President of the United States his relations with the press were far from exemplary as he harassed and persecuted editors.

3

Rapid Growth

With extending impact of media of mass communication on individuals and groups, the Indian society overall is reacting swiftly. The pervasive effects of the various media on the varied spheres of the Indian life-economic, social, cultural, intellectual, religious and even moral values are transforming rapidly.

As a result of this change, what is emerging in the Indian situation is, in DeFleur and Rokeach's words, "a conception of the media audience as a set of individuals who now encounter the media as social beings connected to their social environments." In fact, some two decades before this would not have possible or practicable at all.

India, as is well known, is a nation of diverse and divergent cultures and sub-cultures, languages and dialects that run into several hundreds, varied religions and faiths. An ancient country with civilization some 4,000-year-old, India, now a land of teeming millions, is abounding with challenging themes and problems of development. The 640 million people are waiting for a revolution in all aspects of human endeavour, a rich field for mass media to exert the influence and cast their impact.

It is unfortunate that prior to 1947, when India formed a part of the British rulers acted only in those directions which either aided in extending their influence or perpetuating their power.

With the consequences that no consistent attitudes or patterns of behaviour could be formed or inculcated among the masses. Newspapers were not permitted freedom of writing, radio was under the control of the government, television had not even been conceived, although Britain had a well-established television and radio networks at home, black and white cinema was unaware of developments in colour techniques in the west and other media of mass communication did not progress in any systematic, planned direction to assist the country in any way.

The advent of independence in August 1947 removed the shackles of the colonial era and a new horizon breathed in all aspects of the country's life. The media of mass communication also rose to the occasion. There was a tremendous progress in the fields of print and the broadcast media, the rate of literacy rose, more cinemas came into being, more and more people came in contact with one another in the countryside and the urban areas. The impact of the wide world was beginning to be felt at large.

Most of the laws restriction or controlling the activities of the journalists and writers were either withdrawn or suspended. Freedom of speech and expression (including thereby the freedom of the press) was guaranteed by the Constitution as a fundamental right (Article 19 A). The Constitution also granted freedom of movement, right to profession and property and also to hold meetings and cultural gatherings. All this added to the momentum of growth of mass media immensely. Since the Indian

Constitution recognizes 16 provincial and regional languages, equal opportunities were available to all of them for instituting newspapers and periodicals in their respective regions for their proliferation and development. Radio though remained under the control of the Central Government, but several new stations were planned to give coverage to all national and regional languages including several dialects.

In 1976, twenty-nine years after independence, India had 13,320 newspapers in 65 languages. Of which, 10,947 or 78 per cent were started after independence. The largest number of newspapers was in Hindi—a language spoken by about 40 percent of the country's population, followed by English. The number in Hindi was 3,289 and in English 2,765 next probably only to the USSR. The total circulation of all the newspapers, though not very large as compared to the Western standards, amounted to over 34 million copies. Weekly and other journals in the Indian and regional languages numbered 12,445. The progress has continued unabated, despite several hurdles of low advertising and shortage of newsprint, specially in the field of regional and provincial languages.

Started with only six broadcasting stations in 1947, All India Radio (AIR) has also greatly extended its services and progressively created its impact on the masses. In 1977, 155 radio stations including relay station, were functioning and these stations were broadcasting in several foreign, national and regional languages. A regular feedback was in existence in most languages wherein listeners could have a say in programming and broadcasting scheduled in these languages. AIR went commercial in 1967.

Television arrived in India in 1959, though pretty late and on a rather too restricted scale. The United Nations Educational, Scientific and Cultural Organisation (UNESCO), the USA, West Germany, Yugoslavia and Japan helped India in establishing, extending and programming of the television network in India.

In 1975, the US-loaned satellite enabled India to initiate the SITE (Satellite Instructional Television Experiment) programme. It was the first experiment of its kind ever made in the world. Some 3,000 villages in the six Indian states were brought under the focus of the television programs for four hours every day. This was the greatest achievement for the country's mass media. Although the NASA (National Aeronautics Space Administration of the USA) has now withdrawn the satellite, the Indian Government is determined to establish the television link to the 70 per cent of the 3,000 villages to the television stations to be started in the near by states to these villages. This is being done expeditiously with a view to keeping these villages further exposed to the new medium the "magic box."

Besides the seventeen television stations set up in various towns of the country are now covering 15 per cent of the population, as per the UNESCO figures published in the publication entitled "World Communication."

The Indian cinema has also taken rapid strides: some 619 films in 15 Indian regional languages were produced in 1978 and there were over 8,000 cinemas in the country's various states.

Right now, the Indian mass media are actively involved in the different aspects of national development. After the national emergency declared in India in June 1975, the mass media, especially the press, came under stress. But it should be stated to the credit of the media that in spite of severe restraints, they gave increasingly contributed to improvement of the situation and assisted the government and the masses in social, economic and political endeavour. People are being systematically educated in the new and modern means of production. Much more needs to be done however.

The coming of huge industry and large-scale construction works in India after independence have brought problem: complex working groups human resources mobilisation for national development, which have in turn changed the skill, training and attitudes which usually go side by side. As "the mobilising of human resources requires a great deal of attention of what the population knows and thinks of national development, and especially to the encouragement of the attitudes and social customs and the provision of knowledge, which will be favourable to the development", the mass media have undertaken the job quite competently.

This task of creating and encouraging attitudes and providing adequate information is being increasingly entrusted to the mass media. For, unless, according to Wilbur Schraemm, there is enough information designed to encourage productive attitudes, social patterns and customs, the development process is bound to suffer and be blocked. The individual differences perspective, the social categories perspective and the social relations perspective theories as enunciated by Melvin' De Fleur and Sandra Ball-Rokeach find a fair amount of application in the present Indian situation, if we assess the economic, social and political perspectives in the country in the last three decades or so since the dawn of independence. Terrific changes have taken place in the entire range of human activity in the country.

Schramm notices change in social, cultural, religious and personal attitudes which subsequently have helped change and shape a society completely differently. The Indian society has by and large reacted almost in an identical manner. This has been amply established by some well known studies conducted by Indian mass communication scholars such as Rao, Damle and several others. These researches have proved that mass media have immensely aided and assisted the rate and score of development and the pace of people in absorbing the new media which has completely revolutionised the style of people.

In bringing about these changes in which the various media are fully participating and getting involved include political consciousness, urbanisation, professional mobility, adult literacy, media consumption, and a broad general participation in the nation's reconstruction and similar activities. This has given a new dimension to the media's role in a developing situation and this is media in action in a country well on a road to progress which India presents today in the last quarter of the twentieth century.

Considering its size, swelling population and a fairly developing economy and a comparatively stable political system, India is the largest country in Asia today, second only to China. A great task of building up the country and developing its various latent human and natural resources lies on the head of the people in numerous fields. For its economic recovery and raising a complex infrastructure, India has already executed its four five-year development plans; the fifth commenced from April 1976 and will cost the country about $1,000 billion (Rs. 70,000 crores) on its completion and full execution in 1981. It is a colossal task requiring close cooperation and thorough coordination of the various factors including the mass media.

The Indian people "raised in different social environments" are therefore passing through a series of changes in "attitudes, values and beliefs that constitute their personal-psychological make-up." No system of mass media are "poorly developed." They have not been put to work "for economic development nor have they been used to bring about common anxieties, common concerns, and common emotions for India as a whole."

But it must be recognised that "it is through communication that people can learn about new ideas, can be stimulated by change which is conveyed to them or be cognizant of change and what it means, and can understand what is going around·them." Mass media are essentially agents of social change, and the "specific kind of social change they are expected to help accomplish in the transition to new customs and practices, and in some cases to different social relationships. Behind such changes in behaviour must necessarily present substantial alterations in attitudes, beliefs, skills and social norms."

Thus the carious people would take the perspective that media present to them not in the same uniform way but in varying manners suiting their personal and psychological viewpoints which the media would possibly focus on resulting in individual differences in perspective on the mass communication process.

In fact, the initial stages, as Rokeach and DeFleur point out in their Dependency Model, the cognitive effects of mass media may be creation and resolution of ambiguity which "can occur because people lack enough information to understand the meaning of an event, or because they lack adequate information to determine which of several possible interpretations of an event is correct one." Besides, in such a situation "attitude formation", "agenda-setting," "the expansion of people's beliefs" and "the values" of a society are also affected in a changing situation.

Since the most media messages at present are closely linked to the Indian audience dependence, perceptible influence on their activities, attitudes, values, aspirations and endeavours have been keenly noticed. The active media message reception of the people has been effectively instrumental in changing individual needs, psychological and social characteristics. And in some cases they flow back to alter the nature of social system itself. These factors play an overriding role in shaping the developmental attitudes of a people and which changes the developmental strategy of a nation.

As India is passing through an era of economic transition, people's attitudes and values are changing fast; media use by the people is also going through quick shifts. Although communication facilities prevalent in the urban areas are much more than in the rural areas, villagers are becoming increasingly conscious of the power of knowledge. There has been quite a spurt in the rural press in the recent times in almost all regional dialects and national languages.

This has led in rural families now have one or two members who either subscribe to the newspapers, borrow from others or read in the village reading rooms. More villagers now visit cities, there is more interpersonal communication. The rural people now get more opportunities to see films as cinema houses have been brought to the villages. Actually, the shows are always full to the capacity now than ever.

With transistor revolution, more radios are used by the rural people; there were some 150 million licences issued until December 1973 by the various radio stations in the country. A farmer with a radio transistor tucked on his shoulder working in the fields is a common sight now. As the portable television set has already been manufactured in India itself, the radio transistor would, it is hoped to be replaced by the portable television.

The commercialisation of radio and television in India has brought the whole world of advertising to his door steps. As the messages about the new goods and products reach the rural homes and " if they (the messages) relate to their (people's) interests, consistent with their attitudes, congruent with their beliefs, and supportive to their values", as

De Fleur and Rokeach point out, these are quickly acted upon and "hotly" pursued.

The proof of this, if one were required, lies in the improved living standards of the farmers, their better dressed and well-fed families, their awakening to health and family planning methods, their awareness of modern agricultural techniques and latest innovations. In fact, they are deriving the maximum use of media messages concern directly individually and jointly. But it is true that majority of people are not gaining or are not able to benefit so much from the media messages. "Since there are individual differences in personality characteristics among such members, it is natural to assume that there will be variations in effect which correspond to these individual differences."

Another aspect of the Indian life, an altogether different and novel, is in the urban areas. The journals and periodicals published in most regional and national languages have fairly good circulations; majority of the people have seen television at some place or the other and a good number have them in their drawing rooms. They watch all that this "magic box" has to offer day in and day out.

The programme presented by the SITE offered a year-long contact with the modern information science and technology in kaleidoscopic forms and fashion. People have learnt from media and acquired ability to cope with new ideas and innovative techniques. Most people are acquainted with the human machines called the computers; they are familiar with A-bomb; they try to keep themselves abreast with what is happening in the most important parts of the world through radio, newspapers, journals and television. When they learnt about the murder of John Kennedy, many people stopped work and mourned; news about the forthcoming change in the American administration and Carter's victory were widely acclaimed all over.

Awareness of the media message even among the old people, who were markedly passive to political, social, economic and cultural developments, is also rising. Even a 70-year-old illiterate woman in a middle-class Delhi home knows how to switch on/off radio and television, air-cooler and fan, often enjoys the radio and television programmes that concern her and interest her.

More and more people are being exposed to technical subjects which one can use in everyday life. Some of these include things such as the DDT powder, chemical fertilizers, pesticides automatic machines and the intricate electronic gadgets. This is also raising their general level of understanding and information. The level of knowledge on abstract subjects like the local and national politics, diplomacy, air-carriers, pollution, ecology, elections, dictatorship, democracy, etc. expanding steadily.

The elites are still feetter off: It is, however, interesting and significant that the sense of change separates the elite from the masses most dramatically. Some 30 percent of the Indian people belong to the elite class and these people are as Westernised as could be conceived. They have completely shrugged off old traditional ways, attitudes and customs. And the Western media, newspapers, magazines films and television show have drastically transformed them into entirely new personalities. Living in the urban areas also means frequent mixing with the people from other advanced nations who come there as tourists or on business or in international gatherings and conferences (which are now a common feature). These intercourses have brought them nearer to the people in the United States, the U.K., West Germany, Canada, Australia and the USSR. And this has taken them away from superstitions, obsolete habits and beliefs of the yore. There is a great desire for change in life styles, values, economic status, social position and overall thinking.

Media have immensely contributed to this change and this development taking place in the Indian society. Like a wild magic media have placed the Indian society "up to hill higher than we can see on the horizon and let him look beyond." Media are like magic because "they can let a man see and hear where he has never been and know people has never met."

This indeed is a tremendous achievement for the Indian media and their yeoman's service in concrete terms to the national development and the common man.

Society at Work

It has been prominently borne out by several research studies conducted in the various developing countries that modern communication media have immeasurable potency for improving and changing the face of a traditional society like that of India.

The studies conducted by Lerner, Schramm, Rao, and Doop, etc., have amply demonstrated that the interaction between the media and the society from development point of view is "constant and cumulative." The prominent reason, according to De Fleur and Rokeach, is that "people located at similar positions in a similar social structure would be similar in personality because of similarity of their immediate social environment." And they would naturally react and are most likely to grasp identically the gains in the form of knowledge of new techniques and new ideas have to offer.

Thus with constant communication flow, people will have a great deal in common in setting before them their developmental goals, deciding when and how they should change and what they want their society to be changing when such a communication is available and established in a society, the job of arriving at social consensus, designing a policy and directing action is entrusted to the government, but social and political organisations and the mass media become the most powerful instruments of change and development. The communication is fundamental to all social and development processes.

Development in India has been more or less on these very lines. Media, print and electronic, have played their role in framing economic and development attitudes for the five-year plans, directing and helping action by the government with people's participation, as far as practicable under the existing limitations of literacy and access. Of course, success has been slow and tardy.

Huge economic and development five-year plans for overall economic emancipation, giant industrial establishments and mammoth power works, enormous network of state undertakings, elaborately spread health and family welfare programmes and well-developed telecommunications, air and rail transportation networks and primary and higher education systems would not have been possible without a responsible and responsive mass media asserting their influence. These projects may only have come about slowly in the ordinary course of history by continuing contact with other economic systems through mass media.

It seems to be a simple and straight procedure, but actually it is a long drawn-out programme. To work this out would not have been easy and the process not so smooth. But the media helped expedite it and manoeuvre it through engineering human cooperation, consent and skill.

It is indeed a great task, which media could assist in bringing about in most amiable way. In its drain, change is also introduced in cultural fields and group relationship by participation, decision making and action. India has organised and successfully held six general elections for the 520 seat Parliament and several for the 22 state legislatures, wherein thousands of candidates and millions of electorates had complete liberty of "formulating voting decisions and actually going to the polls" where mass communication media barring radio and television had a full free-play of their potentialities, where people had not only "direction of exposure to mass communicated campaign material, but also the kind of effects that such material would have upon them." The mass media effects on the Indian situation have been indeed invaluable, of late specially.

We therefore, see "communication is a two-way process", as Dube says, "it involves giving as well as receiving information and direction. While this fact has been recognised in defining the role of community development projects (in the rural areas) as agents of communication and change, in actual practice the projects have tended to assume the role of the giver and the village people have mostly been at the receiving end."

In fact, India's swift agricultural progress, commonly termed as the "green revolution" in the late sixties and the early seventies. It is a living tribute to the power of mass communication which has carried the results of the university laboratories to the farmer in the field and has made India almost self-sufficient in feeding its 630 million people.

As social relations perspectives of the Indian people are being progressively altered by the all-pervasive force of the mass media, family system, relations between parents and children, old and young, clothing habits and fashions, dressing and eating, and cultural and moral values are being assessed and reassessed. Large families, arranged marriages, women confining to kitchen drudgery and bearing children, etc. are becoming things of the past. Diehards are losing ground and mass-communicated youngsters with modern ideals are rapidly taking over even in the tradition-ridden homes and changing the society tremendously.

Although the government in India is very powerful in the field of mass communication and has complete monopoly of radio and television, and its films division produces a heavy proportion of the films made in the country, the government also publishes a large number of journals and periodicals-states and the central governments together are certainly the largest publishers in the country-nevertheless other mass communication media too have a heavy impact in the total situation of the nation.

That the mass media are trying to involve themselves and participate in the overall national development process is apparent from glancing through any issue of a newspaper or magazine. There has been an active realisation to the fact that there cannot be and significant economic development without the use of mass media. You cannot increase agricultural yields, convince people about family welfare, persuade them to hold off from buying or to bring their crops to the market, or teach them the value of sending their daughters to schools, without reaching them through radio, television, films or newspapers. Nor can one hope, without better mass communications, to weld together a vast country with many languages; bring about a concern for the same thing, see to it, that the citizens talk about the same national problems and, further take positions about them which are not primarily dictated by regional or other narrow considerations. For this we need, of course, the expansion of media. Mass media in India are therefore striving to perform three developmental tasks (as outlined by Schramm): the populace must have information about national development: their attention must be focussed on the need to change, the opportunities inviting change, the methods and means of change; and if possible their aspiration for themselves and their country must be raised and highlighted.

In the second place, there must be opportunity to participate intelligently in the decision process, and thirdly, the needed skills must be taught: adults must be taught to read, children must be educated, farmers must learn the methods of modern farming, teachers, doctors, engineers must be trained, workers must master technical skills, people in general must learn more about how to keep themselves healthy and strong. The end result of this process in the situation as it develops would ultimately play a very vital role and would lead to the emergence of informal social relationships which would be helpful in "modifying the manner in which given individuals will act upon a message that comes to their attention via the mass media."

As De Fleur and Rokeach have underlined, "conceptually speaking, considerable similarity exists between the case of a farmer being advised to adopt a new form of weed spray via a radio programme devoted to farm problems and the case of a person being advised to adopt a new household detergent (or family planning method as in India) via a radio commercial designed to sell soap (or the family planning device)."

Media in India by and large in the near future would be able to assist in decision-making process which must accompany the country's overall developments and allround progress. The result indeed would be much better if the media get more and more opportunities and their activities have a free, unfettered flow.

There are, however, serious hurdles indeed: financial, technological, political, and social. But these would certainly be overcome as the nation moves further in the realms of development and progresses with the impact of its media of mass communication.

Factors Responsible

Of late, the concept of development itself is undergoing vast changes, and mass media's role in this process is being redefined and reassessed. Everette Rogers of Stanford University has recently tried to improve upon Schramm's concept of development. He states, ".....equality of distribution of information, socio-economic benefits; popular participation in self-development planning and execution usually accompanied by the decentralisation of certain of these activities to the village level; self-reliance and independence in development, within an emphasis upon the potential of local resources; integration of traditional with modern system, so that modernisation is a syncretisation of old and new ideas, with the exact mixture somewhat different in each locale form the essential elements in the new concept of development."

There has already been immense realisation in India of the type of development envisaged by Rogers. With mass communication media constantly "bombarding" these concepts, the rural and urban poor are receiving keen attention, and getting priority audience in development programmes so that the gap between the rich and the poor is being bridged as ably and quickly as possible.

Media have already started giving ample space and time to the villages, which they were earlier either doing casually or not doing at all. And with stimulus and incentives being promised, villagers and people of the lowest rung of the society are themselves being induced to develop themselves. Radio, television and cinema are persistently focussing on the plight of the downtrodden, the underprivileged and the unprivileged. Some old habits and customs are being yoked to reinforce new ideals on development so that every village, township or city may develop in their own way. Newspapers are adopting villages and with their influence, colleges and universities are following suit. As the news media report about the changes taking place in these villages at regular intervals and the spotlight works as a catalyst agent for the development of the entire community, a pattern suited to a particular environment is being worked out. This would also be determined by local and personal behaviour, style of living or community patterns. Thus Indian mass media are striking to focus development as a widely participatory process of social change in a society, intended to bring about both social and material advancement (including greater equality, freedom, and other valued qualities) for the majority of the people through their gaining greater control over their environment. This is Rogers' definition of development given in 1975 which exactly fits the Indian panorama and the mass media's emphasis.

But there are still huge problems awaiting solutions. Agriculture, health and family welfare, education, and adult literacy, obscure habits and outdated customs yet untouched and unearthed. These need media's urgent attention. There is lot to be done to accomplish these problems. This will immensely stimulate the people in their self-development patterns and would provoke them to outline their own achievements and successes in the various fields.

At political plane, masses still need to be educated about the necessity of stable political environments, they require to be enlightened about the importance of a pliable democratic process, and the role of a common citizen in the over-all administration of the country.

As Y.V.L. Rao points out in his study on the role of communication in the growth and development of the various aspects of the village life, the mass media should help the Indian people to raise their economic status, bring about greater respect for human dignity and greater equality among the masses, make cultural, social, political and economic chances a perpetuating process.

It is, therefore, clear that mass media have an eminently significant role in the total development and is "tied inseparably" in the entire process in India. However, as

De Fleur and Rokeach underline that there is need to recognise and establish that "the effects of a given mass-communicated message sent out on a given channel will depend 'upon a large number of psychological characteristics and social categories similarities which audience members bring to their encounters with the quickly gaining momentum of the mass communication function. The method is to involve in the innumerable fields of activity. Communication specialists and researchers over the world are looking at the outcome of media's this involvement in India development with interest, and perhaps with an amount of concern.

Communication, as it is known today, has originated and evolved in the West, particularly in the United States of America. With the development of technologies, the communication methods also developed. The methods became complex and sophisticated. But the concept of 'communication' has been with us since the creation of man. The methods and the process is differ from region to region, country to country. Even now, with the idea of 'global village' becoming a reality, we differ as far as methods and process of communication are concerned.

You must be aware of various seminars and workshops being conducted to formulate a policy regarding satellite communication. Some experts say as a result of exposures to foreign television programmes, our values and culture may be damaged beyond repair. The negative influence of such telecasts may prove detrimental to the development of the nation.

Some scholars say that the Indian tradition has hardly any thoughts on communications. Those who grant such thoughts have negative vies on the issue. 'Communication' is a word coined in the recent past to explain a particular area of study. Therefore, in our ancient literature this view was not dealt with separately. But, a lot has been said on the process and methods of communication is an integral part of our socio-political and cultural life. It was as important then as it is now. It worked according to the social and cultural norms. At present, we must ensure that it works as per the socio-cultural ethos of our nation. Otherwise the fabric of the nation may be disturbed.

Our way of life is influenced by religion and various philosophical teachings. As a God fearing people, we have found various ways to worship. Mysticism is one such way.

Mysticism has given birth to a new method of communicating one's deep realisation and understanding of God and the Universe. Mysticism is centered on oneself. It is a process by which one plunges into the deepest core of one's heart of self. A profound communication takes place in one's innermost core. This communication process can be termed as interpersonal communication-communication with oneself. Mira Bai and Kabir communicated so much in a very easy way because their realisation was clear. We have not explored this mystical process. This mystical approach possibly can help us to communicate with our people more effectively. Interpersonal Communication enriched interpersonal communication. This area of communication has not been sufficiently explored. Some enthusiastic communication professionals take a parochial view and try desperately to invent a communication theory or a model which existed in the ancient times. Having discussed the importance of interpersonal and interpersonal communication, we shall discuss the importance of Indian philosophy in Communication. We come to know about the process of communication in ancient India through treatises on arts, religion, and mysticism. We can also go through Sanskrit,. Persian, Urdu and Hindi sources.

Accounts of Vedanta, Bhakti, Vaishnavism and Sufism speak volumes on communication. To be effective in our communication we should be able to establish their relevance to the people of modern India. This Indian orientation will help us to recast and reframe the whole outlook towards communication concepts norms, and beliefs.

We ought to turn to the Indian philosophical tradition which has tremendous intellectual and spiritual resources and can easily supply us with basic framework for a creative and relevant communication process. The impact of this heritage has been felt through the ages and its richness and university has been acknowledged by the world. Since the present communication concept and discipline has developed in the west, we do get carried away by its Western perception and hence become ineffective in the Indian situation. It is necessary, therefore that we ground ourselves firmly in our culture, beliefs and ethos. We need not copy the western models blindly. And thus consequently suffer the loss of inspiration.

The Assets

In India, communication is inextricably linked with philosophy and religion. Sarvapalli Radhakrishnan says, "the pursuit of philosophy is deemed a religious vocation. Therefore, in order to come to terms with the cultural ideal that animates Indian society, we need to examine, brief though they may be, the outlines of Indian philosophy."

The Upanishads call attention to the value of the knowledge of ultimate truth as a means of liberation. The Upanishads, greatly emphasise the need to look inward for a clearer understanding of reality. The basic tenet of the Upanishads is the need to acquire self-knowledge and thereby liberate oneself from worldly bondages.

With the passage to time, a number of non-Vedic philosophical traditions sprang up. The Charvakas placed heavy emphasis on the material world on the material world and discarded all notions of transcendentality. Jainism was another tradition of philosophy which was non-Vedic in character. In maintained that both the animate and the inanimate world were eternal and independent. Therefore one has to be tolerant to all that exists on earth. Buddhism, another non-vedic philosophy constituted a powerful reaction against the ritualism that characterized the Vedas and the transcendentalism that was associated with the Upanishads. The individual, according to Buddhism, should diligently work out his salvation, from pain and suffering.

Later, Indian Philosophy began to move further and further away from the original ways of thinking and, indeed, split into different and competing systems. Although these systems do not by any means constitute mutually exclusive categories, they display sufficient variation for each to warrant on autonomous conceptual status. Of these, there are six that deserve close attention. They are the Nyaya; Vaishesika; Samkhya; Yoga; Mimamsa; Vedanta and Advaita. These schools, too, contributed to the formation of the Indian tradition.

The Indian schools philosophy originated from the Vedas; two schools are Vedic—the Mimamsa and the Vedanta; the four-Samkhya, Yoga, Vaishesika, and Nyaya-have their base in the Vedas. Therefore, these six schools are classed as Vedic or Astika. The two schools of Buddhism and Jainism are called Nastika as they do not accept Vedic authority. These eight schools are products of the great thought that characterised the post-Vedic age. Each school of philosophy is called a Darshana, meaning a view or a vision of the truth. The aims and aspirations of life are not only the pursuit of material gains and pleasure but also virtue and morality which chasten life and spiritual enlightenment and freedom.

Each school is associated with a sage as its first promulgator—Samkhya with Kapila, Yoga with Patanjali,

Vaishesika with Kanada, Nyaya with Gautama, Mimamsa with Jaimini and Vedanta with Badarayana-Vyasa. Because of their mutual relationship, these six schools fall into three groups of allied systems. Samkhya is accepted by Yoga, with the addition of God as the omniscient first Teacher. The speciality of Yoga is the practical aspect of the methods of mental control by which the philosophical ideal of the Samkhya, namely, the isolation of the Spirit from Matter is achieved. But Yoga as a Sadhana or preparatory discipline and means came to be accepted by all schools.

Today, it has, with the help of science, grown in strength and gained a world-wide vogue. The vaishesika doctrines form the basis of Nyaya, both being schools of realism and pluralism. The Mimamsa and Vedanta go together because of their common Vedic basis but otherwise they differ fundamentally. The former is concerned with Karma and Dharma, the performance of ordained duty, but the latter to the opposite of Karma, namely, renunciation from activity; according to Vedanta, knowledge is the means of salvation. Mimamsa is thus related to the Karma-kanda, and Vedanta to the Upanishads. The Mimamsa also made a valuable contribution to the science of interpreting texts; it came to be known therefore as Vakya Shastra.

But what do all these mean to us today. Our tradition, philosophy, culture, and religion are not dead. We still practice our ancient religion. We do study our ancient philosophy and theology. Our beliefs are largely based on Karma and Dharma. Therefore, these things have meaning in our day to day life. The words coined in various philosophical and theological books are still being used by us to convey the same meaning. Thus, to communicate meaningfully, we must be well grounded in this rich heritage. But a little caution-we must not be so heavily grounded in these, so as not to be able to fly and explore the richness of clear blue sky.

What implication does this survey of Indian philosophy have for communication theory? On the basis of these philosophical tenets, we can construct a workable model of communication for the Indian situation. This may differ substantially from models found in the Western countries. Each culture may have models of communication of its own. What is essential is that any communication model must be based on a cultural context. Otherwise the meaning conveyed may differ from the intended meaning to be conveying in a communication. Many times, we may fail to communicate if we do not take this cultural context into consideration.

In India generally the primary focus of interest in communication is how does the receiver make sense of the stimuli that he receives so as to deepen his self-awareness. In the Western model, the basic question that present themselves are how does the Communicator affect/influence/ manipulate the receiver and how does the communicator and receiver share information and enter into a two-way relationship. According to traditional Indian views, meaning should necessarily lead to self-awareness. Hence the Indian definition of communication would be that it is an inward search for meaning—a process of intra-personal communication.

In the West, communication is seen as the transference of meaning with the intention of influencing the receiver. But in Indian meaning brings enlightenment. Meaning, according to traditional Indian thought, was seen as process which leads to self-awareness, then to freedom, and finally to truth. Here, by freedom we mean the liberation of persons from ignorance, from illusion of the world, and the web of the artificial categories constructed all around us. Indian and the Western ways is that the Indian way focuses attention on the intra-personal dimension as opposed to the inter-personal dimension.

The Western way is expression-oriented but the Indian way is interpretation oriented. The Indian way seems to suggest that what is important in human communication is to find out how a receiver makes sense of the verbal stimuli that are received by him and engages in a search for meaning. This search is an inward one. The traditional authorities maintain that the reality is indeed within man. To know it is to be. In other words, distinction between the knower and the known narrows down considerably. The realization of truth is facilitated neither by language nor by logic and rationality. To know is to be; to know is to become aware of the artificial categorization imposed on the world by language and logic. It is only through an intuitive process that man will be able to lift himself out of the illusory world, which according to the Indian viewpoint, is indeed the aim of communication. People may differ with this view. But we all must agree that in India realisation dawns when we internalise the communication. It needs to be pointed out that one may not understand the current development in communication solely in the light of this model. We are living in a world where the border lines between countries are disappearing very fast. We do know and feel at one with the happenings in other parts of the globe. We are passing though a phase of civilization which could be termed, at best, the transition, and 'chaotic' at worst.

Indian communication centres on the word Sadharanikaran. It is derived from the Sanskrit world Sadharan meaning simple, common or ordinary. Sadharanikaran would thus imply simplification. The word has a familiar ring and is equivalent to the Latin word "communs" that is communication, meaning commonness of experience.

Sadharanikaran has been vividly described in Bharata's Natya Shastra, which though discovered in the 10th century A.D. by Bhattanayak, has now been established to have its authorship in a period as early as 500 BC. It is also known as the fifth Veda, as in it Bharata Muni had condensed the essence of the four Vedas for the benefit of the common man.

How does Sadharanikaran take place? Bharata describes Sadharanikaran as that point in the climax of a drama when the audience becomes one with the actor who lives an experience through his acting on stage and starts simultaneously reliving the same experience. The process has been described as rasa swadan. When Sadharanikaran happens, universalisation or commonness of experience takes place in full form. According Bhattanayak, the essence of communication is to achieve commonness or oneness among the people. Later, this word was extensively used in literacy circles for explaining poetics, aesthetics and drama.

But today, Sadharanikaran is often employed to convey the idea of commonness and simplification. The entire superstructure of Indian aesthetic centres on the act of Sadharanikaran through rasa swadan.

Rasa has been explained thus: man in his essential characteristics is a bundle of bhawa that constitute his being and form part of his total consciousness. These have been categorised as 50 in number. Of these nine are described as Sthai bhawa 33 as Vyabhichari bhawa and the remaining as Satwik bhawa. Bharata, after an intensive study of these moods, has grouped them under one all encompassing expression bhawa for purposes of establishing Sadharanikaran.

Coomaraswamy describes 'bhawa' as springing from aesthetic emotion of person who derives its existence from sensory experience. Each mood is capable of arousing a relevant state of feeling/quality of response.

Bharat Muni also postulated that for Sadharanikaran to take place, Sthai Bhava, that is, permanent moods in the audience, have to be aroused which will result in the unleashing of the attendant Rasas, feeling or aesthetic pleasures, thereby completing the process of communication.

A Bhava is the first reaction or sensation caused in the sympathetic mind by a stimulus called Vibhavas sone, a bird, a picture. A sustained Bhava that leads to Rasa is the Sthayee Bhava. An Anubhava is the physical manifestation that takes place immediately as Bhava registers itself in the mind. The Sthayee Bhava is stimulated by the Vibhava in the mind and is heightened by Anubhavas and Sanchari Bhavas. In this state, the mind will be highly receptive to the Rasa experience.

When a person experiences the intensity of the Bhavas of the Vaibhavas he overcomes his own personality and completely identifies himself with actual state of the Vibhava: This is state of universalisation. The universalisation leads to identification and involvement. Whatever is communicated leaves deep impact. Rasa can be understood only by the Sahridaya the person who alone is capable of rasaswadan. Who is Sahridaya? He/she is person in state of emotional intensity i.e. a quality of emotional dimension coequal to that of the sender of the message of communicator. Both must be sahridayas.

In India, communication lays great stress on the communicator and the one who receives communication belonging to the same cultural group. The same cultural context will help the communicator and the receiver to communicate effectively. The sender and receiver of a communication belonging to same culture, would be able to communicate more effectively. In other world, it is emphasised that communication may be ineffective between an individuals or groups, not belonging to the same culture as total grasp of symbols, signs and meanings are essential for effective communication. The relevance of the message, the code and the experience that the code stands for, to the group with which communication is sought to be established, is an important factor in communication.

In Western societies sources and receivers, at least in principle, communicate as equals, but in Indian society, it is not the case. The source is viewed as higher and the receiver as lower in status. The relationship is a hierarchical one of dominance and subordination. The source is held in high esteem by the receiver of communication, a relationship idealized in the gurushishya relationship. Even though the source and receiver are unequal, they are Sahridayas, having a common cultural orientation. This makes the communication is their unequal relationship satisfying. The hierarchical aspect of Sadharanikaran contributed to the blossoming of Indian civilization through efficient communication. This was, however, later taken to the level of absurdity, resulting in highly rigid and hierarchical society. To some extent, it made Indian society into a more or less closed system and thereby contributed towards its stagnancy and decay. It is true Natyashastra was written by Bharat Muni to simplify the complex Vedas for the benefit of the common man and thereby bridge the gap between the elites, the priests, the nobles and Sudras. However, with the passage of time, Sadharanikaran resulted in divisions within society. Later, with institutionalization of difference the society became stagnant.

Sadharanikaran, through communication, between unequals over a period of time, contributed toward the development of more or less permanent and rigid hierarchical social relationships, as reflected in the caste system. Not only that, it seems that the values supporting the hierarchical nature of social arousal of permanent mood and particular aesthetic pleasure made them natural and acceptable as well as satisfying. Acceptance of this type of communication pattern by the people belonging to different castes, made the system stronger and permanent.

Today, to a great extent, the caste system influences communication patterns, particularly in Indian villages. Within a village community, far more communication takes place among the members of a caste than between castes because of the highly stratified and hierarchical nature of the caste system. People of high and low castes accept their position as natural. The asymmetrical relationship between high and low caste members is hereditary and is accepted by those who are in a disadvantageous position.

It may be pointed out here that in Indian many sages and saints, in different times, launched reform movements against social inequalities. They attempted to further simplify and reinterpret Indian philosophy for the benefit of the common people and thereby bridge the gap between elites and commoners.

However, the question arises: apart from the academic exercise, is there any use of studying of the Indian view on communication? In think, it is necessary and the need is urgent. Some the reasons are as follow:

(a) The Indian view of communication takes into consideration the man and his environment as healthy unit as against the mechanical and quantitative view of man.

(b) The use of technology has added a new dimension to use of world as a tool of communication. The printing press, radio TV and satellite have multiplied words and their use to an immeasurable extent. The knowledge of Indian view of communication may help in minimising the use of words to create a greater effect with aid of visuals.

(c) The emergence and use of large number of words has resulted in the distortion of the meaning or words. Words, however, would continue to occupy primacy in human communication in future despite the expansion of electronic media. "Better than a collection of thousand meaningless words is one word full of meaning on hearing which one becomes peaceful", says the Dhammapada.

(d) The Sadharanikaran theory underlines the role of communication. It is total communication and communication at its best. It is more integrated approach to communication because it seeks to affect the behaviour of human beings by arousing emotional and physical response simultaneously.

Influence in General

Indian society is often characterised as one of "unity in diversity" and its villages as "independent republics." These characterizations have important implications for the patterns of human communication in India.

In ancient India, cultures blossomed in different parts of the subcontinent. These were unique and independent of each other. These cultures derived strength and inspirations from each other. The merits of cultures were communicated through the long established oral tradition.

The roving saints and sufies performed the task of communicating messages. They propagated the gospels of truth enshrined in the Vedas and Puranas, epic stories like Ramayana and Mahabharata and other scriptures. They reinterpreted these messages as per the realities prevailing in the society. In the process, they succeeded in communicating the norms values proper for decent social living.

At the communicating level, known as a class of knowledgeable people, Brahmins enjoyed the highest social status. They played an effective role as "link persons" between the common man of their own community and persons from outside the community.

Village communities were mostly self-sufficient. Each community had strong and extensive cultural links with other communities beyond the neighbouring villages and towns. Administrative contract were minimal, largely confined to revenue collection. Even this task was performed through intermediaries such as the Nawabs Zamindars and Lambardars. Thus, in ancient or traditional India, there existed effective systems of communication which were both local and pan-Indian in character. Such communication provided meaning and justification for the social order. It inculcated the spirit of devotion, love and faith.

Indian society was highly stratified and hierarchical. Communication tended to flow from persons of higher status to persons of lower status. In any communication situation, the relationship between the source and the receiver was that of dominance and subordination. In spite of this there as some dialogue between the two. Both shared a common frame of reference which made communication smooth and effective.

Changed Face

With the advent of British rule in India, there was an increase in administrative links, and physical mobility was encouraged through rails and roads. A new philosophy and culture spread by Macaulay's education system started making inroads into traditional Indian society and culture. The two were incompatible in many ways. However, the communication of foreign concepts, ideas and philosophies was successful as a lot of Indians accepted them. At the same time the conflict between the Indian and British ways of life became evident. As a consequence, there were upheavals, and turmoils, which ultimately led to the birth of independent India.

Free India has adopted democracy based on universal adult franchise as form of government. As welfare state it has opted for planned development. The technological growth and developments, huge development in communication and increases in the scale of economic activities have enlarged the range of choices. The philosophy of equality, irrespective of caste, creed and religion and the compulsions of democratic elections at all levels—village panchayats to the Parliament help to minimise the disadvantages of the traditional social and political relationships.

Communication is not confined only through to religion and practice of social norms. Its task is much more than maintaining the order and stability in society. Though the speaker is till viewed as an authority figure, particularly in rural areas and the listener as subordinate, such a relationship does not go unchallenged in many parts of our country to day. Tensions centred on such relationship do exit and report of social tensions from different parts of the country are frequently published. At the same time, there are situations where communication patterns are more on a basis of equality. Communication is no longer viewed only as a means to stability and harmony but for change as well. Thus communication in India has become a complex subject.

We are well aware of societal conditions that have given rise to various mass media. It is normally assumed that technology has been necessary for the reproduction of communications for mass audiences. Industrialisation, with the division of labour and urbanization, has created mass and heterogenous audiences. The proponents of this idea also hold that in the pre-industrial period, the communication system was restricted to direct face-to-face communication between individuals.

These assumptions, as far as India is concerned, are not wholly true. First, despite passing from the First Information and Communication Revolution, the Indian society has largely retained the traditions of oral and interpersonal communication. Therefore, when we consider the distinguishing features of modern society, it is not the 'mass' of people that constitutes 'a mass society', but the relationships between the members. The western concept of mass society explains its heterogenous nature due to its being alienated by technology, socially differentiated due to occupation and physically separated through expansion of urbanisation. Thus the need to reach out to this highly "impersonalized" mass society, requires various "mass media" not only to bring together its members into mainstream, but also to seek their consent for social action.

Does this portrayal of the "mass" of people provide an accurate picture of present-day Indian society? Clearly it does not. Yes, we have undergone industrialization, urbanisation and modernisation. Yet life in contemporary Indian society is very different, because of these changes. But when we look at the villages in India, we see large "masses" of people living together as homogenized blocks, linked together by their myriad languages, dialects, common culture, traditions and so on. So, what we have today are groups of "masses" linked together by oral tradition, culture and language, giving a picture of homogeneity.

However, in recent years, even among communication scholars, there has been tendency to transplant communication models from the West to developing countries. They have transplanted the idea that rational independent messages beamed at "individuals" will lead to motivation and attitude change. This basically the advertising and marketing model of a society believing in perfect competition.

We are now beginning to realise that there is another model of society in which the indivi-dual derives his legitimacy from the system. In such a society the role of "communication" is quite different. Therefore, attempts to inform, educate and motivate the individual in many a times do not succeed. However, messages with symbols appealing to the "collective" consciousness many times do succeed. The Indian society, with its unique concept of the "collective" nature of interpersonal networks, affirms that while we keep our windows open to the world, our feet are rooted in the innate wisdom that has come down to us over the last 5000 years. It is within these parameters, that India's transition from the oral to the modern mass media-based society, has to perceive.

In India, the print media took roots first in the major provincial capitals of British Indian—Calcutta and Madras and later Bombay. These cities with their surrounding areas accounted for the bulk of their newspaper circulations. Advertising also developed in these metropolitan centres. As the freedom struggle gained momentum, newspapers were published from main centres of the agitation like Delhi, Lahore, Lucknow and Kanpur. Other newspaper centres were concentrated in the princely states of Mysore, Hyderabad, Bhopal and Baroda. These cities also had their own radio stations.

Newspaper readership continued to remain in urban areas. After independence the print medium emerged from its pre-colonial past and spread into the semi urban and rural areas. Advanced technology, better roads and transport helped the press to move into semi urban centres, but they were still rotted in the cities. A new class emerged—the information rich who were already modernised, literate and economically well off. With development and growth of newspaper technology and sharp competition the costs of publishing a newspaper also rose. The advertising world—the backbone of newspaper—hitched its wagon to the highly-circulated newspaper and magazines, fuelling the growing difference between big and small newspapers and magazines. The power of the print media attracted bit industrialists to invest in the newspaper industry. Monopolies and chain newspapers became the order of the day. Suddenly, the missionary zeal of pre-independence days gave away to a competitive frenzy in commerce. Today we have chain-newspapers controlled by business tycoons who run them purely on commercial lines.

What has been the impact of newspapers on Indian society? A difficult question to answer. But a few pointers would give us somewhat clear picture. Newspapers have become a class medium, catering only to the rich and the powerful. However, the language newspapers do cater to the lower levels of society. But their reach and access are linked to literacy and capacity to purchase. According to present estimates, newspapers are purchased and read by less than 20 per cent of India's 900 million population. A wide gulf has been created between the "information-rich" and "information-poor." Instead of a democratising and bringing equity the newspapers have helped to perpetuate a class structure in society.

The broadcasting media though government control, have the capacity to reach out to the people in every nook and corner of the country. While both are highly capital-intensive, it is their capacity to reach out to millions that makes them a people's medium. The development of Akashvani and Doordarshan in India has had its ups and downs, but today we have about 545 TV stations covering about 90 per cent of area and catering to about 60 per cent of the population. Radio has much wider reach and access.

But in case of the two media, it is not the development of infrastructure that we need to look into, but their programme content and how it is being received by the people. It is in this area that both AIR and Doordarshan have not been found wanting. While "news" has been accepted as the important segment in their programme content, other aspects lime development and education have been given adequate attention. However, entertainment has become synonymous with these two corporations.

AIR has opened various channels for entertainment; but has failed to evoke the same kind of audience response to other development-oriented programmes as to entertainment. Even its educational programmes have restricted listenership. Researchers have pointed out to the lack of quality programmes over AIR.

Doordarshan has fared no better. The criticism levelled against AIR also applies to Doordarshan. The criticism levelled against Doordarshan is sometimes more severe as the policy formulated for it says that it should serve the developmental aspirations of the majority. The Doordarshan has ended up with more entertainment than any other type of programmes. Except for news and few current affairs programmes. DD largely depends on films and film-based programmes to fill in its telecast time. Criticism about lack of professionalism, creativity and production skills, have been levelled against DD. What has been its impact on society? People do say that TV is an "idiot box" and has harmful effects on children. But TV is a tool of learning also and so far, has been well-received. Further, information on health, family planning and eradication of social evils like drugs, smoking, alcoholism and dowry, have all been successfully projected over Doordarshan.

Let us take another important mass medium—films. Films can be produced on almost all subjects of human interest and include, broadly speaking, feature films, documentaries and newsreels. The themes may encompass such diverse subjects as industry, agriculture development, education, environment and vital national issues like family welfare, national integration and untouchability. In fact, a large number of films are not commercial in the usual sense.

Contemporary film making more than ever before, is a big financial venture. It is usually controlled by commercial consideration rather than the demands of the art. The star system, lavish promotion and publicity and huge budgets for formula pictures are all frantic attempts to minimise the financial risk involve in film making. No wonder such films aim to please the audience by creating a synthetic world of unreal emotions. They make no demands on the power of thinking and ignores are for the sake of commerce. Films seeks to attract the audience by providing rather glib and naive entertainment in order to covert people's childishness into cash. For the majority of the viewers, a film is day-dreaming device in which they forget their worries and get lost in world of fantasy—full of melodramatic sentiments, songs and dance, violence and sex. In fact, with only a few honourable exceptions cinema in India has been overwhelmingly entertainment-oriented almost since its beginning. The Indian film stars have exerted such a hypnotic hold on the masses that they have made a place for themselves in public life, politics and even influenced the living style of the people. Exceptional Indian Films, with their intense realism and abiding concern for the common man, have found their way to international acclaim. The emergence of the new cinema as a movement, presenting a modern humanistic approach, offered a refreshing contrast to the commercial cinema.

Video has grown to be a very popular mass medium within a remarkably short times. It has endless possibilities for entertainment and education. Video in India in India is largely perceived as an alternative source of entertainment. However, video news magazine has caught the popular fancy and many leading newspapers have come forward to launch news magazines in audio-visual form. Public sector companies have utilised the video medium for bringing out house journals. But video has also come to occupy an important place in political and poll campaigns in India.

A communication satellite is a man-made platform launched into space; it remains relatively stationary over the earth. It serves as a platform for radio relay stations which receive radio signals beamed to it from the earth and relays those signals back to other locations on earth. Satellite communication greatly benefited the newspaper industry. It made possible facsimiles of newspaper pages to be sent electronically via satellite to receiving station anywhere in the world where printing facilities may be located.

The satellite distribution systems give the newspapers a flexibility hitherto not possible. Satellites now link news bureaus all over the country and can instantly transmit news reports to any station. Computers can automatically set the stories in type and start the process rolling. The cable TV system can receive programmes through satellite and deliver them by cable to subscribers' sets. In another form of transmission, called Direct Broadcast Satellite, television programmes are directly received by the dish antenna at home, totally bypassing the cable system.

But the strongest impact of TV comes through the Hong Kong-based STAR-TV, CNN, the BBC and Pakistan TV, using satellites to beam programmes right into our homes. There has been a furore over the role of these foreign satellite broadcasts, referred to as post-colonial cultural imperialism. They have made serious inroads into DD viewership. Innumerable dish antennae dot the horizon of Delhi, Mumbai, Kolkata, Chennai, Bangalore and Ahmedabad and a large number of smaller cities in the country. DD replied to this "invasion from the sky" by opening the 5 Metro channels to Indian viewers from August 15, 1993. It also hopes to use the terrestial links to further upgrade the coverage geographically. Multiplicity of channels has increased the choice for the viewers. The question always is as to which channel will win the audience—ratings race. It has been observed that a large majority of TV viewers seem to be convinced that the foreign-based TV channels, thought better produced, are not culturally conducive to a large number of viewers.

It should be obvious by now that for an Indian approach to communication a sound knowledge of its philosophical, cultural and linguistic traditions is necessary. It is also necessary to go to Sanskrit, as it may provide us with a lot of materials on communication which could be of use to communicate to our people properly and effectively. It is only by undertaking such kind of studies and by relating these to the demands of modern life that we will be able to re-cast and reframe our whole outlook toward communication concepts, norms and beliefs.

In this connection, we have to look at the trends in characteristic of the highly industrialised west and particularly of the USA. There the science of communication have been mastered, but because of a highly materialistic focus, who are losing the true purpose of communication is lost sight of in their eagerness to consume more and provide themselves with more free time and leisure, the listener has unleashed a Frankensteinian unstoppable momentum to the growth of sophisticated technology. The wisdom of the East, from India and China, may help them to reframe their communication priorities.

It is a matter of concern, that the lure of technology is creating a wide gap among various communities and classes in Indian society. We require to prioritize our use of technology, particularly those needs related to the socio-cultural and linguistic demands. According to many scholars, catering to this large number of people with diverse needs has become a problem. Faced with spectre of proliferating communication technology, India is on the threshold of a giant leap forward. Just acquisition of communication technology may not help the Indian society. India has used a lot of communication technology in almost five decades since Independence. But the increase in the use of modern technology for development did not make our communication better. Analysis reveals that during this process of modernisation, very powerful political and economic forces have gained control over the communication system. This in turn had led to either distortion, discrimination of even total obstruction of the communication flow from and to the grassroot level. This has not only resulted in cultural erosion, but at the same time has pushed large masses of people below the poverty line of information. This needs to be guarded against India with its teeming millions cannot afford to sustain an imbalanced system of communication. We have communicated with our people for so long through the oral tradition, now, let us not destroy this tradition.

Long before the mass media were invented, Plato may have provided the opening round in the controversy over the social costs and benefits of mass culture. In his commentary on the training of the children who were to become the leaders of his ideal Republic, he saw the mass culture of his day as posing a threat to the minds of the young.

Then shall we simply allow our children to listen to any stories that anyone happens to make up, and so receive into their minds ideas often the very opposite of those we shall think they ought to have when they are grown up?

No, certainly not [replies, Glaucon].

It seems, then, our first business will be to supervise the making of fables and legends, rejecting all which are unsatisfactory; and we shall induce nurses and mothers to tell their children only those which we have approved.

Most of the stories now in use must be discarded.

This theme-popular entertainment is harmful to the minds of the young has been a consistent one from the beginnings of mass communication. It has been claimed from time to time that such charges can be validated by scientific evidence, but repeatedly this evidence has turned out to be difficult to interpret and therefore controversial.

Social sciences insist that any important conclusions about the effects of the media be supported by solid evidence. Because of such insistence upon data rather than emotion, they sometimes find themselves in the awkward position of seeming to defend the media when actually they are simply refusing to accept the inadequately supported claims of critics.

Nevertheless, the insistence that conclusions be based on adequate evidence has never deterred the literacy critic from charging the media with a deep responsibility for society's problems. Most nineteenth century's American writers at some point in their careers took time to criticize and condemn the newspaper for superficiality and distortion.

Functional Dimensions

The tenacity and stability of the mass media generally in the face of such a long history of criticism by powerful voices needs explanation. The problem at first seems deceptively simple: the media appeal to the masses and the masses want the kind of content they get and so the media continue to give it to them.

Many social scientists, such as Skornia, have exposed the inadequacy of this explanation by nothing the old chicken-and-egg problem. It is difficult at best to know if the public taste determines the media fare or if the media fare determines public taste. The answer probably lies somewhere in between with public taste being both a cause and effect of media fare. The relationship between public taste and media fare thus becomes a circular one which, in terms of the chicken-egg analogy, is an ongoing process of chickens producing eggs and eggs producing chickens.

The structural functional analysis of social systems (or "functional analysis" for short) concerns itself with the patterns of action exhibited by individuals or subgroups who relate themselves to one another within such systems. A social system is, for this reason, an abstraction—but one not too far removed from the observable and empirically verifiable behaviours of the persons who are doing the acting. The social system, then, is a complex of stable, repetitive, and patterned action that is in part a manifestation of the culture shared by the actors, and in part a manifestation of the psychological orientations of the actors (which are in turn derived from that culture). The cultural system, the social system, and the personality systems (of the individual actors), therefore, are different kinds of abstractions made from the same basic data, namely, the overt and symbolic behaviours of individual human beings. They are equally legitimate abstractions, each providing in its own right a basis for various kinds of explanations and predictions. Generally speaking, it may be difficult or nearly impossible to analyse or understand fully one such abstraction without some reference to the others.

But, granted that the term "social system" is a legitimate scientific abstraction, how does this general conceptual strategy help in understanding; the mass media of communication? To answer this question, we need to set forth in greater detail exactly what is meant by the term social system, and what type of analysis it provides. To aid in providing such an explanation we turn briefly to several ideas that are important aspects of the study of social systems. One of the most important of these ideas is the concept of the "function" of some particular repetitive phenomenon (set of actions) within such a system. The fact that such content has long survived the jibes of influential critics was said to require explanation. One form of explanation will be provided by noting the function of such a repetitive phenomenon within some stable system of action. The term "function" in the present context means little more than "consequence." To illustrate briefly, we might hypothesize that the repetitive practice of wearing wedding rings on the part of a given married couple has the function (consequence) of reminding, them as well as others that the two are bound together by the obligations and ties that matrimony implies. This practice thereby contributes indirectly to maintaining the permanence of the marriage—the stability of that particular social system. The practice is in a sense "explained" by noting its contribution to the context within which it occurs. A comparison of a number of such systems with and without this particular item (but in other respects matched) would test the assertion.

In the above example, the social system is a relatively simple one. There are only two "components," and each of these happen to be the behaviour pattern of an individual. Their patterns are derived both from the individual psychological makeup of the partners and from the cultural norms concerning marriage prevailing in their community, social class, and society. It is a miniature system whose stability is dependent upon satisfaction of its "needs." For example, such a system requires that the partners perform roles that meet the expectations each has of the other and the expectations the community has of married couples. This can be thought of as a "need" for adequate role performance, without which the stability of the system would be endangered. Other "needs," related to economic matters and emotional satisfactions, could be cited.

More complex illustrations of social systems can easily be pointed to, where the "components" of the system are not the actions of individual persons but subsystems. A department store, for example, is a complex social system consisting of the actions of managerial personnel, buyers, salespersons, the clerical staff, customers, transportation workers, a janitorial team, and security employees. Each of these components is a smaller system of action within the broader system of the store itself, and it in turn is a complex system of action carried out within the context of the external social conditions of the community. In spite of the complexity, any given set of repetitive actions might be analysed in terms of their contribution to maintaining or undermining the system's stability. Granting to employees the right to buy merchandise at cost could have the function (consequence) of maintaining their morale and loyalty, and thus would contribute fairly directly to the maintenance of the system. Rigid insistence on the observance of petty rules, such as docking the pay of an employee who on rare occasions was late for work, might be disruptive of morale and loyalty, and by contributing to labour turnover it could be dysfunctional. Instead of contributing to the maintenance of the system, it could cause disruptions and instability. Such inductively derived conclusions would be subject to testing for validity, of course, but the functional analysis would have generated the hypothesis to be tested an important role of theory.

The Administration

A "functional analysis," then, focuses on some specific phenomenon occurring within a social system. It then attempts to show how this phenomenon has consequences that contribute to the stability and permanence of the system as a whole. The phenomenon may, of course, have a negative influence, and if so, it would be said to have "dysfunctions" rather than "functions." The analysis is a strategy for inducing or locating hypotheses that can be tested empirically by comparative studies or other appropriate research methods.

The analysis of social system is extremely difficult, no infallible rules specify precisely how to locate and define the exact boundaries of a given social system, particularly if it is relatively complex. As yet, no completely agreed upon criteria exist for establishing linkages between the components of a system, and no standard formulas can uncover the precise contribution that a given repetitive form of action makes to the stability of a system. A functional analysis of the contribution of some item to the stability of a system, then, is a procedure that is somewhat less than rigorous. But in spite of this source of potential criticism, this strategy has proved useful in our attempts to understand complex social phenomena, such as the mass media.

How can this type of analysis be applied to the mass media? First, we can identify that portion of the content of the mass media that is in "low" cultural taste or provides gratifications to the mass audience in such a manner that it is widely held to be potentially debasing as the "relatively persistent trait or disposition" of the mass media we seek to explain. It would be difficult in practice to construct a set of categories under which to analyse the content of the media so that material of "low" cultural taste can be identified readily. It would be difficult, but actually it would not be impossible.

Excessive violence, the portrayal of criminal techniques, horror and monster themes, open pornography, suggestive music, and dreary formula melodramas are typical categories of content that arouse the ire of critics. Considerable disagreement would probably occur as to the exact content that should be included in any given category. There would also be debates over the number of categories used. There would also be debates over the number of categories used. Nevertheless, it is theoretically possible to identify the content of any given medium that is most objected to by the largest number of critics. We will assume that given sufficient time and resources, and using survey techniques, preference scales, attitude measuring instruments, and other research procedures now available that the content of any given medium could be divided roughly into something like the following three categories:

Low-taste Content: This would be media content widely distributed and attended to by the mass audience, but which has consistently aroused the ire of critics. Examples would be crime dramas on television that emphasize violence, openly pornographic motion pictures, day time, confession magazines, crime comics, suggestive music, or other content that has been widely held to contribute to a lowering of taste, disruption of morals, or stimulation toward socially unacceptable conduct. Whether or not such charges are true.

Non-debated Content: This would be media content, widely distributed and attended to, about which media critics have said very little. It is not an issue in the debate over the impact of the media on the masses. Examples would be television weather reports, some news content, music that is neither symphonic nor popular, magazines devoted to specialized interests, motion pictures using "wholesome" themes, and many others. Such content is not believed either to elevate or lower taste, and it is not seen as a threat to moral standards.

High-taste Content: This would be media content sometimes widely distributed but not necessarily widely attended to. It is content that media critics feel is in better taste, morally uplifting, educational, or in some way inspiring. Examples would be serious music, sophisticated drama, political discussions, art films, or magazines devoted to political commentary. Such content is championed by critics as the opposite of the low-taste material, which they see as distinctly objectionable.

Of course, the first of the above categories is the one to which we wish to direct most of our attention. It is the repetitive phenomenon whose contribution to the media (as a social system) needs analysis. Nevertheless, it would also be possible to study the other two categories with somewhat parallel perspectives, but this will receive relatively little attention in the present discussion.

We need now to begin to identify the components and boundaries of the social system within which low-taste content occurs so that eventually the contribution it makes to the system can be inductively hypothesized.

Rather than develop a purely descriptively scheme that will apply only to a single medium, it will be more fruitful to attempt to develop a general conceptual scheme into which any or all media could be placed, with suitable minor modifications in details. Such a general scheme will emphasize the similarities between media, particularly in terms of relationships between the components in the system.

Audiences: The first major component of the social system of mass communication is the audience. This is an exceedingly complex component. The audience is stratified, differentiated, and interrelated in the many ways that social scientists have studied for years. Some of the major variables that play a part in determining how this component will operate within the system are the major needs and interests of audience members, the various social categories represented in an audience, and the nature of the social relationships between audience members. These variables point to behavioural mechanisms that determine the patterns of attention, interpretation, and response of an audience with respect to content of a given type.

Research Organisations: The rough typology of content suggested is in some degree related to the characteristics of the audience. Organizations devoted to research, to measuring the performances of media audiences, or to various forms of market research provide information to those responsible for selecting the categories of content that will be distributed to the audience. There is a link, then, between the audience as a component in the system and the market research-rating service organizations as a second component. In purely theoretical terms, both components are role system themselves and are thus actually subsystems. This is in a sense a one-way link. For very minor (or usually no) personal reward, audience members selected for study provide data about themselves to such an agency, but very little flows back. This linkage between components is by comparison relatively simple.

Distributors: The content itself, of whatever type, flows from some distributor to the audience. The role system of the distributor component varies in detail from one medium to another. In addition, several somewhat distinct subsystems exist within this general component. First, there are local outlets, which are likely to be in the most immediate contact with the audience. The local newspaper, the local theatre, the local broadcasting station play the most immediate part in placing messages before their respective audiences. But inseparably tied to them are other subsystems of this general component. Newspaper syndicates, broadcasting networks, or chains of movie theatres pass content on to their local outlets. The link between these two subsystems is a two-way one. The local outlet provides money, and the larger distributor supplies content. Or the link age may be that the local outlet provides a service, and the distributor (who is paid elsewhere) provides money.

The relationship between audience and distributor seems at first to be mostly a one-way link. The distributor provides entertainment content (and often advertising), but the audience provides little back in a direct sense. However, it does provide its attention. In fact, it is precisely the attention of the audience that distributors are attempting to solicit. They sell this "commodity" directly to their financial backer or sponsor. In addition, the audience supplies information to the research component and this is indirectly supplied to distributors in the form of feedback so that they may gauge the amount of attention they are eliciting. The linkages between components grow more complex as we seek the boundaries of the system.

Producers and their Sponsors: To the audience, the research, and the distributing component, we may add the role system of the producer of content. This component's primary link is with the financial backer (or sponsor) component and with the distributor, from whom money is obtained and for whom various forms of entertainment content are manufactured. A host of subsystems are included in this producer component, depending upon the particular medium. Examples are actors, directors, television producers, technicians, foreign correspondents, wire-service editors, film producers, labour union leaders, publishers, copyeditors, clerical staff, and many many more.

Advertising Agencies: Linking the sponsor, distributor, producer, and research organization are the advertising agencies. Paid primarily by the sponsor, this component provides (in return) certain ideas and services. For the most part, it provides the distributor with advertising messages. It may have links with the research component as well.

Subsystems of Control: Over this complex set of interrelated components, there are other subsystems that exert control. The legislative bodies, at both the state and national level, which enact regulative statutes concerning the media, constitute an important part of such a control component. Another important part of this role subsystem is the official regulative agencies, which implement the policies that have been legislated. The link between the legislative body (control component) and the audience is, course, one of votes and public opinion, to which the component is presumably sensitive and dependent. Information lines between audience, legislative bodies, and regulatory agencies are more or less open. To the regulatory components whose role definitions are found in legal statute can be added the private voluntary associations that develop "codes" and to some degree serve as a control over the distributors. Such distributors provide them with money, and they in turn provide surveillance and other services.

The regulatory subsystems draw definitions of permissible and non-permissible content from the general set of external conditions within which this extremely complicated system operates. Surrounding the entire structure as an external condition are our society's general norms concerning morality, and the expressions that these find in formal law. Similar, although less likely to be incorporated into law, are our general cultural norms and beliefs regarding what will be likely to entertain or otherwise gratify Americans. Thus, we seldom see traditional Chinese opera but frequently see western horse opera. We seldom hear the strains of Hindu temple music but frequently hear the "strains" and other noises of the latest singer whom teenagers admire. If our interests run to more serious fare, we are likely to hear the music of a relatively small list of European or American composers who created their works within a span of about three centuries. Or we are likely to view ballet, opera, drama, and so on, of a fairly limited of artists whose products are defined by our society as classics or as innovative new approaches.

Each of the several media will fit into this general model of a social system in slightly different ways. A complete description of each of the media separately would be tedious. Indeed, each could well occupy the contents of an entire book. Two decades ago, Opotowsky attempted just such a detailed analysis of the television industry, although he did not use the social system concept.

To add to the complexity of this conceptual scheme, it must be remembered that although each medium constitutes a somewhat separate social system in itself, the media are also related to one another in systematic ways. Thus, we may speak of the entire set of communication media, including those which have not been specifically analysed in the present volume, as the mass communication system of the United States.

The structure of this mass communication system has been heavily influenced by the general social, political, economic, and cultural conditions that were current during the period when our mass media were developing and remain as important socio-cultural forces in the society within which they operate. Because of their importance for understanding our mass media as they are today. Our free enterprise beliefs, our views of the legitimacy of the profit motive, the virtues of controlled capitalism, and our general values concerning freedom of speech constitute further external conditions (in addition to those related to moral limits and cultural tastes) within which the American mass communication system operates.

The Power

Within the system itself, the principal internal condition is, of course, a financial one. Most of the components in the system are occupational role structures, which motivate their incumbent personnel primarily through money. To obtain money, they are all ultimately dependent upon the most central component of all the audience. Unless its decisions to give attention, to purchase, to vote, and the like, are made in favourable ways, the system would undergo service strain and would eventually collapse. Almost any dramatic change in the behaviour of the audience would cause the most severe disruption in the system for any given medium. The consequences of attention loss to the motion picture theatre as a mass medium was shown to be severe.

Such disruptions are infrequent, buy they do occur. The key to heading off dramatic changes in audience behaviour, of course, is to provide entertainment content that will satisfy and motivate the largest possible number of audience members to carry out their roles in accord with the needs of the system. Such content will, in other words, maintain the stability of the system. The ideal, from the standpoint of the system, is content that will capture audience members' attention, persuade them to purchase goods, and at the same time be sufficiently within the bounds of moral norms and standards are not provoked.

The entertainment content that seems most capable of eliciting the attention of the largest number of audience members is the more dramatic, low-taste content. Since the most central media system goal is economic profit, sex and violence or any other attention-getting and attention-maintaining content is functional in the sense that even though it may be of low-taste, it maximizes the size of the audience exposed to advertisements. In general, the larger the audience, the more the distributor and producer can charge for advertising. For example, ads in prime-time television periods cost substantially more than those aired during relatively low-audience-size periods, such as early in the morning. The assumption made by many media personnel and advertisers that low-taste content appeals primarily to the relatively uneducated, who still constitute a majority of the potential audience, may be false. In an early study Wilensky found that educated people said that they preferred and exposed themselves to high-taste content more often than did the relatively uneducated. But when observations were made of what the educated and educated actually aid, there was little difference between their levels of exposure to low-taste media content.

There is a great deal of evidence to show that the relatively uneducated spend more time than the educated being exposed to the mass media. It may be misleading to conclude that they do so only because the uneducated relish low-taste content. The relatively uneducated majority also have relatively low incomes, which probably means they have less choice than their more educated and wealthier counterparts in how they spend their non-working hours. The mass media may be more appealing to the relatively uneducated and poor in large part because the media are relatively inexpensive forms of leisure. Moreover, as Baker and Ball point out, it is probably superficial to think that the only reason people in general spend time with the media is because of the inherent appeal of their content. Any number of need-fulfilments and gratifications, over and above those related to entertainment or staying informed, are provided by the media. Babysitting and companionship (even when it is electronic companionship) are examples.

When all is said and done, however, it is still true that low-taste content sells and sells big. This fact establishes it as the key element in the social system of the media. It keeps the entire complex together by maintaining the financial stability of the system. Critics who provoke public attention by denouncing media content or by proclaiming that a casual connection exists between media content and socially undesirable behaviour may temporarily receive some recognition, they may also achieve some temporary disturbance in the system, or if they are persistent enough, they may ultimately even displace some specific from of low-taste content from a given medium altogether. Examples from the past are quiz shows that were found to be "rigged," and popular disc jockeys who were receiving "payola" (a fee for repeatedly playing a song to make it popular). In such cases the audience may be temporarily disaffected, low-taste content comes in such a variety of forms that the temporary or even permanent absence of one minor form does not alter the major picture. Critics have been complaining about newspaper concentration on crime news for a century, yet there has been no noticeable abatement in the reporting of such stories. Critics of the soap opera may have breathed a sigh of relief several years ago when these programs at last disappeared from radio. Their joy must have been short-lived when such daytime serials turned out to be quite popular with television viewers, so popular in fact that soap operas now appear during prime evening hours. Analyses of the level of violent television content show that it goes down slightly after federal government investigations on the effects of television violence or widespread campaigns by voluntary associations (e.g., the P.T.A.), only to return shortly after the public outcry has subsided.

When a formula is discovered for eliciting attention and influencing purchasing decisions from any large segment of the audience, it will be abandoned by the media only with great reluctance, if at all. The broadcast ballgame, the war movie, the star comedian, the family situation comedy, the western thriller, the detective story, the adventures of the secret agent, the drama of the courtroom-all are beginning to rank with such time-honoured formulas as the sob story, the funnies, the sex-murder account, the sports page, and disclosure of corruption in high places as attention-getting devices that can bring the eye or ear of the consumer nearer to the advertising message.

In short, the social system of the mass media in the United States is becoming more and more deeply established. Some future change can be expected in the kind of content it will produce to maintain its own stability. At present, however, the function of what we have called low-taste content is to maintain the financial stability of a deeply institutionalized social system that is tightly integrated with the whole of the American economic institution. The probability that our system of mass communication in this respect can be drastically altered by the occasional outbursts of critics seems small indeed.

Far more likely than media system change brought about by periodic attacks on low-taste media content is media system change brought about by trends in the economic system such as the emergence of a "post-industrial" society. Because the media system is also a subsystem in the larger economic system, it will have to adapt to such changes if it is to survive. If Bell's forecast that systems in the business of producing, processing, and transmitting information will become increasingly involved in key economic sectors of our society is valid, then we would expect significant changes in the nature of the mass media system. One change would surely be a marked increase in the knowledge and technical information of "non-debated" media content will rise sharply with a corresponding decline in low-taste media content.

But as is usually the case when talking about changes in social systems, such future developments in the nature of the mass media are not likely to by that simple. Recall Durkheim's basic principle that as organisms or systems grow, they are likely to become more differentiated or complex. Taking this assumption and combining it with the enormous technological advances in electronic communications technology witnessed in recent years, it may be hypothesized that media systems will become more specialized. Some media organizations, for example, might specialize in low-taste content, others in knowledge and technical information, others in news content, and still others in high-taste content. Such technological developments as closed-circuit and cable television already are making such specialization possible.

4

Basic Concepts

Guidelines for Press : In an annexure, listing guidelines on the right to privacy, the Council pointed out that the Indian Constitution does not expressly declare any right to privacy unlike certain global instruments to which India is a signatory, like the human rights charter. Even so, there is a school of thought which holds the view that the right to privacy is a fundamental right emanating from Article 21.

According to the Press Council, the law of defamation covers certain limited aspects of privacy. Certain countries have, therefore, enacted privacy laws which go beyond the range of defamation or reputation to protect personal interest, grief and the personality or psyche of the individual.

The guidelines laid down by the Council specify that for journalists writing about people in terms of human interest, the litmus test must be in public interest—the person being a public person by some reasonable definition (politician, sportsman, scientist or anyone in the public eye by virtue of his position, achievements or notoriety) and a person whose actions fall within the domain of public interest, as an example or warning to others. Even then, the publication must be justified by the legitimate public interest, not a prurient or morbid curiosity.

The personal and family or social life of a public figure or one who adopts a position of moral leadership can legitimately be open to public scrutiny where the private conduct can adversely affect or influence the proper discharge of his/her public functions and he/she may be setting a bad example where seen as a role model by others.

Any private activity liable to result in the commission, of a crime or result in evasion of criminal liability or in seriously antisocial conduct may also be legitimately exposed in the public interest.

While all individuals are equal, certain vulnerable categories like children, women, the aged, the mentally retarded or handicapped and the sick require added protection.

Rapes and molestation of women, sexual abuse of children etc. are fit cases where privacy should be respected and the identity, photographs or sordid details of the offence should not be publicised to those unconcerned with law enforcement or with administrative jurisdiction in the matter.

A discharged convict has a right to a fresh start in building his/her life anew. It would be an invasion of privacy to recall his/her earlier crime to damn a redeemed criminal in the absence of any public interest consideration.

It would also be an invasion of privacy to name the family or associates of a wrongdoer when they are totally innocent of the crime and no public interest is involved. Suggestive guilt by association would be unfair to the privacy of others.

Even in cases where the reports are legitimate and proper, but the means by which the information has been gained entails an unwarranted intrusion into the privacy of an individual, such reporting is to be eschewed. Such intrusive reporting may be by gate-crashing into a home or hospital room unnoticed to write about an accident or illness, or publishing casual conversation overheard or something told in confidence or in a privileged gathering.

Interception of mail, phone tapping, bugging, photographing people in their homes without their consent or by using telephoto lenses would be invasion of privacy. Breach of fair practice by one journal would not justify publication by another.

The Times of India published the regret on September 27,1991 with the following note from the Editor :

> 'The Press Council has directed this paper to publish the gist of its decision of how the murder of the two nuns in Bombay in November 1990 was reported and has asked us to express our regret, which we now are doing. We are deeply sorry if our report has hurt the sentiments of a section of our readers. However, in the light of the Press Council's findings, we will now review several issues of journalistic ethics which this case has given rise to — Editor.

The Illustrated Weekly of India in its issue dated May 18, 1986, carried an article by its correspondent S.M. Abdi entitled, 'Shocking: The strange escapades of J.B. Patnaik' (Orissa Chief Minister). It dealt with deviant sexual life of the Chief Minister.

This article was followed by another captioned: 'Why is J.B. being allowed to gag the Press? The second supported the first. The first article carried photostats of FIR of complaints against Patnaik. Soon after it was published, Patnaik filed a suit for damages of Rs 1 crore against The Illustrated Weekly of India.

In the suit filed in the Orissa High-Court, Patnaik asked for details about the documents, source of information from the writer of the article and the editor and publisher of the Weekly.

Even as the case was pending in the High Court, the editor and the publisher moved the Supreme Court against the order of the lower court arguing that the application for better particulars etc. amounted to seek disclosure of evidence which was not permissible under Order 6 of the Civil Procedure Code and no journalist could be forced to disclose his source of information.

Advocates for the petitioners also submitted that what was before the court was a libel suit and if anyone of the objection raised was proved, the suit would be decreed.

It is strange that this landmark in journalism should be attributed to The Illustrated Weekly of India. Magazine journalism came of age in India primarily due to this journal. Under Khushwant Singh's editorship in early seventies, the Weekly gained unprecedented heights. Magazine reports had never before been taken so seriously. Also the magazine had never sold so well. The seeds of the magazine revolution, which swept India in the late seventies and the early eighties, were sown in the offices of the Weekly.

It was the Weekly success story which led to the launching of Sunday and India Today in mid-seventies.

It was the first magazine to send its young reporters for field assignments. Investigative reports and human interest stories became the byword for magazine journalism.

As described earlier, the events of 1977 and the subsequent developments saw magazines emerge as a dominant force on the Indian media scene. Indepth reports and investigative stories became the preserve of the magazine. The dominance of the magazines over newspapers continued till mid-80s.

By mid-80s, the newspapers had begun to overtake the magazines in the field of indepth and investigative reporting. Sunday editor M.J. Akbar, who emerged on top of the scene after starting as a brilliant reporter for the Weekly under Khushwant Singh, started concentrating on daily newspapers. Slowly the glamour days of the magazines faded out.

With the sole exception of India Today, which showed a steady upward trend in its circulation figures, magazines by and large suffered considerable loss in circulation. It is said the Weekly story on Patnaik came at this juncture. It started publishing a number of sensational stories, each accompanied with a mark of exclamation.

Soon after the story about Patnaik appeared, Patnaik brought the full force of his office to harass and humiliate Pritish Nandy. He was arrested and interrogated. He was made to appear before the courts time and again and barring a brave but solitary exception, even senior lawyers of the state were reluctant to come to Nandy's help. All those who had filed affidavits against Patnaik retracted.

The Weekly maintained the posture that it had committed no wrong, in fact, done public service by exposing a chief minister who had been using his office for purposes other than administration.

After three years of legal battle, The Weekly's will wilted. It agreed before the Supreme Court to tender an apology to the chief minister. The text of the apology was filed before the apex court, and sealed till it was published by The Weekly.

The apology was published by The Weekly in its issue dated August 27 to September 2, 1989. It ran as follows:

> We Bennett, Coleman and Company Ltd., Pritish Nandy, Editor of The Illustrated Weekly and S.N.M. Abdi, special correspondent of The Illustrated Weekly, had published two articles

> under the captions, 'The strange escapades of JB Patnaik' and 'Why is J.B. Patnaik being allowed to gag the Press,' in the issues dated 18-24 May 1986 and 3-9 August 1986 respectively, based on information available to us. Subsequently, we found that the information on the basis of which these articles were written was not true and was politically motivated. We regret the damage done to Mr. Patnaik's reputation and offer our apologies to him.

Commenting on the Weekly-Patnaik episodes, Khushwant Singh said that he would never have published this kind of an article. He said he had the same kind of material sent to him, when he was the editor of the Weekly, by a senior member of the IAS. It was accompanied with documentary proof as well as a confidential report of the services tribunal which had recommended his dismissal. But he refused to publish it. He said his view was that a person's private life should be his own. A public figure's private life could only be exposed if there was a clear evidence of misuse of power.

An eminent freelance journalist Nikhil Chakravarty said that an apology did not add to the credit of any newspaper or journalist. Therefore, before writing a story, we should exercise a sense of responsibility not only in relation to the question of privacy but on any other issue. He said 'my point about this particular case is that it should not have dragged on for three years. When the case was launched then if those who were responsible for the story found that it could not be substantiated, then they should immediately have moved up and issued a contradiction.

The question of code of conduct has been hanging fire for decades. If you want to have a code of conduct for journalists you cannot have it in isolation from the code of conduct for politicians or public life as a whole. Even if one were to have a code of conduct it will be very difficult to enforce.' *Navbharat Times* Editor Rajendra Mathur said that first it was difficult to prove a case like this when the allegations were made against the chief minister in his home state. Second, there was the question of expenses because the case could go on and on and Bennett and Coleman could not fight these cases in a very pedestrian way.

He thought what could have been awarded as damages if Patnaik had won, half of it or perhaps two-thirds would have been spent in litigating the case. All this might have influenced the decision to apologise.

Inderjit, editor, INFA said: 'When a publication like *The Illustrated Weekly* carried a cover story on Patnaik, I was little shocked. Having been associated with *The Times of India* group for almost ten years, these are not the kind of cover stories one normally carried. I felt that the editor of the paper would have good reason and solid facts to back up the story. Now that he has agreed to apologise I do think that the facts could not back up the story. Therefore, I am a little distressed by this development. It was not in keeping with the character of *The Times* Group. It was scurrilous and highly defamatory.

It is possible as some people suggested that it was not easy to get the required evidence, it was also suggested that people in Orissa were afraid of the consequences, it was also suggested that people who had given sworn affidavits had resiled, but these are the hazards of our profession and all these factors should have been taken into consideration before publishing the story.....'

The Times of India Editor Dilip Padgaonkar offered the following comments:

> '. . .I would say, as a rule, a public official had a right to privacy, but if that privacy is explored without malice for public good, the Press should be allowed to do so. In this particular case, the

> article is not the kind I would have published in *The Times of India,* but if the editor thought it necessary to expose certain aspects of private life of the public official concerned I would have given him the benefit of doubt because the person in power and authority has a far greater room for manoeuvre to get things done to bring subtle or harsh pressures to promote his interests.
>
> I may not agree with the decision of the editor to offer to apologise, but I understand why it was done. If you are going to enter into a very hazy legalistic area and if at the end of it all there would be no victors of any kind then why go into it? This can be one line of argument. I have known people who have filed suits because of intrusion into their privacy and then they find that if they submit themselves to interrogation, then there will be worse defamation.. .not many people want to subject themselves to this.
>
> . . .principles are involved and my hope was that certain professional bodies such as the Editors Guild would take up this matter. I certainly intend to do so because if this becomes a precedent—an out-of-court settlement of this kind—then I am afraid that sooner or later—sooner rather than later—we might end up by curtailing an important area of Press freedom.'

It is worthwhile comparing what happened in Goa in September 1989. Goa Legislative Assembly Speaker Dayanand Ganesh Narvekar, allegedly molested a clerk, Sumita Holdankar. The matter leaked out. Credence was given to it by a political opponent, the leader of the Maharashtra Gomantak Party, Mr. Ramakant Khalap. The latter insisted that the story of molestation was true and that if it was proved to be false, he would quit politics.

The matter was taken up by Goa's English paper, *Gomantak Times.* The paper demanded the resignation of Narvekar. The daily reflected popular sentiment for soon the cry was taken up by others as well.

It is not that efforts were not made by interested parties to silence Sumita. *Gomantak Times* published stories of how attempts were made to buy Sumita Holdankar's silence. Someone, apparently, gave her Rs 11,000 to buy jewellery. *Gomantak Times* published photostats of bills. Sumita still has to explain how she was bribed.

Demands for Narvekar's resignation gathered momentum. The Gomantak Kshatriya Marathis Samaj, which comprises people belonging to the Kharvi and Pagi communities and of which Dayanand Ganesh Narvekar is a member, launched a strong attack on him. Over 6,000 young people from all over Goa converged on Panaji, the capital, to demand Narvekar's resignation.

The protest rally convened by the Students Action Front was addressed by Sumita who braved the wrath of the Speaker. Subsequently, Narvekar resigned.

But in the case of *The Illustrated Weekly* none among the journalist's community came out openly to support it. The key witness disappeared or refused to give evidence against Patnaik. The lawyers in Orissa, with the sole exception of one Ranjit Mohanty were not prepared to take up this case because of the fear of retribution from the Chief Minister.

There might be few politicians whose personal lives are completely above board. The U.K. Prime Minister Harold Macmillan's life was in a mess with his wife Dorothy carrying on for years with another man; so was Lloyd George, US President Franklin Delano Roosevelt, had an affair with a friend of his wife, Eleanor.

S. Gopal, son of India's President S. Radhakrishnan, has

written about his father's liaisons and the affair of Jawaharlal Nehru with Lady Mountbatten has been talked about for years now with everyone from Mountbatten's official biographer Phillip Ziegly down to others less knowledgeable trying to put a kind face on the subject. Only Nehru's personal secretary, late M.O. Mathai, had the temerity to suggest that the emperor had no clothes. But the important thing about these happenings i& that they never arose during the life time of these individuals.

The scandal involving Christine Keeler (U.K. Society girl) and former UK Minister John Profumo is an extreme case. John Profumo had to resign not because he was carrying on with Christine Keeler, but because Keeler also had a Soviet Official as a friend to whom it was suspected, she might' have passed on secrets. Profumo had to quit in public interest.

It is doubtless that the life style of a public official has a tremendous bearing on the administration, but this can be exposed only if it is in public interest to do so.

It is also true that in India, unlike in the West, the public officials do not lead a distinct private and public life. It is invariably mixed up. This, perhaps, requires a close tab on them.

Taking into account the increasing tendency to publish defamatory news in the newspapers and magazines there is a need to strengthen defamation laws in the country. The Press Council indictment of newspapers publishing defamatory news is not a sufficient deterrent to prevent such publications. The Editors Guild and other Press associations should ponder over this problem and suggest steps for self-regulation.

But the move on the part of the Rajiv government to pass Defamation Bill was to gag the Press and stop it from exposing misdeeds of public men.

Defamatory Issue

The idea to enact the Defamation Bill was conceived by the government sometimes in early 1987. It was around this time that media exposures on Bofors, Reliance Industries, and Ajitabh Bachchan's alleged purchase of flat in Switzerland surfaced.

The immediate provocation was the revelations involving Lalit Suri allegedly getting a Rupees Six Crore commission from a Japanese firm on a pipeline deal. This story was carried by *The Statesman.*

On August 29, 1988, the Lok Sabha passed the Defamation Bill putting unprecedented curbs on the freedom of the Press in the post-Independence era, barring the Emergency period. The Bill sought to bring the following changes in the old law.

Old Law

(1) Prima facie onus of proving defamation with the complainant.

(2) Defamation cases to be tried in the judicial magistrate's court.

(3) No deadline for clearing the case.

(4) No minimum imprisonment.

(5) Matters termed grossly indecent, scurrilous and intended for blackmail not covered by law.

(6) No penalty for criminal imputation.

(7) Ten grounds to prove innocence including publication in good faith.

(8) Government departments treated on par with others.

(9) No pre-trial penalty.

(10) Specific exemption from personal appearance.

(11) No provision for summary trial.

New Law

(1) Entire onus of proving innocence on the accused. The prosecution would have the right to lead evidence in rebuttal.

(2) The cases to go directly to the second stage Sessions Court.

(3) 90-day limit for the final judgement.

(4) Minimum imprisonment of one month on first offence, three months to five for subsequent offence. The imprisonment could be up to five years for subsequent offences.

(5) All these terms ware included in the Bill without specific definitions, making it possible to twist their meanings to support trumped up charges. The bill created a new offence of publication of grossly indecent or scurrilous matter intended for blackmailing. The terms grossly indecent or scurrilous were not defined. The bill explained that it was not scurrilous to make true imputations against any person provided it was for the public good, but the fact that it was good for the public had to be proved by the accused.

(6) Criminal imputation was made an offence.

(7) No ground to prove innocence in the case of criminal imputation.

(8) No exemption at all. The editor, printer and publisher to be personally present at every hearing of the case which would proceed on a day-to-day basis.

(9) Provision for summary trial and the proceedings to be held in camera.

The bill was rushed through and passed in a matter of nine-hour acrimonious debate in the Lok Sabha which resulted in the opposition walkout. The government did not bother to consult any professional body of the journalists during the time of the formulation of the bill.

The Home Ministry proposed a policy paper on the Defamation Bill. The then Home Minister Chidambaram played an active role in its drafting and instead of sending the paper to the Cabinet for approval, it was directly sent to legislative wing of the Law Ministry. In mid 1987 when the furore over defence scandals such as Bofors and HDW deals was at its peak, the Home Ministry approached the Cabinet with a comprehensive Bill. The Cabinet appointed an 8-member group of ministers including P. Shiv Shankar, Vasant Sathe, H.K.L. Bhagat, Chidambaram and H.R. Bhardwaj, with Home Minister Buta Singh as its Chairman. The group met at least 20 times to finalise the bill. The final approval was given on August 8,1988.

The Bill evoked angry reaction from the journalists, constitutional experts and lawyers. It soon snowballed into a nationwide agitation.

On September 5, 1988 in an unprecedented show of unity, various sections of the Press from all over the country came together at a rally in Delhi against the proposed Defamation Bill. The journalists were joined in the rally by proprietors, freelancers and press workers. The 800-strong protestors marched down India Gate to Boat Club carrying placards.

Among the prominent personalities present at the rally were Ram Nath Goenka, Proprietor of *Indian Express,* Mr. Rajaji Rao, editor and proprietor of *Eenadu* (A.P.), Mr. Girilal Jain, former Editor, *The Times of India,* Mr. C.R. Irani, Managing Director, *The Statesman,* Mr. Arun Shourie, editor, *The Indian Express,* Mr. N. Ram, Associate Editor, *The Hindu,* Mr. Prem Bhatia former editor, *The Tribune,* Mr. M.J. Akbar, editor, *The Telegraph,* Mr. Aroon Purie, editor and proprietor *India Today,* Mr. Khushwant Singh, Mr. Kuldip Nayar, Ms Amita Malik, Mr. Gour Kishore Ghose, veteran journalist from Calcutta and winner of Magsaysay award, Mr. S. Nihal Singh, former editor of *The Indian Post* and *The Statesman.*

Mr. Ramkrishna Hegde and Mr. Biju Patnaik, also put in an appearance to express solidarity with the journalists.

With the exception of the English daily, *The National Herald* and its Urdu counterpart *Qaumi Awaj* all newspapers and news agencies observed a day's token strike on September 6 as part of the protest at the proposed Defamation Bill. On September 11, seven thousand lawyers practicing in various courts in Delhi, except the Supreme Court abstained from work against the Defamation Bill.

While expressing their solidarity with the agitated journalists, lawyers also warned the government against undue delay in withdrawing, what they said, the draconian Bill which was said to be the worst statutory aggression and onslaught on the freedom of speech and expression.

In pursuit of their struggle against the Defamation Bill, newsmen on September 7 walked out of a Press Conference being addressed by Union Minister for Information and Broadcasting and Parliamentary Affairs H.K.L. Bhagat.

Bhagat's plea that the government was prepared to reconsider all aspects of the Bill could not satisfy the journalists who maintained that they could not offer any cooperation on the issue with the sword of Damocles hanging over their heads.

On September 8, the entire Pune Press and the correspondents of Bombay newspapers boycotted the felicitation of Congress Secretary and barrister V. N. Gadgil. The latter was to be felicitated by Maharashtra Chief Minister Sharad Pawar on his first visit to the city after becoming Congress (I) General Secretary.

To meet out this threat from the journalists, the government worked out a strategy. Meetings were arranged with senior journalists known to be pro-Rajiv, but most of these journalists advised the government against the enactment of the Bill. Rajiv's media managers then tried to create rift among journalists by inviting some of them on the television.

Later, Bhagat wrote personal letters to journalists, inviting them for a dialogue with a 7-member committee constituted by the Prime Minister. But to the government's surprise, all the organisations, except three which are pronouncedly pro-Congress-I rejected the invitation.

Faced with this situation, Prime Minister Rajiv Gandhi and his advisers desperately tried to evolve a face-saving formula.

Shortly after his return from Punjab on September 21, 1988, Rajiv Gandhi summoned the ministerial group for a discussion at his residence. The meeting lasted for over three hours and Rajiv decided to withdraw the Bill.

On September 22, 1988, Rajiv Gandhi announced the Defamation Bill's withdrawal with the following statement.

The Defamation Bill, 1988 was brought forward to protect the individual from defamatory speeches, writings and actions and to provide adequate and timely redress to the aggrieved. The Bill seeks to codify the existing law on the subject and to take it forward in some areas.

Defamation as defined in the Bill is not an issue between government and the Press but an issue between individual and individual, between a person aggrieved and a person accused. The Bill attempts to reconcile the rights of an individual with the right to freedom of expression of another.

A free Press is an integral part of the inner strength and dynamism of our democracy. Without a free Press, there can be no democracy. The imperishable values of our freedom struggle have gone into the making of the Press in India.

We uphold this legacy. We shall continue to do so. Our commitment to this freedom of the Press is total. We have no intention of curbing in any way, the freedom of the Press.

The freedom and rights of the individual are equally sacred. It is this that makes the issue of defamation a serious issue. The bill seeks to resolve the issue in accordance with the basic principles of our Constitution and the laws. It has, however, aroused misapprehensions and misgivings. The Press and section of the public have expressed their concern.

We are alive to these concerns. We draw inspiration from Mahatma Gandhi, Jawaharlal Nehru and Indira Gandhi, who always responded to democratic expression of opinion. We, therefore, offered an unconditional dialogue on the subject. Some organisations and individuals have responded to this offer.

We feel, however, that there should be wider and fuller national debate in keeping with our heritage and traditions.

The issue of defamation remains. It is our earnest hope that the concerned citizens, jurists and media will participate in the national debate on the issue of defamation. In course of time, government may, if necessary, make suitable forum to carry forward the dialogue in a spirit of understanding and cooperation. A solution based on national consensus will strengthen the institutions of our public.

The Central Government has made every effort to manage the Press after managing the other two organs of the government successfully—the Parliament and the judiciary. The Press by and large in India is pro-establishment. Even then the government is not satisfied and wants to choke a few discordant voices in the Press. The passage of this Bill would have scared the Press to do whatever little investigative reporting they are doing. In fact, there was no need to enact such laws if the Press Council in India is adequate to deal with defamation cases.

It is worthwhile examining the laws pertaining to the freedom of the Press and the right to privacy.

The mechanisms that have been evolved in truly democratic countries for achieving the above objectives are generally twofold. One is to make defamation a crime punishable with imprisonment or fine or both. The other is an action in the courts of law for the Tort of defamation in which damages can be awarded.

It is well known that in countries that have followed the civil law system, like France, have favoured the system of subjecting the defendant or respondent to penal punishment.

In those countries where the Anglo-Saxon system of jurisprudence prevails, like the United Kingdom, the USA, Australia and India, there are provisions for imposing penal punishment and/or claiming damages in civil courts.

Although criminal action can be taken in Britain, this is done in very few cases. In the UK there was some thinking whether the law of criminal libel should be drastically reformed and whether a new statutory offence of criminal defamation should replace the old offence.

It was proposed that the offence should be triable only on indictment and the penalty should not exceed two years imprisonment or a fine or both.

In fact, the British Law Commission had made it clear in its report that the offence which it had in mind is the character assassination type. When the Faulk Committee in England considered defamation in 1971, the British Press Council was of the view that criminal libel would have no relevance so far as the Press was concerned.

In the US one hardly comes across any instances where penal punishment has been awarded in defamation cases. But in civil actions the damages that are granted are so heavy that every newspaper has to think twice before publishing a libellous article.

Any student of the law of defamation has to understand its basic object and aim. The question immediately arises as to when interference with an individual liberty can be allowed.

The answer given is that such interference would be permissible when the individual actions cause harm to other members of the society. What kind of harm should the law then punish. As defamation deals with harm, it is necessary for the person who has published a defamation matter to justify the publication by invoking the fundamental right of freedom of expression which would include freedom of the Press as guaranteed by Article 19 (a) of our Constitution.

This raised the point that if something has been done for public good or in public interest or its truthfulness established, the harm to reputation of the person defamed should not attract any such consequences as may be penal or may involve payment of damages.

These as regarded as some of the basis of the defamation laws.

In the US, the decision of the US Supreme Court in *The New York Times*—Sullivan case (1964) has brought about revolutionary changes, especially in cases of action against public officials. In Sullivan case, the court ruled that even erroneous statements about public officials were protected by the constitutional mandate unless a libellous statement had been published with full knowledge of falsity or reckless disregard or its truthfulness.

In Australia, the position seems to be similar to that in the US where if one is wise one would make sure that all assets are in somebody else's name. For if one wants to discuss anything which is even slightly controversial, however small one is, one will be sued for defamation and one will be out of business or bankrupt within months.

Indeed it would not be wrong to say that criminal libel is becoming outmoded in defamation laws even in those developed countries where freedom and privacy of the individual are zealously guarded and highly prized rights.

In most of the countries the right of an individual to privacy has been recognised and it has close connection with defamation. Although privacy has been defined in the US, the best definition appears to be the one given by Thomas Colley. Privacy has not been recognised as a Tort either in India or Britain.

The Second Press Commission in India did not recommend any legislation on the subject. The Commission considered that Section 13 (l) (c) of the Press Council Act, 1978 should be amended by adding the words 'including respect for privacy.'

In our country, any law of defamation has in the first place to pass the test of constitutionality. Article 19 (1) of the Constitution confers on every citizen the fundamental right to freedom of speech and expression.

The Supreme Court has left no one in doubt that freedom of the Press is included in the above provision. The ambit and the scope of the provision is no less wide than what has been conferred by the First amendment to the American Constitution.

Clause 2 of Article 19 indicates the parameters of the right guaranteed under clause (1). Thus, existing or future laws can be made imposing reasonable restrictions on the exercise of the right in the interest set in clause (2) which includes defamation.

One of the most important steps taken for the purpose of preserving the freedom of the Press and of maintaining and improving the standards of newspapers and news agencies was the establishment of the Press Council in 1966 by an Act of Parliament. The Act was repealed in 1976 and there was no Press Council in existence till the end of March 1979.

Our Press Council being a statutory body derives its powers from an Act of Parliament. It has 28 members and a chairman. It is completely independent and the manner in which its chairman and members are nominated is such that no executive or outside interference is possible.

Global Trends

In France the law relating to privacy has been developed largely through interpretation of Article 1382 of the Civil Code of 1859 by the courts on case-by-case basis. There was a spurt in this process during the fifth and sixth decades of the twentieth century as a response to the increasing invasions of personal privacy by the Press. The principles thus evolved, by courts, were embodied in the Law of July 17, 1970. Article 9 of this codified law provides that 'each person has the right to have his privacy respected'.

The law of 1970 does not provide a general definition of 'privacy'. This has been left to be spelled out by the courts. In general, family, personal, and sexual matters are all covered by the right of privacy. 'Public interest', 'good faith', and 'truth' do not in themselves, furnish a good defence in an action for violation of privacy.

In Germany, the Penal Code punishes, as criminal offences, certain grosser invasions of privacy, namely:

(a) trespassing into another person's home, and in certain other private places;

(b) recording private conversation without permission;

(c) eavesdropping using bugging devices;

(d) obtaining certain private information (such as medical records) without permission, and

(e) obtaining any private information which is stored in a computer.

To the above, there are certain exceptions, e.g., pictures within the scope of contemporary history; pictures of public processions, and pictures created for genuinely artistic purposes.

German Civil Courts have, through an interpretation of the Constitution, devised the concept of the 'right of human personality'. Pursuant to this concept, the courts provide a civil remedy in actions for defamation and invasion of privacy in a number of situations, which include:

(i) Where a newspaper publishes inaccurate personal infirmation about a person and then refuses to correct it;

(ii) Where one person makes use of another's picture without his consent in order to advertise the products; and

(iii) Where someone publishes the past misdeeds of an ex-offender, where it is not in the public interest to do so.

Like Denmark, in the Netherlands, apart from defamation, a number of invasions of privacy are criminal offences. These include: trespass into another person's home, to eavesdrop on private conversations, and to take photographs of people on private property, without their consent; publication of such photographs is also an offence.

Several provinces of the Canadian Federation have enacted torts of privacy. The British Columbia Privacy Act has much in common with the laws on the subject enacted by the other Provinces. This Act of 1979 provides that it is a tort, actionable without proof of damage, for a person wilfully and without claim of right, to violate the privacy of another.

Eavesdropping and surveillance are specifically but not exclusively, cited as means by which privacy may be violated.

However, it is not a violation of privacy to publish material that is of public interest or (in) fair comment on a matter of 'public interest'. Unauthorised use of a person's name or portrait is also a tort under the Act.

A similar approach to the subject of privacy has been adopted by the Saskatchewan Privacy Act, 1979.

The Canadian Federal legislation on privacy (relating to information about individuals, held by public bodies) provides by contrast an exhaustive definition comprising 18 paragraphs, of private information. It also includes a general public interest provision to cover matters falling outside the specific criteria. This definition has been widely criticised as too long and confusing.

Professors Philip Meyer and Ruth Walden of the University of North Carolina, Chapel Hill, have conducted research in ethics of journalism. They find that the laws governing the Press in United States of America are frequently confusing and subjective, particularly in the area of privacy law. Walden notes that with a few minor exceptions, there is no federal law governing invasions of privacy by the media. Essentially, every state has its own law. There are 50 different privacy laws as they relate to the media.

Nevertheless, since Warren and Brandeis article of 1890, intrusion upon an individual privacy has gradually come to be recognised as a tort throughout most of the United States, even though its definition and application vary from state to state. According to experts, the tort appears to cover the following four kinds of invasion of privacy, though they are considered distinct rights having little in common:

(a) intrusion into an individual's physical solitude;

(b) publication of private matter violating the ordinary decencies;

(c) putting someone in false light; and

(d) appropriation of an individual's name or likeness (normally for commercial purposes).

It is proposed to elaborate these categories a little.

Intrusion : Intrusion upon the solitude and private life of an individual is prohibited as an actionable wrong. Unauthorised wiretapping, telephone tapping, room bugging, snooping, making illegal searches and breaking into private records of an individual and like acts, without the consent of the individual concerned, are considered torts falling in this category. This legal wrong is committed as soon as the intrusion takes place whether or not the private facts gathered are published. Intruders are liable for this tort regardless of what use is made of the purloined material. This was so held by a California Court in Dietemann Vs Time-Life Magazine Inc, (1971).

However, the whole area of the law relating to intrusion upon privacy has not yet come out of the grey zone. Some kinds of intrusions through new sophisticated devices are hard to define. For committing this tort, it is not necessary for the intruder to enter upon private property. He may commit intrusion from outside, remaining at a distance, with the use of some snooper aids as telephoto lens, hidden microphones etc.

'While the public interest', noted Don R. Pember, 'is the key to defending most privacy suits, it has very little to do with intrusion'. It seems that in U.S.A. public interest defence, normally, does not avail against intrusion.

Publication of Private Information : This category has been defined as 'the disclosure of private, embarrassing, non-newsworthy facts about an individual'.

This may take the form of deceptive or illegal means of obtaining information such as trespassing or unauthorised use of cameras. 'Gossip substances of private conversation, and details of private tragedy or illness', particularly when their publication is repugnant to good taste and sense, are legal wrongs of this category. Truthfulness of the information published is no defence to a suit when this tort constitutes the cause of action.

An example of lapses in ethical standards, akin to this type of infringement of personal privacy, is furnished by the publication of a story in *The New York Times.* In the second week of April, 1991, in which not only the alleged Palm Beach rape victim, who has accused a member of the Kennedy family of the criminal act, was blamed, but also the details of the woman's past, including her alleged 'wild break' in high school, her mother's divorce, and her 17 tickets for speeding and careless driving, were given. *The New York Times* further reported, 'She gave birth to a daughter by a local man she did not marry. In 1989 she had a brief affair with the son of a once prosperous family He was the father of the child, friends say. . . .' Another acquaintance, Nathaniel Read said: 'She liked to drink and have fun with the never-do-wells in cafe society.'

The publication of this story is reported to have brought *The New York Times* into the centre of an embarrassing public debate of its unusual foray into tabloid journalism. The editors of the paper had to face sharp protest from members of its own staff. One woman employee said that 'we don't understand why you have got *New York Times* reports peeping in windows'. Another staffer said the paper had 'crucified' the woman.

The Times editor also faced criticism over the publication on the front page of the newspaper recently, on Kitty Kelley's biography of Nancy Reagan, which contained unsavoury and fallacious allegations against the former First Lady. The Executive Editor of *The New York Times* was reported to have admitted that Kelley piece was a 'mistake' and that 'the story did not live up to our standards'.

The primary defence to an action for this kind of invasion of privacy, is that the published material is newsworthy, that is to say, it is of wide public or general interest. A Newsworthy formula has been devised by American Courts for this purpose. According to this formula, the nature of the story, the status of the subjects, the intimacy of the revelations, and the degree of embarrassment to the plaintiff are all weighed against each other. Publication of information about public officials or public figures, such as Ministers, legislators, entertainers, labour leaders, sport personalities, even "some editors, journalists and broadcasters, normally qualify as newsworthy. But publication of the same kind of information about private persons who are not public figures might not so qualify.

The kind of invasion of privacy, according to some scholars, is an outgrowth of category (d) Appropriation. For constituting a tort under this category, it is not necessary that the published material should be defamatory or has been presented in a derogatory manner.

It is sufficient if the representation of the published material gives a false impression, even though the impression is not unfavourable, of the plaintiff. Photographs, rather than stories are the common source of 'false light' actions in tort. Truth of the report is a valid defence to such an action. The defendant can also use the First Amendment as a defence and maintain that the plaintiff has failed to prove that the material /story was published by the defendant with actual malice knowing it to be false, or in publishing it the defendant exhibited reckless disregard for the truth of the story.

This includes the unauthorised use of individual's name or likeness for trade or advertising purposes. Appropriation is the least ambiguous and the oldest of these four kinds of torts, stated above. The law relating to all the above categories of invasion of privacy, in the USA, is being still developed by their Supreme Court through its adjudications in a manner which seeks to strike a proper balance between the right to freedom of speech and freedom of the Press on the one hand, and the right to individual privacy, on the other. The overall position in USA has been summed up by Calcutt Committee (UK), thus:

> 'Generally speaking, the Press is free to publish almost any true material about public figures on the basis that virtually all human activity reveals the character of the person concerned. In some states, however, the publication of truthful but embarrassing information about individuals who are not public figures, can give rise to a cause of action. The Supreme Court has yet to rule on the constitutionality of this. Where the material published is untrue, some states provide redress on the grounds of false light. Cases on such grounds have been upheld by the Supreme Court.'

Although the English Common Law does not recognise the invasion of privacy as a tort in all cases in which the courts in USA do, yet the development of the law in USA had its impact on British scholars and jurists. Salmond in his Law of Torts, 15th Edition, adopted the view of Dean Prosser, one of the outstanding exponents of this concept. Salmond identifies four distinct kinds of torts recognised by American Courts.

No general right of privacy has been recognised under Common Law of the United Kingdom. However, as invasions of privacy by the media, particularly by the tabloid Press, increased, complaints against these intrusive forays were voiced by several sections of the British public. At the advent of the 7th decade of the Century, Younger Committee on Privacy was set up to study the problem and suggest remedial measures. In its Report rendered in July 1972, the committee recommended, by a majority, against statutory right of privacy for the reason that there was before it no compelling evidence, of a substantial wrong to be tackled.

It noted that since in complaints of invasion of privacy there may be a conflict of interest between the need of the public to be informed and the need to respect the individual's privacy, the balancing of these interests in each case should be left to the judgement of the Press Council. It recommended that the Council should insist that its adjudications be published with equal prominence to the original item. It further recommended that the Council should explore the possibility of codifying its adjudications on privacy to give readier guidance to busy practising journalists and to the interested public and to keep the codification up-to-date. Consequent upon this, the Council began codifying its general adjudications but remained opposed to the publication of a formal code of practice.

In 1976, U.K. Press Council issued the following declaration of principles on privacy, setting out the rules for guidance of editors in deciding when to publish stories about people's private lives:

(i) The publication of information about the private lives or concerns of individuals without their consent is only acceptable if there is a legitimate public interest overriding the right of privacy.

(ii) It is the responsibility of editors to ensure that inquiries into matters affecting the private life or concern of individuals are only undertaken when in the editor's opinion at the time a legitimate public interest in such matters may rise. The right to privacy is, however, not involved if the individuals concerned have freely and clearly consented to the pursuit of inquiries and publications.

(iii) The public interest relied on as the justification for publication or inquiries which conflict with a claim to privacy must be a legitimate and proper public interest and not only a prurient or morbid curiosity. 'Of interest to the public' is not synonymous with 'in the public interest'. It should be recognised that entry into public life does not disqualify an individual from his right to privacy about his private affairs, save when the circumstances relating to the private life of an individual occupying a particular public position may be likely to affect the performance of his duties or public confidence in him or his office.

(iv) Invasion of privacy by deception, eavesdropping or technological methods which are not in themselves unlawful can, however, only be justified when it is in pursuit of infirmation which ought to be published in the public interest and there is no other reasonably practicable method of obtaining or confirming it.

(v) The Council expects the obtaining of news or pictures to be carried out with sympathy and discretion. Reporters and photographers should do nothing to cause harm or humiliation to bereaved or distressed people unless it is clear that the publication of the news or pictures will serve a legitimate public interest and there is no other reasonably practicable means of obtaining the material.

(vi) Editors are responsible for the actions of those employed by their newspapers and have a duty to ensure that all concerned are aware of the importance of respecting the legitimate claims to personal privacy.

The Third Royal Commission on the Press headed by Lord McGregor, in its report of July 1977, adopted an approach similar to that of the Younger Committee. In the Commission's view also, legislation was not necessary because the Press Council could be its appropriate substitute. It, however, recommended that the Press Council should formulate a comprehensive code of conduct for the Press.

During 1988 and 1989 there occurred a number of glaring invasions of personal privacy by a section of the 'British Press, particularly the tabloid Press. As a result, the Press came under severe criticism for intruding upon accident victims and other patients in hospitals, for using stolen private photographs or correspondence and for publishing scurrilous details of individuals' private lives. Matters reached a climax when a million pound out-of-court libel settlement was made following stories in *The Sun* about Eltson John's private life.

In the course of discussions in the 1988-89 session of Parliament, on two private Members' Bills, one introduced by John Brown, MP, and the other by Tony Worthington, MP, on protection of Privacy and Right of Reply, respectively a number of cases of such unethical practices indulged in by the Press were cited.

This led to the appointment by the government of the Committee under the Chairmanship of Sir David Calcutt to consider what measures (whether legislative or otherwise) are needed to give further protection to individual privacy from the activities of the Press and improve recourse against the Press for the individual citizen, taking account of existing remedies, including the law of defamation and breach of confidence, and to make recommendations.

Following the appointment of the Calcutt Committee, there were two major developments. In November 1989 Newspaper Publishers Association, formulated and declared a code of practice. Thereafter, on March 13, 1990 the Press Council in U.K. adopted a revised code after discussion with the interested parties, including Newspaper Publishers Association (NPA).

Para 5 directs Newspapers and journalists serving them to use 'straightforward means to obtain information or pictures. The use of subterfuge can be justified only to obtain material which ought to be published in the public interest and could not be obtained by other means.'

As per para 7, newspapers and journalists serving them were required to avoid intrusion into personal grief and to carry out inquiries with sympathy and discretion.

Para 10 provides that save in exceptional circumstances newspapers should not, even where the law permits it, identify children under the age of 16 as victims, witnesses or defendants involved in cases concerning sexual offences.

Para 11 forbids newspapers to identify victims of rape, or publish material likely to contribute to such identification.

Para 12 provides that newspapers should refrain from publishing pictures which needlessly exacerbate grief or cause distress.

Para 15 directs journalists making inquiries at hospitals or similar institutions, to identify themselves to a responsible official before entering except in very rare cases where information which ought to be disclosed could not otherwise be obtained.

Part of the Committee

The Calcutt Committee accepted that there is little possibility of producing a precise or exhaustive definition of privacy or for that matter public interest. It felt that working definition of privacy, however, is nevertheless needed as a yardstick against which to measure complaints and solutions. It, therefore, adopted the following working definition:

> Privacy could be regarded as the antithesis of what is public hence everything concerning an individual's home, family, religion, health, sexuality, personal legal and personal financial affairs. The formulation 'the right to be let alone' is too simplistic. There is a mismatch between

> what an individual might regard as private and what might be regarded as such by his neighbours, including the Press....
>
> ...our formulation is the right of individual to be protected against intrusion into his personal life or affairs, or those of his family, by direct physical means or by publication of information.

The Committee emphasised that individual privacy is not to be considered in isolation. It must be weighed alongside freedom of speech and expression. In balancing these two factors, the Committee preferred to be guided in its approach by what the European Court of Human Rights, when interpreting Article 10 of the Convention, in its judgement in *The Sunday Times* vs United Kingdom (1979-80) 2 EHRR 245: (the Thalidomide case) emphasised that it was faced not with a choice between two conflicting principles but with a principle of freedom of expression that is subject to a number of exceptions which must be narrowly interpreted. 'Thus, the Committee professedly started from a position that freedom of expression is preeminent. Certain exceptions protecting individual privacy may then prove to be necessary.

The Committee conceded that it is not possible to devise a simple criterion of what constitutes a justifiable intrusion into an individual's privacy, it may have to be recognised that not all people are entitled to expect the same degree of privacy. A distinction may have to be drawn between what is justified in respect of public figures and what is justified for other people. Nevertheless, a public figure should not be required to surrender his right to privacy over every aspect of his life when he takes up public office or pursues a career which brings him into the public eye.

The committee emphasised that 'Public interest' in bald terms is not helpful in determining whether an intrusion is or is not justified.

In general terms, the Committee accepted that any conduct which impinges upon the public, might reasonably be made public. An individual who publicly claims to practice certain special or religious principle or adopts a position of moral leadership, can reasonably be subject to greater public scrutiny than his fellow citizens.

The committee opined that (generally) the revelation about the private life of a public figure are justified only:

(a) to protect the health or safety of the public, or

(b) to expose crime or seriously antisocial conduct, or

(c) in his behaviour if his private life adversely affects his public duties or is so hypocritical that the public is likely to be seriously misled.

The Committee concluded that just as it is impossible to define privacy other than in terms of a series of general values, so what constitutes an unwarranted intrusion into an individual's privacy can only be set out in terms relative to that person's status and conduct in the context of what is socially acceptable at the time. It is inevitable that decisions will be based on a series of value judgements. 'We consider', said the Committee, 'that every code of practice likely to be of practical use in newspaper offices must take account of these complexities.'

A number of witnesses urged that the Calcutt Committee to recommend the introduction of a statutory tort of infringement of privacy. There was also a suggestion that the civil law might be evolved in relation to privacy by courts on case-by-case basis. In this context, the Committee observed:

> 'A Common Law right to privacy could possibly develop in Scotland, where there is more general concept of Culpa (wrongful behaviour) compared with the more narrowly-drawn English torts. But in its judgement on March 16, 1990 in Keyer

> Robertson and Sport Newspapers Ltd., the Court of Appeal clearly ruled out the development of such a tort in English Law. Any remedy of this kind would now have to be provided by Statute.' The Committee then quoted from the judgement of Glide-well and Legatt L. JJ. in the said case where this point was raised.

After examining the five Bills introduced on this topic from time during the period 1961 to 1989, as also the draft Bill produced by Justice and the Natural Council for Civil Liberties and all other material and suggestions before them, the Committee concluded:

> '... an overwhelming case for introducing a statutory tort of infringement of privacy has not so far been made out and that the better solution lies with the measures set out elsewhere in this report. We, therefore, recommend that such a tort should not presently be introduced.'

The Committee made it clear that they were making their recommendation on the assumption that the improved scheme for self-regulation of the Press recommended by them in Chapter 15 of their report, will be made to work.

The Committee Recommended: 'The Press should be given one final chance to prove that voluntary self-regulation can be made to work. However, we do not consider that the Press Council even if reformed as proposed in its internal review, should be kept as part of the system. We, therefore, recommend that the Press Council should be disbanded and replaced by a new body, specifically charged with adjudicating on complaints of Press malpractice.

This body must be seen to be authoritative, independent and impartial. It must also have jurisdiction over the Press as a whole, must be adequately funded and must provide a means of seeking to prevent publication of intrusive material.

We consider it particularly to emphasise the break from the past. The new body should, therefore, be called the Press Complaints Commission.' (Hereafter called PCC.)

It is further recommended by the Committee that the PCC should publish, monitor and implement a comprehensive code of practice for the guidance of both the Press and public. The PCC should operate a hot line for complaints on a 24-hour basis. The PCC adjudications should in certain cases, include a recommendation that an apology be given to the complainant. The precise form of the apology, including whether it should be given publicly or privately, could also be prescribed.

The PCC should have an independent Chairman and not more than 12 members, with smaller subcommittees adjudicating on complaints under delegated powers.

Appointments to the PCC should be made by an Appointment Commission with explicit freedom to appoint whoever it considers best qualified. The Appointments Commission itself should be independently appointed, possibly by the Lord Chancellor.

Complaints Committee should have delegated power to release adjudications subject to a right of appeal for either party to the full Press Complaints Commission before publication.

The PCC should not operate a waiver of legal rights. If the industry wishes to maintain a system of non-statutory self-regulation, it must demonstrate its commitment in particular by providing the necessary money for setting up and maintaining the PCC.

The Calcutt Committee has recommended that the following acts should be criminal offences in England and Wales:

(a) Entering private property without the consent of the

lawful occupant, with intent to obtain personal information with a view to its publication;

(b) placing a surveillance device on private property without the consent of the lawful occupant, with intent to obtain personal information with a view to its publication; and

(c) taking a photograph or recording the voice of an individual who is on private property, without his consent, with a view to its publication and with intent that the individual shall be identifiable.

The Committee has further recommended that it should be a defence to any of these proposed offences that the act was done.

(i) for the purpose of preventing, detecting or exposing the commission of any crime, or other seriously antisocial conduct; or

(ii) for the protection of public health or safety, or

(iii) under any lawful authority.

The Committee further suggested that the individual having a sufficient interest should be able to apply for an injunction against the publication of any of these criminal offences or, if the material has already been published, for damages or an account of profits. It also recommended that further considerations should be given to the extent to which the law in Scotland needs to be extended to cover the proposed offences and civil remedy and how this might best be done.

The other important recommendations made by the Committee, are as follows:

Legal Restrictions on Press Reporting

(a) The statutory prohibition on identifying rape victims in England and Wales should be extended to cover the victims of the sexual assaults (such as procurement of intercourse with a woman by threats, or by false pretences or by administering drugs, intercourse with girls under 16 or with mental defects, incest, buggery, indecent assault on female or male etc.).

(b) In any criminal proceedings in England and Wales, the court should have the power to make an order prohibiting the publication of the name and address of any person against whom the offence is alleged to have been committed, or of any other matters likely to lead to his or her identification. This should only be exercised if the court believes that it is necessary to protect the mental or physical health, personal security of the home of the victim.

(c) After consulting the Press and the broadcasting authorities, Press Complaints Commission should issue early guidance on jigsaw identification.

Right of Reply

(d) A statutory right of reply should not be introduced.

Tort of Infringement of Privacy

(e) A tort of infringement of privacy should not be introduced.

Statutory Complaints Procedure

(f) If the Press fails to demonstrate that non-statutory self-regulation can be made to work effectively, a statutory system for handling complaints should be introduced.

(g) If maverick publications persistently decline to respect the authority of the Press Complaints Commission, the Commission should be placed on a statutory footing. It should be given sufficient statutory powers to enable it to require any newspaper, periodical or magazine to respond to its enquiries about complaints and to publish its adjudications as directed. It should be able to recommend the payment of compensation.

(h) The Government should set the budget for any statutory Press Complaints Commission and provide the money which it should then reclaim from the industry. The industry should set up a funding body which would apportion the cost between and collect the money from, various industrial bodies or individual publications.

Press Complaints Tribunal

(i) Should the Press fail to set up and support the Press Complaints Commission or should it at any time become clear that the reformed non-statutory mechanism is failing to perform adequately, this should be replaced by a statutory tribunal with statutory powers and implementing a statutory code of practice.

(j) There should be two separate triggers for the replacement of the Press Complaints Commission by a Press Complaints Tribunal.

(k) A Press Complaints Tribunal should perform two distinct functions. First, it should attempt conciliation and investigate complaints. Second, where necessary, it should resolve disputes by ruling whether there had been a breach of the code of practice. This should be reflected in its structure and procedures.

(l) The Press Complaints Tribunal should be able to award compensation. Unless the complainant can show financial loss, the amount of compensation should be limited by statute. This limit should be periodically reviewed.

(m) In privacy cases, the Press Complaints Tribunal should be able to restrain publication of material in breach of the code of practice by means of injunctions. No injunction should be granted if the publisher could show that he had a good arguable defence.

(n) The Tribunal Chairman should be a judge or senior lawyer appointed by the Lord Chancellor. He should sit with two accessors drawn from a panel appointed by the Home Secretary.

The Calcutt Committee has also proposed a code of Practice for the Press. Since infringement of privacy cannot be considered in isolation from other norms of ethics.

Grand Analysis

Some aspects of the Calcutt report have been the subject of worldwide criticism. The chief target of criticism is that part of its recommendations as a result of which the new body i.e., The Press Complaints Commission which has replaced the erstwhile British Press Council has not been entrusted with the responsibility to preserve the freedom of the Press. This recommendation rests on the specious argument that defending the freedom of the Press and adjudicating on complaints are distinct functions which sit uneasily together, there being an inherent conflict between the two.

Mr. Blom Cooper, Chairman of the erstwhile Press Council, maintained that the twin functions are not merely compatible but also interlocked. He submitted that in this respect the report of the Calcutt Committee was fundamentally flawed. In support of the view that these twin functions were inextricably linked with each other, Mr. Blom Cooper referred to a passage in a speech delivered by Lord Devlin, the first independent Chairman of the British Press Council, that to censure effectively misconduct by the Press, it is essential that the Council seeks to preserve the established freedom of British Press and work as to maintain its character in accordance with the highest professional standards.

At the international Conference held in Stockholm on 11-15 June, 1991 on the occasion of the 75th anniversary of their Press Council, delegates from several countries assailed this recommendation of the Calcutt Report and consequent debarment of the new Press Complaints Commission from entertaining complaints of infringement of Press freedom. Eminent among those critics included, Mr. Olle Stenholm, former Chairman of the Swedish Newspaper Publishers Association, Mr. Kenneth Morgan, Director of the British Press Complaints Commission and Professor David Flint, Chairman of the Press Council of Australia.

All of them were firmly of the view that preserving Press freedom and maintaining Press standards, were inseparable as two sides of the same coin. Professor David Flint described the British experiment in setting up the Press Complaints Commission as an ill advised attempt to divorce Press freedom from Press responsibility.

Since Mr. Kenneth Morgan was the best informed person about these developments in UK it will be worthwhile to refer to some of the points made by him in his speech.

In his opinion, the main contributory cause of the death of the British Press Council, was 'that characteristically English disease, obsession with privacy and obsession with privacy in two paradoxical senses'.

Explaining the background of this development, Mr. Morgan said '...the British have no law at all protecting personal privacy. In, say the last twenty years, there has been recurrent concern among politicians, but among others too, about whether she would have such laws, particularly to curb intrusion into people's privacy by the Press, or rather part of the Press, bent on gratifying other peoples' curiosity. The developing chorus of criticism at newspapers during that time has not been directed at all newspapers though its effect may be felt by all of them....

'It is a paradox that while condemning newspapers' focus on private lives, the public rushes out in millions to buy these very newspapers. The argument of proprietors and editors—and it has some force—has been that the sales figures demonstrate that they have been giving readers what they want, whatever politicians, pundits and moralists may say they ought to have. Wearing its Press freedom hat, the Press Council shared the Publishers' antagonism towards new legislation which would be likely to inhibit proper investigation and inquiry by the Press as well as curbing the improper intrusion into private lives at which it is aimed.

Mr. Morgan further reported: 'The Council's view like that of many similar bodies elsewhere, was that while new restrictive laws were undesirable, individuals had a moral right to privacy about their private lives and affairs which editors ought to recognise. The right extended not only to wholly private citizens but also to the people in public life unless what they were doing in private bore directly on their ability or fitness for their public role.

Mr. Morgan lamented that while the Calcutt Committee's report adopted many of the Press Council's own proposals, it suggested the Council's abolition and replacement by the Press Complaints Commission having no role as the Press Council had in defending the freedom of Press. The lopsided suggestion by the Calcutt Committee in Mr. Morgan's view 'was the most significant central flaw in a report which contained many valuable suggestions'.

Mr. Morgan criticised the Calcutt proposal to create the new criminal offences of which in practice only journalists could be guilty.

He further disclosed that the new body, PCC has a code of practice to enforce but not one of its own making. The code, 16 points running from accuracy through privacy and harassment to protection of confidential sources was devised for the newspaper and magazine industry by a Committee of editors led by Miss Patricia Champan, editor of *News of the World.* Commenting on this code, Mr. Morgan said: 'It cannot be denied that a code of this type presents problems. It is to be applied in the spirit not merely in the letter but it is taken to be comprehensive and it thus restricts criticism of conduct which was not thought of by the authors of the code. We cannot all hope to be as farsighted as the Almighty at Sinai when trying to envisage possible human fraility and sin or editorial responsibility. The code will require extension or its restriction of what complaints may be made will have to be relaxed as the years go by.'

Incidentally, these comments are in line with the view consistently taken by successive Press Councils of India, that it is neither necessary nor feasible to formulate a rigid exhaustive code of conduct for journalists. In Press Council of India's view, any attempt at framing a code of this kind would result in a mere enunciation of a few basic principles only in general terms which would be of little help in applying them to individual cases: Because of their elusive, variable nature, these moral principles cannot be reduced into rigid formulas. Ethics being dynamic principles, abhor Procrustean approach.

Questioned as to whether the new Press Complaints Commission on probation was working more effectively than the erstwhile Press Council in ensuring high professional standards of newspapers on self-explanatory basis, Mr. Morgan felt that it would be difficult to devise a more severe test of the new system in Britain than that this commission faced in its first month. He illustrated this point by referring to the complaint of Ms Clare Short, MP, before the PCC, alleging infringement of her right of privacy by the *News of the World.* The complaint 'combined a minefield of issues which are, some of them both in public interest, of interest to the public and crucial to the operation of a system of self-regulation of the Press running alongside the law'. Facets of that single case included:

The question arose whether the private life of a politician, and a leading woman politician at that, was a legitimate subject for newspaper inquiry and report?

The suggestion in the newspaper report was that nearly twenty years ago she had a relationship with a man with a serious criminal record who was eventually shot dead in the street in what may have been a gangland killing. Did the newspaper, as she asked, 'to crawl over' her private life of long ago, invade the privacy of her former husband, a former psychiatric patient, and intrude on the privacy of her present husband, himself a former Member of Parliament and a seriously sick man? Was what emerged an information which ought to be disclosed in the public interest or no more than information which might interest the public?

Should newspapers publish pornographic or near nude pinup pictures? Was this newspaper pursuing Ms Short as part of a vendetta because she had led a campaign to ban by law the publication of page-3 type pictures, an art form made famous by its sister newspaper?

Part of Ms Short's complaint was the way the newspaper reported a speech she made about it and newspaper ethics in Parliament. Part of its case was that she misused her privilege in Parliament to attack the paper and its reporter. She complained of a breach of Parliamentary privilege.

Was the *News of the World's* source for some of its material about Ms Short's private life, information from disaffected members of the West Midlands Police Serious Crime Squad whose record she had attacked in the House of Commons? She complained about this to the Chief Constable and the Police Complaints Authority.

Could the new Press Complaints Commission be expected to deal with her complaint against the paper when her lawyers were already in correspondence with the paper and a legal action looked imminent? The old Press Council had asked complainants to waive their legal rights. The new Commission was not going to do that. Then the overall question that arose was: Could the self-regulating Commission hope to deal fairly and squarely with all these issues on a complaint that the *News of the World* broke the industry's own code on privacy and accuracy? The editor of the Paper, Miss Chapman, was a member of the Commission and Chairman of the Committee which framed the code.

The Commission dealt with these issues, upheld the complaint and the *News of the World* published it's condemnation fairly and in full, taking up a whole page.

'The new Commission has no more sanctions, no more penalties at its command than the old Council. Its greatest strength has in two factors—commitment and fear. Commitment by newspaper and magazine owners and editors to support it and make it work and fear of the threat by government and opposition of what will befall the Press if the test of the last chance is failed.'

Communication comes from the Latin word *communism* meaning 'common'. When we communicate we are trying to establish commonness with someone. That is, we are trying to share information, an idea, or an attitude.

Communication always requires at least three elements: the source, the message and the destination. A source may be an individual (speaking, writing, drawing, and gesturing) or a communication organisation (like a newspaper, publishing house, and television studio or motion picture studio). The messages may be in the form of ink on paper, sound waves in the air, a flag in the hand, or any other signal capable of being interpreted meaningfully. The destination may be an individual listening, watching, or reading, or a member of a group, such as a discussion group, a lecture audience, a football crowd, or a mob, or an individual member of the particular audience we call the mass audience, such as the reader of a newspaper or a viewer of television.

Now what happens when the source tries to build up this commonness with his intended receiver? First, the source encodes his message. That is, he takes the information or feeling he wants to share and puts it into a form that can be transmitted. When it is coded into spoken words, it can be transmitted easily and effectively, but it can not travel very far unless radio carries them. If the coding is in written words, they go more slowly than spoken words, but they go farther and last longer. Indeed, some messages long outlive their sender. Once coded and sent, a message is quite free of its sender and what it does is beyond the power of the sender to change.

Substitute 'microphone' for encoder and 'earphone' for decoder and you are talking about electronic communication. Consider that the 'source' and 'encoder' are one person, 'decoder' and 'destination' are another, and the signal is language, and you are talking about human communication.

Now its perfectly possible by looking at those diagrams to predict how such a system will work. For one thing, such a system can be no stronger than its weakest link. In engineering terms, there may be filtering or distortion at any stage. In human terms, if the source does not have adequate or clear information etc., then the system is working at less than full efficiency.

If the coding is good (for example, with no unnecessary words) the capacity of the channel can be approached, but it can never be exceeded. You can readily see that one of the great skills of communication lies in knowing the capacity to operate a channel.

This is partly determined for use by the nature of the language. English, like every other language, has its sequence of words and stands governed by certain probabilities. We can calculate the amount of freedom open to one in writing any language. For English, the freedom is about 50 per cent.

So much for language redundancy, as communication theorists call it, meaning the percentage of the message, which is not open to free choice. But there is also the communication redundancy, and this is an important aspect of constructing a message. For if we think our audience may have a hard time understanding the message, we can deliberately introduce more redundancy; we can repeat or we can give examples and analogies. In other words, we always have to choose between transmitting more information in a given time, or transmitting less and repeating more in the hope of being better understood. And it is always a delicate choice because too slow a rate will bore an audience, whereas too fast a rate may control them.

The human communication system can be no stronger than its weakest link. If the source does not have adequate or clear information then the system is working at less than full efficiency. Perhaps the most important thing about such a system is that receiver and sender must be in tune. This is clear enough in the case of a radio transmitter and receiver, but somewhat more complicated when it means that a human receiver must be able to understand a human sender.

Let the two big circles represent the accumulated experience of the two individuals trying to communicate. The source can encode, and the destination can decode, only in terms of the experience each has had. If we have never learned Russian, we can neither code nor decode in that language. If an African tribesman has never seen or heard of an airplane, he can decode the sight of a plane only in terms of whatever experience he has. The plane may seem to him to be a bird and the aviator a God born with wings.

If the circles have only a small area in common, that is, if the experiences of source and destination have been strikingly unlike, then it is going to be very difficult to get an intended meaning across from one to the other. This is the difficulty we face when a non-science-trained person tries to read Einstein.

This source, then, tries to encode in such a way as to make it easy for the destination to tune in the message to relate it to parts of his experience which are much like those of the source. What does he have to work with?

Messages are made up of signs. A sign is a signal that stands for something in experience. The word 'dog' is a sign that stands for our generalised experience with dogs. The word would be meaningless to a person who has come from a 'dogless' land and has never even heard of a dog. It is obvious that each person in the communication process is both an encoder and a decoder. He receives and transmits.

Therefore, it is possible to describe either sender or receiver in a human communication system.

If you have learned the sign, you have learned certain responses with it. We can call these mediatory responses, because they mediate what happens to the message in your resource system. These responses are the meaning the sign has for you. They are learned from experience, but they are affected by the state of your organism at the moment. For example, if you are hungry, a picture of a steak may not arouse exactly the same response in you as when you are overfed.

But subject to these effects, the mediatory responses will then determine what you do about the sign. For you have learned other sets of reactions connected to the mediatory responses. A sign that means a certain thing to you will start certain other processes in your nerves and muscles. A sign that means fire, for example, will certainly trigger off some activity in you. In other words, the meaning that results from your decoding of a sign will start your encoding. Exactly what you encode will depend on your choice of the responses available in the situation and connected with the meaning.

Whether this encoding actually results in some overt communication or action depends partly on the barriers in the way. You may think it better to keep silent. And if an action does occur, the nature of the action will also depend in the avenue for action available to you and the barriers in your way. The code of your group may not sanction the action you want to take. The meaning of a sign may make you want to hit the person who has said it, but he may be too big, or you may be in the wrong social situation.

But whatever the exact result, this is the process in which you are constantly engaged. You are constantly decoding signs from your environment, interpreting these signs, and encoding something as a result. In fact, it is misleading to think of the communication process as starting somewhere and ending somewhere. It is really endless. We are little switchboard centres handling and rerouting the great endless current of communication. We can accurately think of communication as passing through us—changed, to be sure, by our interpretations, our habits, our abilities and capabilities, but the input still being reflected in the output.

We need to add another element to our description of the communication process. Consider what happens in a conversation between two people.

The return process in communication is called feedback, and it plays a very important part in communication because it tells us how our messages are being interpreted. Does the bearer say, "yes, yes that's right," and try and persuade him? Does he nod his head in agreement? Does a puzzled frown appear on his forehead? All these are feedback. So is a letter to the editor of a newspaper, protesting an editorial. An experienced communicator is attentive to feedback, and constantly modifies his message in light of what he observes in or hears from his audience. There is another kind of feedback also—the feedback we get from our own selves, for instance, we can hear our own voice and correct our pronunciation. We see the words we have written on paper and can correct spelling or change the style.

In any kind of communication we rarely send out messages in a single channel. When you speak to anyone, the sound waves from your voice are the primary message. But there are others. The expression on your face, your gestures, the relation. The primary message conveys information on several levels. It gives me words to decode. It emphasises certain words above others and presents the words in a pattern of intonation and timing, which contribute to the total meaning. This multiple channel situation exists even in printed mass communication where the channels are perhaps most restricted. Meaning is conveyed not only by the words in a news item but also by the size of the headline, the position of the news item on the page and that of the page in the paper, its association with pictures, and the use of boldface and other typographical devices.

All these tell us something about the item. Thus we can visualise the typical channel of communication, not as a simple telegraph circuit, in which current does or doses not flow, but rather as a sort of coaxial cable in which many signals flow in parallel from source toward the destination. These parallel relationships are complex, but you can see their general pattern. The secondary channels of the sight-sound media are especially rich.

5

Fundamental Elements

'Communication' (together with its twin 'information') is perhaps one of the most hyped words in contemporary culture. It encompasses a multitude of experiences, actions and events, as well as a whole variety of happenings and meanings, and technologies too. Thus, a conference or a meeting or even a mela or procession is a 'communication event', newspapers, radio, video and television are 'communication media', phones, pagers, and email are 'communication technologies', and journalists, advertisers, public relations personnel, and even camera crew and news-readers are 'communication professionals'.

Further, the contemporary percccciod has come to be labelled variously the 'Information Age', the 'Communication Age', and most recently, the Cyber or Networking Age. The uses and understanding of Communication have come a long way from its original association first with 'means of transport' and later with 'transmission'. The English word 'communication' is derived from the Latin noun 'communis' and the Latin verb 'communicare' which means 'to make common'. Terms closely related to communication and with similar etymological origins include community, communion, commonality, communalism and communism. The closest Indian language equivalent to the original concept of communication is 'sadharanikaran'.

Communication, in its simplest sense, is a human relationship, involving two or more persons who come together to share, to dialogue and to commune, or just to be together say at a festival or a time of mourning. Communication is thus not so much an act or even a process but rather social and cultural 'togetherness'. Communion with oneself, with God, nature, the world of spirits, and with one's ancestors are also forms of communication.

Various Offshoots

The study of Communication in its multitudinous forms, whether in its human or technological dimensions, has now taken on the characteristics of an inter-disciplinary and multi-disciplinary social science. To begin with, Communication Science or Communication Studies was based in university departments of Sociology or Psychology or Political Science, and it borrowed heavily from these social science disciplines. In its turn, Communication Studies has led to a re-orientation in the disciplines themselves, a greater involvement with popular cultures, and with men and women as communicators at home and in the work-a-day world.

Studies of propaganda by social scientists resulted in greater interest among governments and academicians in the 'power' of communication strategies. Government departments of defense provided generous funding for propaganda research, and business and industry promoted media research so as to better exploit communication for advertising and marketing their products and services. The United States' government departments, private companies and the media themselves were the prime supporters of university courses and research in the mass media.

Communication Studies was largely influenced by such needs and such research, as well as the rapid growth of the press, and later of the cinema, radio and television. The discipline of Communication owes its origins to the United States of the 1930s, a time when Nazi propaganda was a source of great concern; the US government established an Institute of Propaganda Research to develop techniques for influencing public opinion. In Britain and France, the discipline had its roots in literary and linguistic studies, while in Germany the origins are traceable to the Institute of Social Research (the Frankfurt School) and to Freudian psychoanalysis.

In India, the discipline of Communication came into its own with the Government's need for propagating family planning, social development and national integration throughout the land. The Indian Institute of Mass Communication was established in 1965 by the Ministry of Information and Broadcasting to provide training and conduct research to assist in this effort. University departments of Journalism joined in this effort as well, but continued for the most part to be no more than trade schools for the print media.

Conveyance of Reality

Communication is a fact in the world of human beings, animals, and plants, and is an ever-continuing process going on all the time. It is as necessary to human, animal and vegetable existence as life itself. Halt communication and the life processes wither and die. The need for communication is as basic as the hunger for food and drink, perhaps even more so. In the beginning after all was 'Aum' or the 'Word', the first sound ever made or heard. In Indian tradition the 'Word' is the Shabda Brahman, the divine word.

'Communication is the name we give to the countless ways that humans have of keeping in touch-not just words and music, pictures and print, nods and becks, postures and plumages; to every move that catches someone's eye and every sound that resonates upon another's ear.'

This observation is true also for animals, birds and bees, and other land, sea and air creatures too. The singing and chirping of birds, the croaking of frogs, and the many visual and olfactory signals among bird and beast are forms of communication; some simple, others very highly sophisticated. The dance of the honeybee, for instance, is an advanced means of communication for it conveys to other bees the precise direction and distance of the place where nectar will be found.

Communication Needs

A human being's need for communication is as strong and as basic as the need to eat, sleep and love. It is both an individual and a social need. It is both a natural individual demand and a requirement of social existence to use communication resources in order to engage in the sharing of experiences, through 'symbol-mediated interaction'. The severest punishment for a child is to be isolated, to be left alone, not to be spoken to. North Indian children mete out this punishment when they say 'kuttie' to their playmates, holding out their thumb as an accompanying gesture.

Grown-ups too and especially the aged need company, need to communicate. Society punishes criminals by locking them up in solitary cells, thus starving them of the basic need, and indeed the fundamental right to communicate. Communication involves active interaction with our environments-physical, biological and social. Deprived of this interaction we would not be aware of whether we are safe or in danger, whether hated or loved, or satisfied or hungry. However, most of us take this interaction and this relationship for granted, unless we experience some deprivation of it. When that happens we adapt ourselves to the environment so that we don't lose touch, in both the literal and figurative senses. For, to lose touch is to suffer isolation.

The basic human need for communication can perhaps be traced to the process of mankind's evolution from lower species. Animals, for instance, have to be in sensory communication with their physical and biological surroundings to find food, protect themselves and reproduce their species. A loss of sensation-the inability to hear a predator, for instance, can mean loss of life. Similarly, to be lost from primitive social communication from the pack, from the herd or the tribe is to be condemned to death.

What happens to a person who is 'excommunicated'-literally, cut off from communication by his group or his society? Malcolm X, the Black Muslim leader, described the experience of being expelled from his group as 'a state of emotional shock'. Elaborating, he said that this state was like that of someone 'who for twelve years had an inseparable, beautiful marriage partner and then suddenly one morning at breakfast the marriage partner had thrust across the table some divorce papers. I felt as though something in nature had failed, like the sun or the stars. It was that incredible a phenomenon to me-something too stupendous to conceive.

Others who have been isolated for a period of time from human company are known to have experienced nightmarish hallucinations. Indeed, social isolation can also be hazardous to the heart as much as to the mind. It is estimated that single men without close friends run two or three times the risk of developing heart disease as their more sociable counterparts.

However, lack of communication can be as disorienting

an experience as too much of it. Indeed, the apparent effects of sensory deprivation and sensory overload are frequently similar: anxiety, apathy, impaired judgement, strange visions, and something akin to schizophrenia. The 'information explosion' brought about by satellite television, the internet and other technologies is an instance of this sensory overload.

Importance of Language

But sensory communication alone was not enough for man to survive. Hence the evolution of symbolic communication called language from non-verbal gestures, grunts and grimaces to the verbal, and then to the written and printed word. Language is inseparable from culture which is its very source of sustenance; language embodies and expresses a community's culture. The 'arts' have grown out of this same fundamental desire and need to express oneself and to reach out to others. Cro-Magnon men and women adorned their caves with paintings of animals and hunters; the modern artist shows a preference for the abstract and 'pop', for the electronic and computer arts, for 'virtual reality'. But the human need to communicate has remained the same; only the forms and languages have changed.

A Firm Base

Communication and information are not similar concepts or experiences. Communication is not the mere sending or receiving of information in whatever form. Rather, it is a whole situation and an experience; a human relationship, in sum. Information, on the other hand, is made up of bits of messages, verbal and non-verbal, and is essentially unilinear. Significant information can bring about a communication relationship, but not when the exchange of information is on an unequal or commercial basis.

Then information turns into a 'commodity', an item to be bought and sold in the market place. A commodity, by definition, has a price attached to it. Authentic communication is not helped but rather distorted by such 'commodotized' information. Business communication thus, is a contradiction in terms; when communication becomes a business it turns into a commodity with an exchange value.

An Argentinean scholar, Ricardo C. Noseda, distinguishes between communication and information thus: Communication is not an act but a process by which an individuality enters into mental co-operation with another individuality until they come to constitute a common conscience. Information, instead, is just a unilateral translation of a message from an Emitter to a Receiver.

Basic Rights

The right to information has been declared a fundamental right by a United Nations Charter (and such a right is to recognised in the Freedom of Information Bill introduced in Parliament in May 1997), but what human beings need much more fundamentally is in fact the right to communicate. It is such a right that gives men and women their dignity and their freedom, as well as the ability to participate in the social, religious, economic and political life of a nation.

The right to communicate is now seen as a fundamental human right, much more comprehensive than existing freedoms of speech, the press, etc. It is the basic right of an individual and it extends, in some degree at least, to groups, nations and the international community, and to have important legal, economic and technological implications. It is closely related to the democratisation of communication within and between countries, and to concepts of 'access', 'participation' and the 'two-way' flow.

Interaction, interchange, transaction, dialogue, sharing, communion and commonness are ideas that crop up in any attempt to define the term 'communication'. According to Denis McQuail, communication is a process which increases commonality-but also requires elements of commonality for it to occur at all. This is an ideal worth striving for, but communication by itself does not increase commonality nor does it need commonality for occurrence. A common language, for instance, does not necessarily bring people together. There are other factors too at play such as a shared culture and a common interest which bring about a sense of commonality and more significantly, a sense of community.

The Sanskrit term 'sadharanikaran' in Bharata's Natya Shastra comes closest to the sense of 'common' or 'commonness' usually associated with communication. Sadharanikaran is a social process which can be achieved only among sahridayas, people with a capacity to receive messages. This is an innate ability acquired through culture, adaptation or learning. The focus here is not on the sender but the receiver of the message. Moreover, communication according to this Sanskrit concept is a relationship based on common and mutual understanding and feeling, for sahridaya literally means 'of one heart.' The derivation of this ancient Indian concept of communication from the aesthetic theory of 'rasa' will be examined in a later section.

Communication thus presupposes a shared symbolic environment, a social relationship among those who participate. What it leads to is social interaction, and in combination with a set of other factors, contributes to a sense of community. Since the world of man, bird and beast too possesses and communicates such a social relationship, the need arises to speak of 'human communication' rather, than 'communication' alone in our study, though many communication researchers do not like the distinction.

Denis McQuail sees 'human communication' in linear terms as the sending of meaningful messages from one person to another. These messages could be oral or written, visual or olfactory. He also takes such things as laws, customs, practices, ways of dressing, gestures, buildings, gardens, military parades, and flags to be communication.

Ashley Montagu and Floyd Matson go a step further. In their view 'human communication' as the saying goes, is a clash of symbols, and it covers a multitude of signs. But it is more than media and message, information and persuasion; it also meets a deeper need and serves a higher purpose. Whether clear or garbled, tumultuous or silent, deliberate or inadvertent, communication is the ground of meeting and the foundation of the community. It is, in short, the essential human connection.

W.S. Cardon, a leading exponent of kinesics, the science of body language, develops the argument still further. He stresses that interaction within a culture is governed not so much by language, but by 'body synthesizers' set in motion almost immediately after birth and thereafter conditioned by culture. Communication, therefore, is not a matter of 'isolated entities sending discrete messages back and forth, but a process of mutual participation in a common structure of rhythmic patterns by all members of a culture'.

Various Types

Communication has been classified into several types: in terms of the verbal and non-verbal; the technological and non-technological; the mediated and non-mediated, the participatory and the non-participatory, and so on. Most of these typologies, however, are mainly for pedagogic or instructional purposes; in actual practice, there is much overlapping and mixing of the various types. The typologies must be seen as attempts at coming to grips with the apparently simple but really complex phenomenon of communication.

One common typology relates to the size of a social group

or the number of people involved in the experience of communication. Such a typology ranges from the intrapersonal and interpersonal and transpersonal to the group and the mass.

Two-way Communication

Intrapersonal Communication is individual reflection, contemplation and meditation. Transcendental meditation, for instance, is an example of such communication. Conversing with the divine, with spirits and ancestors, may be termed 'transpersonal' communication. This is a vital experience in the religious and monastic life, in ashrams and places of prayer, and among aboriginal and tribal communities.

Direct Connection

Interpersonal Communication is direct face-to-face communication between two persons. It is, in other words, a dialogue or a conversation without the intervention of another person or a machine like the telephone or a two-way radio or television set-up. It is personal, direct, and intimate, allowing for maximum interaction and exchange in word and gesture. Indeed, it is the highest, the most perfect form of communication that two persons can attain. It is more persuasive and influential than any other type of communication such as group communication or mass communication, for it involves the interplay of words and gestures, the warmth of human closeness and in fact all the five senses. All interpersonal exchange is, therefore a communion and a sharing at the most intimate and open level. It is total communication for it takes within its compass words, body movements, physical characteristics, body odours, and even clothes. This is not to deny that interpersonal exchanges can be used by confidence tricksters and conmen to throw wool over people's eyes. A man may smile and smile and yet be a villain for all we know. That perhaps explains why we cherish our privacy, and are constantly on our guard in face-to-face encounters, much more so than in group or mass gatherings. Only the ones who have our trust, and have proved themselves are allowed to cross the barriers of an intimate relationship. Most are kept at a distance.

In the area of business communication that distance is ritualized. For instance, interpersonal exchanges between a medical representative and a doctor or that between a manager and a clerk, are generally carried out on a professional level. As the saying goes they usually 'talk shop', but on occasions, even business charter can lead to close and abiding friendships. That potential lies in the nature of interpersonal communication; hence the frequent barriers we raise lest people invade our space, our 'territory.'

According to Konrad Lorenz and Desmond Morris, the ethologists, animals and birds often turn aggressive when their territories are invaded by outsiders. This is because of the 'territorial imperative"-the obsession with protecting one's space. The elephant has his herd, the lion his pride, the wolf his pack, and the birds and bees their nests and hives. Any encroachment from other groups is resented, and fought off, sometimes violently. Human beings react in an equally savage manner when their spatial privacy is encroached upon. In European cultures, it is considered bad manners and bad communication to get too close (literally and figuratively) and too intimate unless you have been permitted to enter the sanctum sanctorum of another. Among Indians and Arabs, however, physical closeness in Interpersonal Communication does not generally imply intimacy, nor does constant gazing into each other's eyes. This is a part of West and South Asian cultures. According to Buddhism, the four social emotions that should guide interpersonal communication are: metta (loving kindness), karuna (compassion), murdita (sympathetic joy) and upekkha (equanimity).

The Interrelationship

Interpersonal communication is conducted on the basis of focussed and unfocussed interactions. In his book Behaviour in Public Places, Erving Goffman argues that most interpersonal communication is of an unfocussed nature. It takes place whenever we observe or listen to persons with whom we are not conversing, for instance in buses, trains, lifts or in public places like stations, bus stops, or on the street. It's the kind of activity we indulge in when we are 'people watching' without their being aware we are doing so. And what do we come to know about them? Our inferences may not all be valid or meaningful, but the fact remains that we do make inferences all the time about people.

The young man who passes us by in a street dressed in pyjama and kurta evokes different associations from one clad in jeans and a jazzy shirt, depending of course on our own background, and the location of the street. The girl in a simple cotton sari, with her hair tied in a 'plait' say in a city like Bombay, conveys different impressions from the girl in a dress and with her hair bobbed. Additional sources of information about these persons are height, weight, and build. For instance, a well-built tall man is regarded as handsome, a stout fat woman as ugly, a thin wiry figure as athletic. Body movements such as gestures, the manner of standing, sitting or walking too convey certain meanings to us. Very broad gestures and loud talk, for example, are considered uncouth in polite society, but not necessarily so among working class groups. Thus it is that we draw conclusions on a person's qualities, cultural and religious background, socio-economic status, political ideology and other preferences without ever speaking to him or to her.

Focussed interactions, on the other hand, result from an actual encounter between two persons. The persons involved are fully aware that they are communicating with each other. Sitting or standing face-to-face either close or distant, they know fully well that they are exchanging both verbal and non-verbal messages, though they may not realize how these messages are being interpreted. Also, they are generally not conscious of the meanings they are conveying through 'body language.' An unfocussed interaction usually is set off by eye contact. The meeting of eyes indicates that both parties are willing to have an interpersonal exchange. The turning away of eyes, on other hand, cuts off the attempts to come together and start a conversation. It shows lack of interest. Similarly, reduction in eye involvement during a conversation is a non-verbal signal which indicates that it is time to bring the conversation to a close. Indeed, there is no more effective way of ending a face-to-face interaction than refusing to continue eye contact.

Various Stages

The Phatic Stage : The initial exploratory stage of communication determines the course conversation will take. This first stage is known as the phatic period (from the Greek "phasis", an utterance). It begins with a "Hi!" or a "Hello! How are you?", "Good Morning" or even a simple 'namaste' or 'vanakkam' or 'Jairam'. The accompanying gestures are the meeting of the eyes, a smile, perhaps a handshake, and moving in closer to a talking distance. In a formal encounter, the distance is greater (though not among all cultures) than an informal friendly meeting. The conversation then may veer to talk about the weather or queries like "How's life?", "How are things with you?" What have you been doing with yourself?', "What's the news?", "How are the folks at home?"

The Phatic stage is, therefore, a warming-up time during

which ritualized greetings are exchanged. In themselves, the words and gestures exchanged during this period do not mean much. Indeed, the questions asked are not meant to be taken literally. They are only a formalised manner of showing interest and attention. They are a way of saying "I am glad to have met you. Let's have a chat". The answers we give to the queries made are equally formalised. "I'm fine, thank you", for example is a stock reply even if you're not doing too well.

No deception is involved at all: what we are doing through words is merely sending signals that we would like to have a conversation. So at this stage we don't literally mean what we say, but we mean well. It's the meaning after all, and not the words that really matter. The words are only symbols or ways of getting across. The meaning is more often than not behind the words rather in them. More accurately, meaning lies in a situation and a context, seen not so much in isolation but in a social and cultural environment. This is as true of verbal as of non-verbal communication. For instance, the North Indian's gesture of touching an elder's feet connotes respect and reverence among people of that culture, but is considered a demeaning gesture in the cultures of the south and the north-east. The phatic stage then is patterned according to social and cultural norms and rituals.

The Personal Stage : The second stage, called the personal stage, introduces a more personal element into the conversation. During this period we generally lower our social guard a little and are prepared to take some risk in exposing ourselves and our feelings. Having moved on to this personal stage, we are likely to be willing to talk about personal matters such as one's profession, the family, health problems and the like. If, on the other hand, we were hesitant to enter this stage, we would have broken off the conversation at the phatic stage itself or continued talking in a formal manner. Professional discussions rarely go beyond the personal stage. Most business communication, therefore, takes place at this level, for it does involve personal interests and we are ready to go along to promote them.

The Intimate Stage : This stage is reserved for friends and relatives, the degree of intimacy depending upon the closeness of the relationship. To some we open our hearts out completely; to others, though good friends, we are reluctant to tell all. Nevertheless, it's a stage when social barriers fall and we are at ease; interpersonal communication achieves its highest form in this mode, and words seem inadequate. Says Robert Shuter, "In this period, communicators reveal their innermost thoughts and feelings-their fears and joys, weaknesses and strengths. Marked by intimate revelations, this stage is reserved for individuals who have established a deep union, one based on love, respect and understanding."

Cumulative Communication

Group communication shares all these qualities, though in a much less measure. The larger the group the less personal and intimate is the possibility of exchange. In fact, as the group grows in size communication tends to become more and more of a monologue, for participation becomes problematic. The degree of directness and intimacy, therefore, depends upon the size of the group, the place where it meets, as also the relationship of the members of the group to one another, and to the group leader. Group communication is thus a more complex process than interpersonal communication.

The level of mutual participation and understanding among the members suffers as a result. In Interpersonal Communication too understanding and participation may not be complete, especially if the non-verbal cues and the socio-cultural contexts are not paid attention to. However, the possibility of checking up and correcting misunderstanding is much quicker and easier in much interpersonal communication.

Feedback is the key word here. While in interpersonal communication, feedback is instantaneous, it is not so in group communication. What is more, it allows for instant response to feedback received. In Group Communication, on the other hand, feedback is more difficult to measure, and to respond to. It takes time before meanings are clarified and responses assessed. That explains why the art of effective public speaking (an example of one-way top-down communication) is more necessary at the group level than at the interpersonal level. Feedback is a term from cybernetics, the study of messages, particularly of effective message control. When feedback is employed for this kind of social engineering, as in advertising, it is no more communication but propaganda and manipulation.

Face-to-face communication, nevertheless, is more persuasive and influential, particularly in an unequal communication situation. It involves the interplay of words and gestures and above all, the warmth of human closeness. No wonder, advertising people still depend on door-to-door salesmen and sales-girls even where the mass media such as radio, television and the press are widespread.

Sincerity and enthusiasm are far easier to convey, and to react to in a face-to-face situation. In Group Communication, particularly where the group is large, deception and pretence cannot be detected immediately. That must be the reason why 'acting' is associated with Group Communication.

The theatre, religious services, dance performances, carnivals, the Kumbh Mela, Ram Lila, Ras Lila and other folk events, are examples of Group Communication. Village markets, bazars and melas too are instances of informal Group Communication. Then there are 'gossip groups' and other informal traditional groups that come together either regularly or occasionally for sharing information. These are 'micro-groups' that communicate among and within themselves in terms of their status and the nature of their relationships.

Ways of Communication

Group Communication has now been extended by the tools of mass communication: books, the press, the cinema, radio, television, video and the Internet. Mass Communication is generally identified with these modern mass media, but it must be noted that these media are processes and must not be mistaken for the phenomenon of communication itself. Exaggerated claims have been made for the 'power' of the mass media. Daniel Lerner terms them 'mobility multipliers' and Wilbur Schramm considers them to be 'magic multipliers.' Indeed, both the terms 'mass communication' and 'mass media' are inappropriate in the context of developing societies. None of the 'mass media' reach the masses of people in these societies. So in every sense, these are 'minority' or 'elite' media, or even 'class' media, for only those who have the wherewithal can afford to purchase receivers for them. Where access to, and distribution of, the mass media in India is concerned, only the comparatively well-off in urban and rural areas are at an advantage.

Newspapers, transistors, films and televisions are still beyond the economic reach of the majority of our people. Traditional community media like the keertana and yakshagana, and the whole treasure-house of folk song, folk dance and folk theatre are the real organs of mass media in India. They are far less expensive organs, are easy of access, are frequently participatory in nature and communicate much more effectively than the electronic media and at a direct and personal level. Their reach too is far and wide in the country. However, the modern mass media are produced and distributed like other consumer and industrial products on a mass scale.

Mao Zedong, who led the Chinese Cultural Revolution, used a type of communication to talk to the masses. He termed it 'mass-line' communication. Mahatma Gandhi too employed a similar type of communication, the essence of which was personal example, respect for the peasant's knowledge, and non-manipulative information. Kusum J Singh's comparison of the two leaders' use of the mass-line type of communication brings out the relevance of this type of grass-root level communication even today for mobilizing the masses in developmental efforts.

Many Types of Communication

Communication via the 'new' media such as video, cable, videotex, teletext, video-on-demand, tele-shopping, computers, and the Internet is usually termed 'interactive communication'. Telecommunication-based services such as telephones, pagers, cellular or mobile phones, electronic mail are also considered to be 'interactive'. They are point-to-point communication systems, and can approximate to the interpersonal (as in the basic telephone and the various 'value-added' services), the group (as in tele-conferences and video-conferences) or the mass (as in the Internet's World Wide Web) where companies or people with their own web-sites can reach millions of individuals across the globe at their own convenience. A major characteristic of interactive communication is 'asynhronicity', that is the sending and receiving of messages is at one's convenience, rather than at the same time, as in radio, television. Audio and video recording facilitates listening and watching at a time later than the time of transmission; voice mail, electronic mail and pager messages, can be sent and accessed at times convenient to communicators.

European Method

Western theories and models of communication have their origin in Aristotle's Rhetoric. According to Aristotle, rhetoric is made up of three elements: the speaker, the speech, and the listener. The aim of rhetoric is the search for all possible means of persuasion.

Perhaps the most widely quoted definition of mass communication in terms of Aristotelian rhetoric is that of Harold D. Lasswell, the American political scientist. He stated that 'a convenient way to describe an act of communication is to answer the following questions:

Who

Says What

In Which Channel

To Whom

With What Effect?

Lasswell saw communication as performing three functions: surveillance of the environment, correlation of components of society, and cultural transmission between generations. Such a mechanistic and 'effects' approach to communication was to influence communication theory for decades to come. Essential to this understanding were the notions of transmission and transfer of information for intended effects.

A definition on similar lines was given by Berelson and Steiner: 'The transmission of information, ideas, emotions, skills, etc., by use of symbols-words, pictures, figures, graphs, etc. It is the act or process of transmission that is usually called communication'.

The primary goal of communication, according to Western communication theory, is influence through persuasion. Osgood's definition is an illustration. In the most general sense, he explains, we communicate whenever one (the system), (the source), influences another, (the destination), by manipulation of alternative signals which can be transferred over the channel connecting them.

Various Patterns

The effects-oriented models or approaches to mass communication derive from Shannon and Weaver's Mathematical model of communication. Shannon and Weaver conceived of communication as a system composed of five essential parts plus 'noise': (1) an information source, (2) a transmitter, (3) a channel, (4) the receiver, and (5) the destination. As engineers during World War II at the Bell Telephone Laboratories in the United States, their primary concern was finding out the most efficient means of using the channels of communication (the telephone cable and the radio wave) for the transfer of information. They, however, claimed that the mathematical model they worked out as a result of their research at Bell, was widely applicable to human communication as well.

Wilbur Schramm, whose theories have influenced much Indian planning on the role of communication in development, adapted Shannon and Weaver's model to human communication, but stressed the encoding-decoding aspects as crucial. He defined communication as 'the sharing of information, ideas or attitudes'. He endorsed the Aristotelian principle that communication always requires at least three elements—source, message and destination.

The encoding and decoding of the message were the most important components to him. As he explained: Substitute 'microphone' for encoder, and 'earphone' for decoder and you are talking about electronic communication. Consider that the 'source' and 'encoder' are one person, 'decoder' and 'destination' are another, and the signal is language, and you are talking about human communication.

In a communication model he developed with Charles Osgood, Schramm suggested that communication was circular in nature, where both the sender and the receiver were involved in encoding and decoding, and were equal partners in the exchange. Berlo, on the other hand, saw communication as a 'process' and the events and relationships of this process as dynamic, ongoing, ever-changing, continuous.

He argued that you cannot talk about the beginning or the end of communication or say that a particular idea came from one specific source, that communication occurs in only one way and so on. He termed this the 'bucket' theory of communication wherein ideas were dumped from the source into a bucket, such as a film, a lecture, a book, a television program or what have you and shipped the bucket over to the receiver and dumped the contents into his head.

In sum, Western communication theories and the models (especially of development communication) built on them have been largely unilinear, wrongly postulating a mechanical notion of communication as the transmission of information from active sources to passive receivers. Further, these individual-based models wrongly assume that communication is an act, a static phenomenon privileging the source, not a dynamic process involving all elements in a social relationship.

In recent years, however, the focus in Western communication theory has shifted from mechanistic 'effects' models of communication acts to those concerned with communication relationships and the communication 'experience'. Semiotic models look at communication as 'social interaction through messages.' The focus of attention in these models is language (both verbal and non-verbal) as a sign-system; how 'meaning' is generated and understood is central to this approach. The crucial questions the semiotic approaches address are: What is a Sign? What is the Meaning of Signs? What is the relationship between signs, users and external reality? The user is seen as active, as a creator of meaning, as one who makes his or her own meaning. Meaning is thus not so much in the words, gestures or symbols (the 'text') but in the cultural interpretation of the participants (the 'readers') of the communication experience. The semiotic approaches to communication are based on the work of C.S. Pierce, who established the American tradition of semiotics; C.K. Ogden and LA. Richards of Britain; and the Swiss linguist, Ferdinand de Saussure.

James Carey, the American anthropologist, has been foremost in promoting a 'ritual' model communication. Horace Newcomb, Robert Alley and others also promote this perspective. They base their approach on Victor Turner's extensive anthropological studies of the role of ritual in societies. 'All members of the public, not just message senders, are considered to be actors contributing in some way to the pattern of meaning of a nation or region.'

They object to a 'transportation' model which defines communication as the 'transmission of messages for purposes of social control.' Public communication such as television is more closely analogous to the moment of ritual in which myths, values and meanings of life are recalled and re-enacted. Communication is thus a process of creation, representation and celebration of shared beliefs.

Communication as a dialogic and 'participatory' relationship is at the heart of the South American perspective. The key elements of the perspective are 'liberation', 'participation' and 'conscientization' derived from liberation theology and the writings of the late Paulo Freire, the Brazilian educationist. This perspective of communication challenges the traditional Aristotelian model of communication as 'transmission' and 'transportation'. Much of South American research in communication is based on this model.

Sign of Authority

In some situations, Communication is an exercise in power-relations, the power of one individual over another, of an individual over a group, and of mass media owners and producers/professionals over audiences. This perspective of Communication focuses on the inequality among people involved in a communication experience: the inequality in class, caste, economic and social power. This perspective has its basis in Marxism which sees 'conflict' and class differences rather than consensus as the function of communication. Communication is a relationship of power in the family, the classroom, the work place, and the mass media situation.

6

Motives and Purposes

Public opinion is like an iceberg. We know only the tip of this iceberg, while a large part remains submerged. Hence, simple observations may not suffice. Hence, the importance of fact finding as the starting point of any PR programme. It is a battle for men's minds which can never be considered to have ended. Its aims are:

(1) To convey to the public the policies and programmes of the organisation.

(2) To interpret the external world to the top management and interpret top management's decisions and policies to the external publics.

(3) To change people's attitudes.

(4) To overcome people's prejudices, suspicions and dislikes.

(5) To establish goodwill and understanding between organisation and public.

(6) To bring about an adjustment between the organisation and the socio-economic environment.

(7) To build an image of the organisation as a dynamic forward looking organisation.

Public relations thus serves as a detector, evaluator, interpreter and communicator.

Various Channels : The basic tool is communication, to inform and persuade the Public by providing the right kind of information to remove misconceptions, if any, and to promote understanding and to establish the credibility of the organisation.

The publicity department prepares a brief factual account of events like annual accounts, progress made in the year, opening of new offices, launching of new plans, diversification of activities and circulates it to the media.

The chairman and others give an opportunity to the media people to seek information through questions, thus exposing the institution to critical evaluation. This also indicates the willingness of the management to share the information frankly and freely.

Sponsored visits of media men to offices.

Sponsored article by executives of institutions in newspapers and magazines.

Insurance week, claims and deposit clearance campaigns etc., create favourable public opinion.

Elements of Necessity

It is getting along well with the 'Public,' both internal and external. No man can work in a vacuum. Each person who works in an organisation has to get along with the other; he should be aware of the other and show interest in his progress as he does for his own.

Empathy is feeling with the other person. Feeling sorry for him is sympathy. Empathy can be regarded as the primary prerequisite for a satisfying experience in any relationship where a certain degree of depth of understanding is expected.

There are two forms of intercourse between individuals and between groups: force and persuasion. If one party compels another to do something instead of persuading him, this is despotism, it is against the principles of proper conduct, sanctioned by society. A sense of human interest on the person who is being persuaded will understand and appreciate the cause and effect of his action.

It is conversation with a purpose. It is 'reason's only weapon. 'It is not a bargain-basement transaction with haggling and bickering; it is a low form of negotiation.

Dialogue is a reasonable exchange of ideas bringing into being a new form of knowledge: the use of dialogue is for influencing behaviour, selling goods or inspiring ideas.

Calm and Alignment

These are generally involved in dialogue. When speaking to an unfavourably disposed group or person, the first talk is to conciliate people and breakdown prejudice. He is a clever person who, under the circumstances, succeeds in bringing a state of urbanity into a gathering that is marked by discussion.

Public is a group of similar individuals, an assortment of persons having the same interests, problems, circumstances, goals. Public is a varied creature and it comes in many forms and sizes. It has a multitude of wants and desires, and has its own likes and dislikes. It is a source of opinion.

Human wants create the need to establish relations with one another. The respective wants of two individuals will profoundly affect their relationship. To understand any relationship, therefore, one must understand the wants and desires of those involved.

Relationships are of every possible type. We have relationship by rank: superior to inferior: equal to equal. We have relationship which may be neutral. At any rate, it is there, to be accepted, ignored or altered, as desired.

For this purpose we may classify our universe into three groups of people: Those who know you and like you. Those who know you and do not like you. Those who neither know you nor care for you. The third is usually the large majority.

Now the aim should be to reach a position where those who know you and like you stay that way. Where those who know you and do not like you, change their opinion, and those who neither know you nor care for you, wish they could meet you and do business with you. The techniques to be adopted here can be likened to a fisherman. By selecting the worm as the bait, the fisherman goes by the taste of the fish—not by his own taste.

Thus the interlinking of the two human elements, viz., Public and Relations becomes Public Relations — which has now become a profession, and accepted as an arm of all management functions.

We live in an inter dependent world: developing countries depend on the developed countries for technological, economic and other kinds of assistance. For example, oil-less countries depend on oil-rich countries, and oil-rich countries, in turn, depend on oil- less countries to export their surplus of food and allied items of production. And oil-producing countries have necessarily to depend upon others as they cannot produce in their own lands other items required by them — industry, commerce and business depend upon those who could help run their affairs by employing their skills and knowledge and vice versa. Government depends on the public for men and money as well as public acceptance of their policies and programmes. Politicians depend on the citizenry for money and votes, and the citizenry, in turn, depends on the politicians to represent them in the Parliament and State Assemblies.

Public Relations can help win friends and gain their goodwill and that of the community at large: help build favourable image of an organisation or individuals; promote products and services: goodwill of employees; overcome misconceptions and prejudices; forestall attacks by interested groups or individuals; educate the public to a viewpoint; national integration; international understanding.

Public Relations is a profession which will not make you consent without your consent. A public relations professional is fundamentally a catalyst. Upon his initiative, management takes action to obtain a favourable consensus from the various publics. The fact remains that what is best for the shareholders may not be best for the society, and conversely, there are situations where what is best for the society may be incompatible to the interests of the company and its shareholders. The skill at resolving such a conflict is really what public relations is all about.

A public relations professional is not a magician nor will he white-wash a spotted image. Nor is he the good-natured fellow who will keep the inquisitive newspaper reporters away from the management. Nor is he the man who churns out the goodwill of the company year after year even if the origin of good does not exist.

Mutual understanding is the core of public relations. There can be no mutual understanding without communication. For, while the number of 'publics' we recognize has increased over the years, the people who make up these groups have also changed in at least two specifics. They are more *sophisticated* and they are more *involved.* Both of these sophistication, and involvement, can be attributed to the present phenomenon known as the communication or information explosion.

The Interrelationship

Ultimately recognizing that it is not the be-all and end-all of the constant search for wealth only, man's mind eared for something which will bind humankind as a community, and that is Public Relations.

Public Relations is everyone's business: dating back to Adam and Eve. The 'forbidden fruit' would have remained uneaten but for the good PR effort of 'Satan'.

Again, but for sage Narada, the greatest PR personality, gods like Lords Shiva and Vishnu would not have accepted the responsibility of annihilating the evil force in the Asuras and deliver the Devas from their clutches.

(1) Public relations begin when we come in contact with people.

(2) Public relations is based on human relations, a helpful attitude knowledge of one's own subject, ability to generate confidence in one's organization, sticking to the truth, balance in the presentation of controversial issues and fair minded impartiality in dealing with men and matters.

(3) Public relations is a profession which does not make you consent without your consent in that it considers all its 'publics' as relations and all its relations (with the publics) is public.

(4) Public relations highlights the rewards of mutual understanding and the risks in misunderstanding between individuals, groups, governments, by "deliberate, planned and sustained efforts to establish mutual understanding".

(5) The public relations profession demands of the practitioner the skills of a general who knows how to make war, the talents of an advocate who can speak for his clients, the strategy of a politician who

knows what strings to pull and the knowledge of a psychiatrist who understands how crazy people are and why craziness is not bad.

(6) What the management defines... public relations refines.

There are two newspapermen, three personages of particular distinction in history: Edmund Burke, the great parliamentarian, flattered the press gallery by pointing to its members and naming them the Fourth Estate, far more important than the other three estates in Parliament.

Thomas Jefferson said that he would prefer newspapers without a government to a government without a newspaper. Incidentally, it is he who struck the words 'state of thought' and wrote 'Public Relation' instead in his 7th Address to the Congress.

Voltaire set a standard for freedom of speech by telling Helvetius, "I disapprove of what you say, but I will defend to the death your right to say."

Against this backdrop what is expected of newspapers and reporters notably in our country:

(1) The produce of their work is vitally important to the readers and the country.

(2) Should justify their freedom to report by writing accurately and interestingly and by interpreting fairly and intelligently the significant happenings and truths of their time.

(3) They must know their public; it will help if the reader knows something of the problems of the reporter and the editor, and they go about solving them.

(4) If a newspaper is published to advance a cause, it is only a house journal, not a newspaper.

(5) A perfect newspaper will be the voice of the lowly and oppressed and forgotten people, champion of the

underdog. The chief function is to hold up a mirror to the happenings of the day.

(6) Appraise your report, is it a statement of fact, interpretation, opinion, arguments or special pleadings? In an important report is some one named as authority?

(7) An editorial page which offers genuinely worthwhile fare will not have to worry about lack of readers.

(8) A courageous publisher supported by an inspired, intelligent and dynamic reporting and editorial staff might find his great fulfilment as a newspaperman and as an Indian in making his publication desired by the public outside its present circulation and because of its authentic and well-written reports about national affairs.

(9) To sum up newspapers should consider themselves as tenants of society.

Inter Communication

(1) One of the functions of a PR person is to edit a house journal. This is industrial journalism. An editor of a newspaper conforms to the highest standards of journalism—informative, educative, instructive, stimulating, interesting and generally inspiring. The PR executive who edits the house journal also follows standards of the newspaper editor.

(2) The aim of a newspaper is to bring the citizenry and the government closer to each other. Similarly the PR department of a business corporation strives to bring the corporation closer to its related 'Publics'.

(3) If, say a new policy evolved by a company is likely to affect the morale of the employees, the PR executive discusses the pros and cons of the policy with the Board of Directors. Likewise, the editor of a newspaper

has a conference with the editorial staff to analyse any measures adopted by the government which are considered not in the interest of the public at large in the long run; then the 'editorial' is framed accordingly.

(4) How Public Relations comes face-to-face with journalism:

(a) When a 'press release' has to be made.

(b) When a press conference is convened.

(c) When open house, plant tours and exhibitions are organized, good relations with the working journalists, feature columnists, editors has to be developed to keep them informed of the significant features of each event pertaining to the company.

(d) As and when Companies, Chambers of Commerce, Trade Associations... organise Seminars relevant to the larger interest of business and with particular significance to the well-being of the nation, e.g., National Integration, 'Ecology and Environment', Export Promotion... public relations plays a dominant role in getting the press persons involved with a view to making them interested in the proceedings so that conclusions/recommendations/decisions reached will be duly highlighted in the columns of the newspaper and a suitable editorial is also written.

(5) In the following areas of public relations profession, the practitioner has to follow the editors governing;

(a) Dedication to objective and reality,

(b) Social responsibility,

(c) Professional integrity,

(d) Public interest.

International Code of Ethics for Public Relations as adopted by the Public Relations Society of India at the 1st All India Public Relations Conference, New Delhi, April 21, 1968. Considering that all member-countries of the United Nations Organisation have agreed to abide by its Charter which reaffirms "its faith in fundamental human rights, in the dignity and worth of the human person" and that having regard to the very nature of their profession, Public Relations practitioners in these countries should undertake to ascertain and observe the principles set out in this Chapter.

Considering that, apart from 'right', human beings have not only physical or material needs but also intellectual, moral and social needs, and that their rights are of real benefits to them only in so far as needs are essentially met.

Considering that, in the course of their professional duties and depending on how these duties are performed, Public Relations practitioners can substantially help to meet these intellectual, moral and social needs.

And lastly, considering that the use of techniques enabling them to come simultaneously into contact with millions of people gives Public Relations practitioners a power that has to be restrained by the observance of strict moral code.

On all these grounds the Public Relations Society of India hereby declares that it accepts, as its moral charter the principles of the following Code of Ethics, and that if, in the light of evidence submitted to the Society, a member of this Society should be found to have infringed this Code in the course of his professional duties, he will be deemed to be guilty of serious misconduct called for an appropriate penalty.

Importance of Society

(1) To contribute to the achievement of the moral and cultural conditions enabling human beings to reach

their full stature and enjoy the indefeasible rights to which they are entitled under the "Universal Declaration of Human Rights".

(2) To establish communication patterns and channels which, by fostering the free flow of essential information, will make each member of the group feel that he is being kept informed, and also give him an awareness of his personal involvement and responsibility and of his solidarity with other members.

(3) To conduct himself always and in all circumstances in such a manner as to deserve and secure the confidence of those with whom he comes into contact.

(4) To bear in mind that because of the relationship between his profession and the public, his conduct—even in private—will have an impact on the way in which the profession as a whole is appraised.

(5) To observe, in the course of his professional duties, the moral principles and rules of the "Universal Declaration of Human Rights".

(6) To pay due regard to, and uphold, human dignity, and to recognise the right of each individual to judge for himself.

(7) To establish the moral, psychological and intellectual conditions for dialogue in its true sense, and to recognise the right of the parties involved to state their case and express their views.

(8) To act, in all circumstances in such a manner as to take account of the respective interests of the parties involved; both the interest of the organisation which he serves and the interests of the publics concerned.

(9) To carry out his undertakings and commitments which shall always be so worded as to avoid any misunderstanding, and to show loyalty and integrity

in all circumstances so as to keep the confidence of his clients or employees, past or present and of all the publics that are affected by his actions.

(10) Subordinating the truth to other requirements.

(11) Circulating information which is not based on established and ascertainable facts.

(12) Taking part in any venture or undertaking which is unethical or dishonest or capable of impairing human dignity and integrity.

(13) Using any 'manipulative' methods or techniques designed to create subconscious motivations which the individual cannot control of his own free will and so cannot be held accountable for the action taken on him.

Global Picture

* I believe in public relations as the determining factor that brings about harmony of understanding between government and government, government and people, group and the public, and individuals and the public.
* I consider the practice of public relations as based on broad general knowledge; logical and objective thinking; discretion; tact; imagination; talent of expression; an active desire to understand and help people; and, above all, absolute integrity.
* I will maintain as essential to the successful practice of public relations a working knowledge of all avenues of approach to the public such as books, pamphlets, magazines, newspapers, trade and employee publications, house organs, annual reports, brochures presentations, letters, speeches, proceedings, lectures, motion pictures, photographs, radio, television, the drama, the school room, and all events that shape

and symbolize given activities and by which they are known to the public.

* I shall keep faith with the individuals or activities I represent, with the means of communication with the public, and with the public itself; I will not accept assignments that are antagonistic to each other or those that are anti-social and I will shun activities that deviate from the highest ethical standards.
* I shall be alert to public trends, motives, thought, action and reaction so that I shall be a propagandist only in the finest sense of the word.
* I shall collaborate in assuming constructive civic and social responsibilities.
* I shall not obtain any business by means of fraudulent statements or by use of implications unwarranted by fact or reasonable probability and shall comply, both in spirit and letter, with all the rules and regulations prescribed by law and government agencies for the health, safety, and progress of the public.
* I shall not perform, or cause to be performed, any act which would tend to reflect on or bring into disrepute any part of the practice of public relations.
* I believe in public relations as the liaison between the fibre of the nation and the ideas, products, and services that make it strong and I subscribe to these standards as the Code of Public Relations.

Behavioural Norms

As Members and Associates of the *Public Relations Society of America,* we share a responsibility for the good character and reputation of the public relations profession. Therefore we will adhere to the following principles and standards of practice:

(1) We will keep our objectives in full accord with the public welfare as well as the interests of our clients or employers.

(2) We will be guided in all our activities by the standards of accuracy, truth and good taste.

(3) We will safeguard the confidence of both present and former clients or employers.

(4) We will not engage in any activity in which we are directly or indirectly in competition with a present client or employer without the full knowledge and consent of all concerned.

(5) We will cooperate with fellow practitioners in curbing malpractices.

(6) We will support efforts designed to further the technical proficiency of the profession and encourage the establishment of adequate training and education for the practice of public relations.

To the extent that we live up to these principles and standards of practice, we will be meeting our responsibilities for making the profession in which we are engaged worthy of continued public confidence.

7

SYSTEM AT WORK

An ongoing media information service is very much the backbone of any media relations programme. It supports the publicity for important activities and launches and provides the day-to-day contact which is so essential in ensuring that the organization and its activities, services and products receive a steady stream of coverage throughout the year.

Unfortunately this is the least glamorous of any of the activities of a busy public relations office and it tends to receive the least attention. Everyone is happy to jump-to and work hard on a new factory opening or a big product launch, but they are not so eager to rush off and fulfil the everyday requests which come in from the media. Yet service given to the media at this level can determine the outcome of much more important media decisions in the future.

Most editors and journalists are perfectly honest about the fact that when they need help they tend to go to those PROs who have been helpful in the past. A transparency sent round by cab or a special piece of artwork produced at short notice can be just as valuable as an exciting launch or a slap-up launch. Indeed it will contribute to a better relationship.

Nor is the role of an efficient information service purely a passive one. An imaginative PRO or press officer will be thinking up new and useful angles for in-depth feature material suitable for specific programmes or publications and will be spending a good proportion of his or her time selling them. Unfortunately, not enough thought is put into this area and many editors complain about the lack of creativity displayed in the ideas put to them.

Basic Needs

The degree of formal organization given to the media information service depends to some extent on the size of your organization or, for a consultancy, on the size of the fee paid by the client. Some large organizations have specially designated press officers working within a press office which, though coming under the surveillance of the public relations department, is separate from it. Other organizations designate a press officer within the PR office and others simply expect all the PR staff to act as press officers as the need arises.

It probably does not matter what title is held by the people who will be dealing with media enquiries, but what does matter is that they should be reasonably au fait with the company and its products. The lack of even basic knowledge is probably a fault encountered more when dealing with a consultancy than with in-house PROs. If the query is of a complicated or technical nature it is quite acceptable to pass it on to the expert. And you really should have price lists and stockists handy.

As well as having a good working knowledge of the subject with which you are dealing, you, as an efficient PRO, should also have at your fingertips the names and telephone numbers of people within the organization who are competent to speak to the media on specialist subjects, and this list should include others apart from the brand managers and marketing department personnel. It is annoying to a journalist who is working on a story to be told that the PRO will ring back with the relevant numbers and then not to get them for another two or three days.

If the queries coming into the public relations or press office are short questions they can usually be answered on the spot, but quite often they will be in the form of a general request for information on a specific topic and it could be that your organization has in its files material which could be sent out. Do make sure that all this material is filed in such a way that it is easy to find and is related to any photographic or other reference.

Some information services are organized in such detail that they have a grandiose title such as 'The Barbed Wire Information Bureau', information sheets and a direct telephone line. However, such a detailed service is usually organized primarily for the consumer rather than for the media, though answering press queries will be part of its function.

If you do have a fairly sophisticated information service it is easy to think that you have all the answers to hand, but this may not be the case. So when taking down details of media enquiries don't just record them: listen, be constructive and ask questions. If you know what the story or feature is to be about and the angle from which the producer or journalist is approaching it you will be able to be more helpful. There may be a booklet on the subject, a special expert in the technical department who has sat on the relevant government fact-finding commission or a market research survey giving the latest market trends, any of which would help the journalists far more than the standard handouts.

Way of Working

Most journalists agree that the telephone manners of some PR departments leave much to be desired. Some of them leave the impression that they are really too busy to deal with media enquiries and unless the journalist can use the name of a welt-known programme or a national daily the service is grudging to say the least.

However, there are other PROs who are extremely friendly and helpful on the phone. This immediately puts their organization in a good light and the journalist is disposed to feel that this outfit may be a useful source of information in the future. If this friendly attitude is followed up with prompt service the good impression is stamped even deeper. Too often the executive forgets to phone back until the next day. Or even worse, the material promised does not arrive until the end of the following week. It has even been known for a company to respond to a request for information six weeks after the initial query and then to complain that their product had been left out!

There also sometimes seems to be a feeling that the media could have got themselves better organized and asked for the material earlier. There is occasionally some truth in this, but very often the journalist's deadline is looming close, and the PRO is supposed to be providing a service not a favour.

Checklist for an Efficient Enquiries Procedure

1. Be friendly and helpful throughout; do not give the impression that it is all too much trouble.
2. Record the details of the request and ask for further details about the proposed story so that you can dig out the most useful in-depth material. Indicate that this is the reason for your questions.
3. Drop everything and treat the request as extremely

urgent Even if you know that the answer can wait until the next day it is far better to deal with it at once. It may be forgotten later on.

4. If you need to phone back, do so as soon as possible. Phone back within hours to report progress even if you do not yet have the answer.
5. If you leave a message for someone else to phone the journalist back, check to see that they have not missed the message or forgotten to fulfil it.
6. If the request is for an expensive sample use tact in discovering whether it has a genuine background. You may not have heard of the journalist or author concerned but that does not mean that they are not engaged on a bona fide testing programme or working on a first-class magazine feature.
7. Where necessary send material by cab or messenger.
8 Check to see that both postal or hand-delivered material has arrived and whether the journalist needs any more material.

Daily Working

Getting the enquiries procedure right is only the first stage in setting up a good media relations programme. The second stage is the much more active one of going out and securing a steady stream of coverage for the company and its products or services. Start by making a list of the areas in which you think you might be able to generate coverage over a three-month period. Such a list of objectives for the PR department of a food manufacturer might look something like this:

1. Feature material on cooking with a variety of the products in women's magazines and in regional media.
2. A series of radio interviews on local radio.

3. A feature on the use of some of the products in pubs for a catering trade magazine.
4. An in-depth feature on the new soup production line in a leading food production magazine.
5. An in-depth feature on the work of the new product development team in a food technology publication.
6. A visit to the Peterborough factory-where new jobs are coming on-line-by the industrial editor of one of the national newspapers.
7. A feature on the activities of the Skelmersdale fac tory social club in the local media and a possible visit by the local radio station disc jockey to a social evening.

A Similar List for a Heavy Goods Vehicle Manufacturer might Look Something Like this

1. A release on the year's export success for both the heavy goods vehicle publications and all the publications covering the industries to which the goods were sold.
2. Local radio sponsorship of a motoring and good driving show.
3. An in-depth feature on the conversion of a stand ard line for use in a mountainous area for a leading magazine in the field of civil engineering and for publication in the country concerned.
4. An on-site demonstration of the current range of earth-diggers for publications covering public works and civil engineering generally.
5. A feature on the new managing director for the heavy freight publications.
6. A feature on safety aspects of carrying chemicals and other dangerous substances for a lorry drivers' magazine.

To achieve the list of objectives set you will need to be in constant contact with the leading media in your field and in occasional contact with all the other publications which might be useful. This contact may be by post, by telephone or by personal meetings. Some enterprising PRs have also used humorous tapes and promotional videos to put their ideas over. The choice will depend on how important you are to a magazine or radio and the magazine or radio to you and thus how often you are likely to be working with this particular publication, how physically near you are to each other and indeed how well you get on at a social level.

However, if you have creative ideas and good material, face-to-face contact is by no means necessary. Unfortunately many editors feel that this kind of creativity is absent from the activities of a number of PROs. The only material they receive is the syndicated material which is sent out to everyone on the mailing list, and there is little attempt at placing original and exclusive material.

Syndication of material can work quite well at a regional level, though even here blanket coverage can be a real waste. If for example, you are running a recipe or a beauty information service you will be able, over time, to build up a list of regional dailies and weeklies who use the material regularly. Some sophisticated services send out portfolios of material to selected users and these are updated from time to time. If the subject is one which is likely to be covered fairly regularly the expense of such an operation will be recouped. But for most products and services this sort of exercise would be too expensive. Others run food and cookery programmes on their local radio stations or even sponsor national radio slots. The success rate for syndicated material can also be increased by sending out material with themes which are relevant to the local area or which are topical.

For national media the approach must be rather different. Monthly mailings are no use at all, and ideas are needed in the first instance rather than completed material. Once you have sold an idea to an editor you can then discuss how much material you will supply and how much the newspaper or magazine will want to write or photograph for itself. Some magazines are pleased if you can produce an illustrated feature to an agreed plan. Others have a large enough budget to be able to retain their independence, and these publications will probably ask for background material only or will send a journalist to cover the story on the spot.

However, if you are to write the feature remember to check on the editor's requirements as to length, the number of illustrations, the date of issue of the article and the copy deadline. Sometimes it is worth thinking about getting a well-known person in the field to write features for you or at least to suggest his or her name to the publication. This will be a more expensive way of producing feature material but it may also make it more acceptable.

If your work is mainly in the trade and industrial area it is even more important to keep in constant touch with the leading publications in the field. An editor will appreciate it if you supply him or her regularly with information about the company, giving advance warning of changes and additions to the product range, the factory or indeed any aspect of the company's activities.

A good relationship in this area can mean extra coverage since the editor will be more inclined to ring your company for quotes or for filler items. Editors have also been known to remind PROs that their exhibition details have not yet been received. Nor should you forget the media local to your offices and factories. Community relations can be extremely important but they are often relegated to the bottom of the list of PR activities.

Checklist for Active Day-to-day Contact : List areas which are likely to generate coverage during a set period. Look at this list in terms of the relevant media and make a list of objectives to achieve within the period.

Send out syndicated material to specially selected regionals and place specific features ideas with nationals and specialist magazines. Be as original and creative as possible by letter or phone.

Once features have been placed take care to fulfil the editor's requirements.

The Pamphlets

Some PROs like to put together a newsletter to send to the media, outlining all the things that have happened to their company over the previous three or four months. These are often quite stylishly produced with a scanner and desk-top publishing packages. The idea is that journalists will pick up just those stories which are of particular interest to their publications.

The problem is that these newsletters are often so well produced that they look far too much like sales promotion material and they may indeed be of use in selling-in to the trade. Journalists are likely to bin this type of material before they even read it, assuming that it will be full of puffs and exaggerated claims.

Far better to forget the clever design and pretty colours and stick to the news. Write up the facts following the Who? What? Why? Where? When? If possible include some information on forthcoming events as well as past history and make sure that the latter is not too out of date. It is quite permissible to include ideas for features, but it is a waste of time to write the whole piece. It is better to negotiate the placing of the complete material into those sections of the media that are likely to use it.

Different Sides

Though entertaining is not an essential part of the media relations programme it can help to smooth the way. Discriminate in your entertaining. If you are taking a journalist to lunch you should know exactly why you are doing it and what you expect to achieve from it. Even more important, you should know what you have to offer. Journalists will not appreciate your wasting their time, however good the lunch. Indeed 'launching' in the old-fashioned sense is on the decline. So do not be surprised if a journalist simply cannot find the time to join you.

Reasons for individual entertaining might include any of the following:

- Briefing editors or journalists on changes and developments within your organization which could affect the industry as a whole.
- Briefing a newly-appointed editor or specialist writer on your company and its activities and the service you have to offer.
- A 'thank you' for successful cooperation throughout the year, usually coupled with a briefing on the coming year.
- An introduction for yourself to editors or specialist writers in an area of the media which is new to you.
- A general briefing for editors or journalists with whom you are not often in contact, usually coupled withideas for specific features.
- To introduce new senior members of your organization to key journalists.

The question of where to entertain is a function both of your budget and the inclination of your guest. It might be a pleasant gesture to ask your guest where he or she would like to go. On the other hand, if you have reasonable in-house facilities this might be a better venue as it will be free from distraction.

It is sometimes even more valuable to entertain a group of journalists together. This can serve both as a briefing meeting and as a discussion group. It is a good idea, for example, to gather together representatives of your immediate trade or industrial publications, together with specialist writers from the national media, at a briefing lunch on the forthcoming year. Such an event enables the senior personnel within your company to meet the leading journalists in the field and to tell them first hand of the company's plans for the coming year. The journalists can ask their questions direct and can also air any grievances or problems in an informal atmosphere.

It is important that the senior management is briefed to be as open as possible at such meetings, otherwise the value of them tends to be diminished. The representatives of the media should see the meeting as a constructive activity and not just a propaganda exercise.

Another example of extremely useful group entertaining is illustrated by a luncheon arranged by an organization which was moving into sports sponsorship for the first time. Leading journalists covering the particular sport were invited to attend the lunch and to give their views on how the sponsorship could best benefit the sport and on how they would like to be kept in the picture. The lunch also served the purpose of introducing the company's executives to this particular section of the media, and much was learnt about how to get the most out of the sponsorship.

Some companies operating in the consumer field have also seen the value of group luncheons in generating special features around products which are not very exciting and which do not really merit a series of individual lunches. Journalists must be told that this is a speculative lunch with only a small information content and that the genera! intent is to discuss the subject in broad terms with the injection of a few ideas from the PROs. The discussion around the table often generates even better feature ideas which can be taken up by one of the journalists present. The trick is to ensure that there are no magazines represented which compete directly with each other. A luncheon to talk about nail care and nail care products might take in one representative of each of the following types of publication: general women's interest magazines, teenage publications magazines, holiday magazines, regional newspaper, London office women's editors, retirement publications and secretarial magazines. There is very little clash of interests here and it will be quite obvious which magazine will be interested in which idea.

Checklist for Informal Entertainment

1. Entertain only if you have a good reason for doing so and only if you have something of value to impart to the guest.
2. Decide whether it will serve your purpose better to entertain individually or in a group.
3. Make sure that colleagues who are to be present from sections other than the PR department are fully briefed on their role and on what can and cannot be said.
4. Have a variety of ideas ready to throw into the conversation and listen carefully to the resulting discussion. Make a note of all requests made for further information and of any interest expressed in ideas for features.

Whatever the means of communication has been, it is important to follow up properly. If a specific idea has been discussed over the phone confirm the details in writing. If an outline idea has been discussed over the lunch table ring up to carry it further, and if you have floated an idea by post and heard nothing phone up to see if it has fallen on stony ground. And when an idea has been fully agreed make sure that you deliver on time. But whatever you do, do not send out a general mailing and then ring up and ask whether the recipient is going to use it or not. If they are, your phone call will merely be a slight irritant, but if there is no appropriate slot at that particular time your call could cause enough irritation to prevent the material ever seeing the light of day.

It is worth mentioning here that the PRO's job should be a two-way one. So far we have been talking about the flow of information from the company, but it can be equally important for management to receive information on how the world is thinking about the company and its activities, about rival companies and about the industry in which it operates. Thus a press monitoring service becomes even more important. If your organization is involved in foreign markets then reaction in these countries would also be important.

The Media Relations department may also be called upon to act as a general information service, in addition to media directories you may need to keep company and financial directories- *Who's Who* and the like. These may be physical or electronic.

The choice of electronic reference works includes CD-ROMs such as *Microsoft Encarta.* This is a kind of electronic encyclopaedia which you can use to find all kinds of facts and figures. Your electronic database might also include the *Oxford English Dictionary, Grolier's Academic Encyclopaedia* (US) or *Microsoft Bookshelf* (half a dozen standard US reference books).

Alternatively you can subscribe to a variety of services such as CompuServe which provides access to large commercial databases such as Reuters News, Associated Press On-Line and Dun and Bradstreet. Others include the Financial Times 'Profile', British Telecom's 'Gold', 'Prestel' (which will also get you into the French 'Mintel') or 'Gateway' the international airways guide, all of which offer a variety of services. 'Profile', for example, holds every word published since the early 1980s in every national newspaper save a couple of tabloids and a few of the more important regional newspapers. BBC Enterprises have also made their database available.

The Internet is another vast source of information and it is growing all the time. Whole newspapers and magazines, complete books, hotel and restaurant guides, tourist information, weather forecasts-the list is endless-can all be downloaded from the Internet. A useful book which will give you some idea of what is available on the Internet is *The New Rider's Official Internet Yellow Pages* published by New Riders Publishing.

The choice of which kind of electronic reference base to use will depend upon the time taken to access it and the cost. The Internet is often the cheaper option but it can take a long time to find the information you need.

Basic Norms

In essence, the mass media are the tools or technologies that facilitate dissemination of information and entertainment to a vast number of consumers. They are the tools of large-scale manufacture and distribution of information and related messages. These tools 'mediate' the messages; they are not the messages themselves. However, Marshall McLuhan, the media prophet, liked to proclaim that 'the medium is the message', though the title of one of his books suggests rather that 'the medium is the massage.' The media are technologies; they are also messages and massages. They can also be looked at as industries, as cultural or entertainment industries. While cinema, radio, television, cable, and the press can easily be recognised as 'mass media', it requires some stretching of the established meaning of the term to include recent technologies (sometimes termed the 'new media') such as pagers, cellular phones, satellites, computers, electronic mail and the internet as 'mass media'. More correctly, these new media may be termed 'interactive media' for they are not as much transmission technologies from one source to many receivers, as interactive technologies, which involve feedback, exchange and participation.

'A mass medium' says Wilbur Schramm, 'is essentially a working group organised round some device for circulating the same message, at about the same time, to large numbers of people.' Such a definition excludes the folk media, group media, and interpersonal communication such as rumour, education and preaching, where communication is not 'mediated' by a 'device'. Further, the pejorative term 'mass' (a way of looking down at people as 'masses') suggests that the modern media are 'experienced' not by individuals and groups in terms of their own cultures but as part of the 'mass' and as 'mass culture.' The term 'mass' also suggests that people's interaction with media is homogeneous, inactive and unquestioning. In communication studies today, however, the term 'mass media' has come to be a useful collective phrase, though it slurs over the distinctions among the various media.

As generally interpreted the 'mass' media are the press, cinema, radio and television. But books, magazines, pamphlets and direct mail literature and posters also need to be included in the label. They are so termed because their reach extends to vast heterogeneous masses of the population living in a wide and extensive area of a country. The means they employ to communicate messages to the masses are technological—printing machines, records, cameras, cable, modems, computers and satellites. Their communications are thus interposed and mediated; they are not as direct or face-to-face as in interpersonal exchanges.

The organs of the mass media are technological means of transmitting messages to large numbers of people. Indeed, they are much more than that. As they are very expensive media, (particularly the cinema, radio, television, video, cable, computers, and satellites) they have to be run by institutions like the Government or well financed private commercial bodies. They require a group of people to organise and administer, to produce, distribute and constantly maintain in working order the whole set up of, say, a studio, a transmitting centre, or a publishing house.

Yet another feature of the mass media is that they are founded on the idea of mass production and mass distribution-the marks of an industrial society. Copies of newspapers and magazines, for instance, are printed in thousands (some national and regional dailies in India have a circulation of over half a million) and are circulated over a vast area. But to enjoy a mass audience, the media have to cater to a taste that is not very 'cultured' or sophisticated. What the mass media therefore reflect and propagate is a popular culture. The culture made popular by Hindi films in our cities is a case in point. With the rapid expansion of television and video in cities and towns, popular culture is likely to take on new forms; the 'myths' of our culture will find expression in ever-new ways.

But the mass media in India are in fact a minority media as access to them is still restricted because of poverty, low literacy levels, and familiarity with Hindi and English, the major languages used in the various media; moreover, reach is limited to populations living in metros and large cities. The folk media, in contrast, have a wide audience; they are media close to the hearts and minds of the people, suited to a poor country, and help facilitate identification and participation.

Modern mass media serve functions very similar to those fulfilled by traditional media in some ancient societies, and in some developing countries today. Western media theorists generally identify three major functions; surveillance of the environment, interpretation of the information and prescription for conduct, and the transmission of heritage. The developmental and liberation or empowerment functions, or even the ritualistic or celebratory functions of the media rarely find mention in Euro-American media theory. South American media theorists have contributed to our understanding of media for 'liberation' while African and Asian scholars have explored the relevance of media to 'national development.'

Various Codes

Surveillance of the environment relates to information or 'news' about happenings in society. The mass media carry out this function by keeping us posted about the latest news in our own region and around the world. In rural societies, however, the word-of-mouth method is still the most credible means of spreading news.

Consensus : But the mass media cannot or should not stop at watching the horizon for us, through news bulletins or through advertisements of documentaries. They need, and often do help us to correlate our response to the challenges and opportunities which appear on the horizon and to reach consensus on social actions.

In rural India, the panchayat meetings help the village elders to decide on the challenges and the opportunities.

The mass media help us to keep the culture and heritage of our society alive, and to transmit it to others. This is what the media should ideally do, but often don't. Folk media serve a similar purpose in developing countries.

A fourth function is the vital function of entertainment. Entertainment has been a legitimate function of the traditional folk media, but the mass media provide it with a vengeance. They help to pass the time, and to relax with family and friends.

Symbolic Function : Anthropologists of culture and communication discern a symbolic function of the media: the media provide a 'shared symbolic environment.' George Gerbner, for instance, sees television as the central symbol of American culture today. Horace Newcomb and other 'culturalists' (such as James Carey and Robert White) perceive the media as providing a ritualistic and 'liminal' experience.

An equally vital function is that of the mass media helping to sell goods and services through sponsorships and commercials. The commercial function has indeed been served well, perhaps too well, especially in the United States, where the networks would have to close down if the support from commercials were to dry up. At the same time, it would be suicidal to let this function dominate the mass media at the expense of the other four functions. India too promotes the commercial function, and though it has not allowed its representatives to take over the programming of radio and television, the influence is still strong. This is equally true of the press and its dependence on advertising.

Developing Values : In the developing countries of Asia, Africa and Latin America, the mass media, which include traditional media have a different function to perform. In a word, development communication i.e., communication that focuses on the information needs of the poor and the oppressed, and their socio-economic and cultural interests.

While these may be the five functions of the mass media,

it does not necessarily follow that audiences go to them for the same reasons. In his book The Play Theory of Mass Communication, William Stephenson argues that fun is both the greatest impact and the greatest public service of the mass media. Audiences use them as a form of play, or lila. Victor Turner, the anthropologist, believes that the media provide a 'liminal' ritualistic experience. James Carey, Horace Newcomb and others of the 'culturalist' school have developed this approach further by analysing the television experience in terms of 'ritual.'

So, for a good number of the audience, the mass media may be marvellous time-fillers, like listening to the radio while cooking or while driving, or reading during a long train journey. Further, some people use the media to fulfil psychological and social needs. They perhaps get vicarious enjoyment out of sex and violence in the media, and use the media to get topics for conversation at work, or to solve their own problems.

Still others might seek information, merely to be well informed, or perhaps to learn how higher-status people dress and live. Or, they might watch advertisements on TV not so much to know more about a product as to assure themselves that they have bought the best product. These are the 'uses and gratifications' of the media.

So whatever functions the media pundits say the mass media have, the people will continue to use them in the way they (the people, not the pundits) like. It is in this sense that audiences are 'active' rather than 'passive' receivers.

Etiquettes of Journalism

Western theories of the mass media (particularly of the news media) were first propounded by Fred Siebert, Theodore Peterson and Wilbur Schramm in their book Four Theories of the Press.

These theories have now come to be termed 'normative' in the sense that they 'mainly express ideas of how the media ought to, or can be expected to, operate under a prevailing set of conditions and values.' So, strictly speaking they are hypotheses rather than theories. These 'theories' were first enunciated in the United States during the height of the 'cold-war' against communism and the Soviet Union. They were thus part of American propaganda and only loosely based on actual practices in the media. They idealise the American practices, which are touted as being democratic and socially responsible, and deride 'Soviet' and 'Communist', practices as being 'dictatorial' and 'authoritarian.' They do not take into account the 'public service' models of print and electronic media widely accepted in Western Europe, and in many countries of Asia and Africa.

The 'original' four theories of the press/media are authoritarian theory, libertarian theory, social responsibility theory, and Soviet media theory. Each of them suits particular political and economic circumstances, and focuses not so much on the relationship between the press and readers as on the relationships between the press and Government. The major concern is with ownership and control rather than with different perspectives of Journalism or the people's right to information. Siebert, Peterson and Schramm limit their analysis to 'four' theories; three more need to be added to the original four to take account of circumstances in the developing countries of Asia, Africa and Latin America. The last three could be termed 'Developmental or Alternative Theories' of the media.

Authoritarian Theory : According to this theory, the mass media, though not under the direct control of the State and the ruling classes, must do their bidding. The press and other media are expected to respect authority, to be always subordinate to established power and authority, and therefore should avoid offending the majority or dominant moral, political and economic values. Journalists lack independence and freedom; their reports have to be submitted for advance censorship. This censorship is justified on the ground that the State must always take precedence over an individual's right to freedom of expression. Such censorship is more rigidly enforced in times of war and during 'internal' and 'external' emergencies. It needs to be noted that both dictatorial and democratic regimes resort to such authoritarian control of the media. The strictness with which the Official Secrets Act is enforced in Britain and in India is a case in point.

Libertarian Theory : The basis of this 'free press' theory goes back to 17th century England when the printing press made it possible to print several copies of a book or pamphlet at a comparatively low price. In contrast with the authoritarian theory, libertarianism is founded on the fundamental right of an individual to freedom of expression. Western liberal democracies swear by this belief. The First Amendment in the American constitution is an embodiment of this theory; it flows from the individual's right to life, liberty and the pursuit of happiness. The individual, not the State or society, is supreme, and popular will (vox populi) is granted precedence over the power of the State. The argument is that 'truth' can be arrived at only through the free expression of diverse points of view, no matter how erroneous. The great apologists of this theory were John Milton, the epic poet (in his Aeropagitica) and John Stuart Mill (in his essay, On Liberty). A free press is seen as essential to a free society and the dignity of the individual. Moreover, the freedom to publish is often linked to the right to property, and the free market system.

In practice, however, the theory provides the prerogative of free speech only to the rich and the powerful elites of a society. The marginalized groups do not have access to, and indeed, cannot afford the means or the tools of free expression.

What happens on the ground is that media merchants and media monopolies (e.g. the big newspaper chains, the television companies) exploit that freedom to expand their empires. Market forces rather than public good mould the kind of information to be purveyed. The theory thus protects media owners rather than the rights of editors and journalists, or of the public. What the theory offers, in sum, is 'power without social responsibility'.

Social Responsibility Theory : This theory can be said to have been derived from the Hutchins Report (entitled 'A Free and Responsible Press: A General Report on Mass Communication: Newspapers, Radio, Motion Magazines and Books'). The Hutchins Commission on Freedom of the Press (1947) was established and financed by Henry Luce of Time Magazine at a time in the history of American Journalism when press barons like Luce sensed that government regulations on 'yellow journalism' were round the corner. Moreover, the years following the Second World War witnessed the rise of the Democratic Party in the United States, the restraints on business under the New Deal, and the strengthening of the trade union movement. The American press (which was known to be largely pro-Republican) feared that the federal Government would issue legislation to regulate the 'freedom of the press', despite the First Amendment.

Robert Hutchins, the Chairman of the Commission, was the Chancellor of the Chicago University at the time, and he was assisted by twelve others who were experts in different fields. The Report appeared in two volumes: the first on newspapers, the second on the other media.

The Commission found that the free market approach to press freedom had not met the informational and social needs of the less well off classes; in fact, it had increased the power of a single class. There was little expression of diverse views; the emergence of radio, film and television also suggested that some public control and some means of accountability had become necessary.

Thus, the theory had its roots in the view that the media had certain obligations to society-to serve its needs, rather than that of the free market. Hence the need for high professional standards; of truth, accuracy, objectivity and balance. Self-regulation and also state regulations were imperative. Public interest was a greater value than unregulated freedom of expression. So news offensive to religious and ethnic minorities, or news likely to lead to social violence needed to be underplayed. The Hutchins Report led to the establishment of Press Councils, the drawing up of codes of ethics, anti-monopoly legislation, and to press subsidies to small newspapers. State and public intervention in the exercise of free expression was therefore considered legitimate under certain circumstances.

Soviet Media Theory : This theory is derived from Lenin's application of Marx and Engel's dictum in The German Ideology that, 'the ideas of the ruling class are in every epoch the ruling ideas.' The media are thus a means of 'mental production' of the ideology. Hence the need for their control by the working class, that is, through the Communist Party, so that the interests of the working class rather than those of the ruling or elite class are projected. In a Socialist society, therefore, the media should be used as tools to 'socialize' the people; the primary functions of the media are to educate, inform, motivate and mobilize citizens, and to support 'progressive' movements everywhere. What is expected is 'objective' (or 'scientific') presentation of society. Censorship and restriction on the media are legitimate for the media are accountable to the State, to the public and to the Party. The public is encouraged to provide feedback, as it is only in this way that the media will be able to serve the public interest.

Development Communication Theory : The 'four theories of the press' are not fully applicable to the experience of the non-aligned countries of Asia, Africa, and South America. While in most Asian and African countries, the media (especially the broadcast media) are owned and run by the State, in Latin American countries, commercial ownership of all the mass media is the norm. A common factor in the experience of the majority of the non-aligned countries is the dependence on industrialized countries for both hardware and software. Another common factor is the commitment of these nations to social and economic development on their own terms; they would like to employ the mass media as tools for 'development', for 'nation-building.' The larger national interest and the public good are of paramount importance to them. So certain freedoms need to be curbed in the interest of say national integration, and economic and social development. Hence the stress on 'development communication' and 'development journalism'. According to development theorists, journalists have the responsibility to support national governments in their efforts at eradicating illiteracy, promoting family planning, promoting national integration, and increasing production and employment. The weakness in the theory is that 'development' is often equated with government propaganda.

Democratization Theory : Latin American critics (notably Paulo Freire, Reyes Matta, Luis Beltran, Diaz Bordenave and Valerio Fuenzalida) of commercialized ('commodotized') media have come out strongly against the top-down, one way and non-participative character of contemporary mass media. Like the development theorists, they lay stress on the positive uses of the media, on the need for 'access' and the 'right to communicate.' They insist on the need for local and community participation in media and news production. The people must speak for themselves, they argue, not through professional journalists and producers.

What is vehemently opposed also is commercial, political or bureaucratic control of the media, which exist to serve audiences, not the interests of government or commercial enterprises. The 'demassification' of the media, according to this theory, is as vital as 'democratization.' The ultimate purpose is to put the media in the hands of communities (as in people's radio) for their own 'liberation' through a process of 'conscientization.' Thus is created, in Reyes Malta's words, a 'critical national audience.'

The Interconnectedness

Successful media relations involves understanding the media, how they work and what their requirements are. It also involves relating this knowledge to the needs of your own organization and the objectives of its media relations programme. It is important to work out the best strategy and to plan accordingly.

This book is essentially practical. It is concerned with the tools, the organization and the planning of the media relations programme. But it also seeks to show how a thorough knowledge and understanding of the media can make your efforts more effective.

There is, after all, no point in spending a fortune on trying to communicate an important story if you are telling the wrong people, in the wrong way, at the wrong time. Putting yourself in the recipient's place and deciding exactly what will be of interest and what will not will be much more useful from everyone's point of view.

This kind of practical knowledge of the media will put you in a better position to build up a harmonious and helpful relationship with those sections of the media which cover your organization's particular activities. And this relationship will in turn help you to establish a smooth communications channel between media and management.

Unfortunately, the senior managements of some organizations tend to view the press or media relations department as a buffer between the media and themselves. This can only lead to trouble. Very often the Public Relations Officer (PRO) is not qualified to answer detailed and possibly highly technical questions. Nor does he or she have the authority to answer for the company on important issues. Such an attitude inevitably leads to an unnecessarily bad press and a lack of cooperation by the media on future occasions.

Rather, the PRO should be the means by which the two sides can talk to each other more easily and with more understanding. You must stick to your professional guns in telling senior management what the consequences of their actions in the media relations field are likely to be. You must, however, also follow up such a stand with sensible advice on dealing with the media and be on hand to see fair play.

Of course, there are occasions when certain sections of the media behave with some dishonesty and as PRO you must watch out for signs of such a situation arising and warn your management in time. But the vast majority of dealings with the media will not be like this, and management must be encouraged to be as open as possible.

Building up a favourable relationship with the media often involves building up a good personal relationship with key journalists in your field. You cannot hope to achieve this if you are not convinced yourself. If you do not think you can be committed to an organization's activities, do not work for it. Honesty is as important at this level as it is on individual issues.

This applies equally whether you are planning to work directly for the organization or for its PR consultants. Indeed everything in the book applies to both situations, for they differ only in their organization and lines of control. To all intents and purposes a PR consultant must act as though he or she works directly for the client organization. 'Public Relations Officer' has also been taken to be synonymous with Press or Media Relations Officer' for the purposes of this book.

Of course a harmonious relationship with the media does not mean that everything will always go smoothly. Sometimes your objectives and those of your media friends will be in conflict and this is where your powers of diplomacy will be tested to the full. Competent journalists will be probing critically. That is their job. Yours is to present the facts in the most favourable light for your organization and, if the problems are severe, to ensure that ultimately your organization's worst story receives the best hearing.

A good example of successful media relations concerns a multinational oil company, one of whose oil tankers was wrecked, causing extensive spillage along the Californian holiday beaches. Sales at petrol stations immediately started to fall. The company instituted an expensive and wide-ranging mopping up programme including very quick cleaning of the popular beaches and a bird sanctuary, a marine life survey and a restocking operation. Full details of the disaster and the company's prompt action were relayed to the media at once and this, coupled with the previously good relationship between the oil company and the media, ensured that most of the coverage was concentrated on the mopping up operation. This resulted in the company being seen as a responsible, socially conscious organization rectifying an inevitable disaster, rather than as an irresponsible multinational with no concern for the environment. Sales not only recovered but exceeded the previous norm.

There are times when the disaster is less obvious to the public view and this is when there is a strong temptation to deny everything. The short answer is, don't allow your management to do so either. If you or any of the representatives of your organization do lie, your reputation in the media will be shattered and its loss will precede you into whatever industry you go. It is very rare for the truth not to emerge, given time, and once a journalist has been castigated by his or her editor for believing your lies the journalist will, understandably, never trust you again. In future, the journalist will be suspicious of everything you and your organization have to say and will tell associates to be wary too.

Successful media relations, then, means understanding the people with whom you want to communicate-producers, editors and journalists-appreciating their problems, needs and audiences and treating them with honesty, efficiency and common sense. It is this principle that underlies all the detailed information and advice.

The term 'media relations' refers to the communication Pattern between an organization and those sections of the media which are interested in its activities. Such communication may be concerned with anything and everything which happens within and around that organization. It may also be concerned with local and national issues, with finance and legislation and with public opinion.

Communication between organization and media may be initiated by either side, but from the organization's point of view media relations is concerned with achieving the most favourable coverage possible. This can sometimes be achieved by reacting to individual happenings or to media enquiries, but at best this approach is haphazard and at worst it is inefficient and potentially dangerous.

It is far better to plan a media relations programme within the framework of your organization's objectives as a whole. This not only helps to channel your efforts into the most effective areas, but also ensures that everyone who comes into contact with the media knows what their organization is trying to achieve.

Functional Dimensions

The first step is to define and analyse the problems in order of priority and then to set objectives to be achieved. The problems will, of course, vary according to the field in which your company or organization is operating and what it is trying to achieve. However, for a manufacturing company the problems might include any of the following:

- The product range is seen as too expensive.
- The proper use of a new product is not really understood.
- The company has a reputation for bad service.
- The company is moving into a new high technology field and needs to upgrade its scientific image.
- The company is not thought of as a good employer.
- The more expensive end of the product range is not being retailed through the right kind of outlets.
- There is an important technical development behind the introduction of a new product which is not fully appreciated.
- The company is thought of as being old-fashioned.

All these and other problems will come in as feedback from the marketing and other departments. Obviously they need to be countered and an objective must be set. Ideally objectives should be measurable and achievable. If you set unobtainable objectives you will be seen to have failed even if you do a wonderful job. To some extent this is also true if the objectives are not measurable.

Whatever you do, do not try to link your objectives to

sales. There may be a great temptation to do this as part of a justification for the very existence of the media relations programme. But you are unlikely to be able to show a link which is directly attributable to your activities and you will be encouraging the view that media relations is simply a cheap form of advertising.

If an objective is to be measured effectively it needs to be defined clearly. There is no point in stating that the objective is 'to increase awareness' or 'to change an attitude'. This is not enough. You must include the answers to the questions 'of what?' and 'by whom?' which will lead you into defining your target audiences. The answer to 'who are you trying to influence?' will in turn lead you on to 'how are you going to reach them?', and once you have reached this stage the programme starts to become viable.

Analysis : Here is a very simple example of the start of a media relations programme for a small company producing torches.

The Problems : Market research has shown that the company's torches are seen as dependable but rather old-fashioned and there is little awareness of the newer products which have been introduced to fit the contemporary life-style.

Objectives

1. To increase awareness of the more recent products.
2. To show that these products are up to date and invalu able to the modern man or woman.
3. To give the company a more go-ahead image, while retaining the dependable aspect.

Ultimate Target Audience : The torch-buying public includes the following markets:

- Women buying torches for domestic and car use.

- Men buying torches for similar uses.
- Industrial buyers, for security services.
- The police and the armed services.

Intermediary Target Audience : The media reaching the ultimate target audience include the following groups:

- Women's interest programmes and publications.
- Men's and general interest programmes and publications.
- Motoring programmes and press, and the caravan and holiday press.
- Security and safety publications (both consumer and trade).
- Police and armed services press.

Planning : This sort of analysis makes the rest of the programme much easier to plan. Working against the background of known developments and plans for the torch company for the coming year a single idea for each area will start the programme off. There may, for example, be plans to launch a new pocket or handbag version of one of the company's torches; if it is sufficiently different from anything else on the market this could form the basis for an onslaught on the women's interest press.

The frustration of life without a torch, illustrated by either a feature or a demonstration, could interest the men's press, and special car fitments for fixing a torch inside the car would be of great interest to the motoring media. Similar ideas for features, visits and events could be thought up for the remaining areas.

A plan like this not only shows up the priority areas and assists a sensible organization to plan its workload; it also shows where effort should be concentrated and helps in the measurement of success.

Massive coverage may look good but it is less valuable if it appears in media which are not seen by your ultimate target audience. There could even be occasions when extended coverage in a large number of regional and provincial newspapers is much more useful than a short piece in *The Times.* The temptation is, of course, to impress management with national press coverage, but this may not always be the most effective approach. It may be good for your ego, but is it good for the company?

Once you have an outline of your media relations programme worked out, and preferably written down, you will be ready to start thinking about the detailed use of tools such as media lists, press releases, competitions, press receptions, workshops, visits and special events.

Evaluation : However, the media relations programme does not end here. It must be assessed. Is the right message reaching the right people in the right volume or are you wasting your efforts talking to the wrong audience or giving the wrong signals? There are various ways of evaluating a media relations programme.

8

PRACTICAL ASPECTS

A professional journalist is easily identified: he is on the payroll of a journal; he reports for his paper, or he may write features or editorials or edit copy. He is known by different names: Reporter, Feature Writer, Special Correspondent, Sub-Editor, Assistant Editor, Sports Editor, City Editor, Commercial Editor, News Editor etc.

The range of work he does is as wide as the world around him. He may report on crime, law and order, political developments, the courts, the Executive, the Legislature, people, fashions, art, music, drama, literature indeed, whatever makes news.

A journalist does more than that he edits what others write, he comments and criticizes and he puts together the news.

Primarily, it is a profession for the man trained to do the particular job in the complex business of bringing out a journal. It is definitely not for amateurs.

Time was when it used to be said that a journalist is born, not made, that you could not push a man through a journalism school and he would emerge at the other end a journalist. Mahatma Gandhi never saw the inside of a journalism school. Neither did Bal Gangadhar Tilak. Nor did a score of distinguished editors since James August and Hicky brought out the first full-fledged printed newspaper in India, *The Bengal Gazette* on 29 January, 1780. Yet, they were men who brought much honour to the profession.

But those were different times. It was sufficient, then, for any one with a sense of mission, to declare himself a journalist, buy or hire a printing press and bring out a journal. Today, however, things are quite different, more complicated. And while, no doubt, some are born journalists, they would be even better if they attended a course in journalism.

This fact, indeed, was recognized as early as in 1920 by none other than Dr. Annie Besant, founder of the National University at Adyar, Madras. The University was launched under the auspices of the Theosophical Society and its first chancellor was Rabindranath Tagore. Dr. Besant was the Pro-Chancellor and Sir C. P. Ramaswamy lyer, Vice-Chancellor. The University had courses in arts, science and commerce and the subject of journalism was added to the Arts Faculty and was part of the English Department. Dr. James H. Cousins was the Head of the Department of English and Journalism.

The subjects taught were: History of journalism, press laws, editorial practice and newspaper administration. Though the Degree Course was closed down at the end of five years it is interesting to note that the importance of adequate training had been recognised as long ago as 1920 and that among the first teachers of journalism were such men of note as N. S. Rama Rao, C. S. Trilokekar, Yadunath Sarkar, and Seshagiri Rao.

We may, therefore, concede for the moment that to be a good journalist it is important to receive adequate and obviously the right kind of training. But-and here we may enter a caveat-not everyone who aspires to be a journalist necessarily becomes one merely by receiving a diploma. Which makes us turn to the next question: What makes a journalist?

There are as many answers to the question as there are leaders of journalism.

"Vitality" according to James Reston of the *New York Times.*

"Hustling" according to Paul Miller of the Gannett group of newspapers in the United States.

"Ferreting out the truth" according to another distinguished editor, Herbert Brucker.

Of course, a journalist should be fun of energy, must be able to get at the truth, if necessary by hustling, but these are partial answers. More things go into the making of a journalist than mere energy or the drive to do a job. Yet, there is much sense in what Mr. Reston once said in a talk to the Columbia School of Journalism: I am a strong advocate of education and specialized training for newspapermen. Yet on the Washington staff of the *New York Times* we have men with multiple degrees from universities.and other men who did not complete their higher education for-one reason or other... Both do well. In going over their records, I am struck by the fact that all of them have this one great quality-vitality, drive, aliveness-call it what you will.

It occurs to me, therefore, that the most thorough education and the finest training in some speciality are of no avail to make a newspaper man outstanding unless he also had the necessary vitality to get on with the job.

S. Sadanand, founder editor of the *Free Press Journal*

fits Reston's description to a T. Sadanand never went to college and yet-all those who knew him would concede that he was a great journallst. He was a man of tremendous vitality and what Reston called "aliveness" and "drive". And what he was, he sought in others. The point about such a man is that, while he may not have come to his profession with a university degree, he would have enough-energy and initiative to provide himself with the kind of education needed to be a good-and successful-journalist. In the old days men with the necessary drive got themselves jobs as journalists and educated themselves as they went along. They were largely self-taught men. Today, however, with competition being what it is for the few openings available to aspiring men and women, the wise among them would acquire the necessary preeducation before applying for a post.

The student of journalism must have, to start with, a good degree whether it be in the arts, sciences or commerce. This presumes that he can write grammatically and is familiar with the structure of a sentence. It is advisable that a student who had graduated in a non-English medium take a special course in English to get the utmost benefit from studies in jonrnalism imparted in that language.

This does not mean that a student not proficient in English cannot benefit from a course in journalism. The essentials of journalism hold good whether the future journalist works for an English or an Indian-language newspaper. Accuracy, honesty and sensitivity to news are universal assets. In the absence of journalism courses in the Indian languages there is only one way in which an aspirant can learn his trade: by attending courses in the English language.

What is essential is that whichever be the language in which the journalist intends to pursue his calling he be well versed in it. Journalists deal in facts; but facts are expressed in words, whether they are in English, Hindi, Marathi, Malayalam or Tamil. A journalist who is not proficient in the language of his choice cannot possibly hope to make an impact on his readers.

This leads to the issue of proficiency not just in one language, but several. The more languages one knows, the more one's chances of landing a job, especially these days when states vie with one another to conduct their business in the regional languages. Even in the thirties, forties and fifties, the reporter who understood and was conversant with Hindi, Urdu, Gujarati and Marathi, not to speak of Telugu and Tamil had a head start over others, especially while covering All India Congress Committee meetings. What was true of past years is even more true today.

As an addendum it may be stated that the journalist who is conversant with a foreign language such as French, German, Russian or Arabic stands a better chance of being selected for posts abroad than one who knows only English. Is journalism a business, profession, craft or trade? It is fashionable to say that journalism is a profession like law or medicine or engineering. A profession it is, but, at the same time, it is a craft that has to be learnt. And woe to the publisher journalist who is ignorant of the principles of business management. Sadanand was a great journalist but a poor business manager and, in the end, was a sad failure. He would' have been a better journalist if he was a better business manager.

Successful journalism is not necessarily good journalism but good journalism needs to be successful journalism as well. The primary purpose of a journalist is to communicate and a journal that does not sell is a journal that fails of its primary purpose. To say, therefore, that journalism is a lofty profession and not a trade or a craft is a bit of snobbery that one can usefully do without.

Good writing is taught not only because excellence by itself is a desirable asset but also because it sells. And a sub-editor who is sound lay-out man is worth his weight in gold. To say that making a lay-out is a profession and not an art is not to understand the meaning of words. Journalism no doubt is a profession, but a journalist who limits himself to his profession is more likely to find that he has that most unenviable of talent un saleable Knowledge. The history of journalism is littered with the lives of men whose snobbery would not permit them to see themselves as businessmen and traders as well.

A professional is a man who has had training in his particular field. An individual is not allowed to practice medicine unless he is certified by a duly recognized medical school. Lawyers, chartered accountants and in some countries even barbers and "beauticians" have to acquire a certificate that recognizes their competence. It would be in the fitness of things, therefore, if news papermen too acquire adequate recognition of their professional talent from their competeters. However, in the absence of institutional recognition a journalist in India acquires professional respectability by the very fact of being on a journal's payroll. The belief, obviously, is that if a person is on the payroll he must be-competent.

In the circumstances the only way to distinguish a professional from the amateur is to find out whether the person is actively employed on a full-time basis by a newspaper or journal. If he is, he literally qualifies himself to be known as a professional. The free-lance journalist-one who is not regularly employed but is a frequent contributor-is just that a free-lance journalist.

The Random House Dictionary of the English language defines a free-lance as a person who works as a writer, designer, performer etc., but not on a *regular* salary basis for anyone employer, organization or the like. The description or definition obviously stems from the fact that in the middle ages, military adventurers,.often of knightly rank, offered their mercenary services to who ever paid them best. Their lances were, so to speak, available to the highest bidder.

The term is now applicable to writers, designers and all who sell their work to whoever offers them the best terms. They may be amateurs or professionals who have retired but whose work is deemed worthy of acceptance. Among the best-known freelancers, surely, is Ruskin Bond, the short-story writer who contributes widely and is considered a success.

Free-lancing, however, is not an easy way to make a living, especially in India where magazines and journals are not known to be good paymasters. The free-lance writer with demonstrated ability to produce acceptable work, of course may eventually hope to reach the status of a contract writer, assured of a regular in come. Such a status assumes that the writer is on contract to write a set series of articles for editors. Should a writer be commissioned to do a piece, the editor would be morally bound to accept it, unless it is downright hopeless. An editor, however, is not bound to print the piece though he is bound to pay for it. Frequently editors accept articles "for possible use" or lay down their own conditions beforehand that give them freedom to reject a commissioned article.

Free-lancing for a beginner is a precarious way to make a living. A person willing to free-lance must either be willing to live on a subsistence level or have sufficient financial means to stay alive without having to depend on income from writing. Many free lancers have regular jobs that guarantee them their bread and butter Jagjit Singh, the distinguished science writer, was a railway administrator.

Few writers can expect to launch a successful full-time

career in free-lancing until they are thoroughly competent and *well-known.* Too often competence is not enough; they must be recognised as competent. The recognition factor, in the case of freelancers is just as important as the competence factor. A. G. Noorani, the lawyer is frequently commissioned to write in-depth articles from as varied a lot as *The Illustrated Weekly of India* or *Sunday* because he is a regular writer for the *Indian Express.* N. J. Nanporia is, similarly, a frequent contributor to various magazines on the strength not only of his unquestioned competence but because he is recognised as an authority on international affairs.

Another free-lance writer of repute is Chanchal Sarkar who is a Director of the International Press Institute. *Science Today* has an entire stable of free-lance writers who write knowledgeably on science subjects.

Unless he is very well known, a free-lancer is wise to specialize in a field where he has little or no competition. Noorani is a lawyer who can write competently on law-he has few competitors in his particular field. Many astrologers in India make a respectable earning by turning out astrology columns which are invariably popular. A free-lancer who is in great demand rapidly acquires status. Requests have gone to them from editors to produce quick copy when regular staff members are fully engaged or are not adjudged sufficiently competent to contribute on special subjects. On the roster of the *Illustrated Weekly of India's* contributors are such distinguished names as K. P. S. Menon, C. N. Vakil or Nikhil Chakravarthy.

There is one note of warning to the young man or woman who wants to be a journalist. You will not from your first week in office be writing stories which make politicians humble and governments shake. It will be a long time before you get a by-line. The only way up is hard work and merit will first have to be proved. Because you write good essays in school is no guarantee that you will make a good journalist.

Career in Reporting

The career of a journalist is very interesting and full of vast opportunities. It is gaining much importance and prestige in the modern society. With the manifold increase in the circulation of newspapers and magazines as well as start of newspapers and journals, there is a great scope for the young men and women who want to join the profession of journalism.

There are hundreds of openings each year for the new entrants. The increase in the circulation of newspapers has created the need for the addition of more staff, both for the larger and the smaller newspapers. The proliferation of magazines and periodicals has also led to the proliferation of jobs in the field of journalism. There is no doubt that an ambitious man or woman possessing the necessary qualifications, can find a suitable opening in the newspaper media.

The career of a journalist demands a wide range of qualities and skills. There is no doubt that this career is highly rewarding, but a journalist has to work very hard for this. He has to know something of everything. The person who wants to reach the top has to master the techniques of journalism and go through the mill. He should also possess a flair for writing, sound judgement, personal integrity, yearning for facts and an expert knowledge of all branches of journalism.

The men or women who work for newspapers, come from many backgrounds and are of many temperaments. Those in the editorial departments, need a strong sense of curiosity about their fellow-beings and a sympathy for them. The other qualifications include a good command of English (or any other language in which the paper is printed), an interest in politics and the government, a desire to know why things happen, a high respect for accuracy and an aptitude for personal communication with other people in order to obtain news from them. A reporter must be both a willing listener and an alert poser of questions.

Now-a-days newspapers generally seek employees for all editorial and journalistic jobs, who have had at least some college education. Many editors insist upon a graduation degree as the minimum educational requirement for all reporters they hire. The diploma in journalism is desirable, but is not absolutely essential. Nevertheless, an applicant who is well trained in liberal arts, with emphasis on English (or the language of the newspaper) and political science, is welcome in most newspapers. Some of those who join this career can also specialise in a particular branch of journalism like news reporting, editorial work, photography, feature writing, sports, writing for T.V. or Radio, criticism, magazine writing etc.

In fact, there are two main divisions of newsroom work, reporting and desk-work. Reporting includes gathering and writing news and feature stories. Desk-work includes the selection and preparation for printing of the written material and photographs submitted by the reporters, photographers and the news agencies. The men who do the desk-work are called the editors.

Use of Sense

Some men and women find their greatest satisfaction in being reporters all their lives probing for information, being close to events as they happen and mingling with the people who make news. Few laymen have any concept of the inside workers of a newspaper who really put the paper together. In fact, even the desk experience is quite necessary for the top jobs. Similarly, few desk men are successful unless they have had a thorough grounding in reporting. Only in this way they can know the problems—a reporter faces on a story and can give him useful suggestions.

A beginner can start as a city hall beat reporter for small daily, he may also start as the telegraph editor handling the news wire and writing headlines. If he chooses the reporting path and sticks to reporting, then he may graduate eventually to a metropolitan reporting staff. If he selects the editing path, he may advance to a large paper copy desk. Or, in either capacity, he may remain with the small daily and soon rise to the editorial management status.

Some persons prefer to become specialists and do their reporting in one specific field itself. The women's page of a modern daily offers many opportunities for stimulating writing; the sports page has also been a great attraction for young reporters. Business news is also a speciality of many papers. Some big papers also offer oportunities to critical reviewers of film, television, the drama and books. There are also many opportunities to specialise in one of the broader general news areas; politics, science, labour, religion, urban problems, social work and public help. Although news reporting is the most glamourous and best publicised part of newspaper work, there are many other opportunities available for young men and women on the editorial page, advertising and sales, copy-writing, circulation, photograph, promotion, public relations etc. in a newspaper.

Many youngmen and women join certain small newspapers or magazines even to do the subordinate or secretarial work. After obtaining a foothold in the newspaper work they rise up to high posts due to their merits and qualifications, because after working in the offices of these newspapers or magazines they acquire a lot of practical experience in the field of journalism. Some persons, while working in subordinate positions, increase their educational and professional qualifications by attending part time evening courses or through correspondence courses.

Although academic or professional education is not an essential requirement for a successful career in journalism, yet some academic qualification is desirable as a minimum so that a person can write correctly and fluently. Possession of a university degree may be quite advisable for those who want to achieve rapid progress in the field of journalism or who want to reach the top jobs. Some newspapers also demand a minimum qualification of B.A.. degree or its equivalent for the new entrants.

Functional Side

A young man or woman who possesses the minimum educational qualification and the aptitude for journalistic-work should apply for a job to some newspaper or magazine office. If a person has already done some writing work, it will be considered as an additional qualification. There is no doubt that a brilliant person possessing a good educational qualification and an aptitude for writing work, will not find much difficulty in securing a position or job in some newspaper or magazine office. Some newspapers may also offer the post of a trainee or a junior reporter in the beginning for six months or one year. If you want to join this profession, you may accept even this offer. To start with the salary offered may not be very high, but as a person gathers experience and proficiency in writing, he will be able to obtain rapid promotions and a good salary due to his ability and hard work.

Trends in Career

A successful journalist has to know something of everything and in a way everything of something. He should have some knowledge of law, religion, war, science, business, politics, economics etc. He should also be interested in philosophy, music, painting and other cultural activities. In fact, a journalist should have a vast general knowledge, because the more the general knowledge he possesses, the better equipped he will be for the journalistic work.

A journalist should be a voracious reader of newspapers, journals, periodicals etc. In fact there is no end to the knowledge and as far as the knowledge of a journalist is concerned, sky is the limit. Therefore, he should try to learn every new thing which comes in his way. He should have a very strong desire for learning new subjects and new things to increase his knowledge. Only then he can go far in this profession.

Farsightedness and Resourcefulness : A person who wants to become a successful journalist must be far-sighted and resourceful. He will also learn a lot by experience. But he should try to develop the qualities of tact, diplomacy and remaining alert all the time from the very beginning. He should also possess the quality of perseverance which will help him greatly in achieving success in his career. He should be mentally prepared to work for long hours and do hard and tedious work.

A person who wants to join the profession of journalism should also have a sound body. A good health is very necessary, for a person who gets tired after a little extra exertion or suffers from headaches and bodyaches, very often may not be able to remain long in this profession, because a journalist has to undergo the strain of long hours of arduous work. Thus, a journalist must have a sound mind and a sound body.

In this profession, he may have to travel a lot, in the city, in the interior areas and may be in different parts of his country. Sometimes, he may also have to travel to foreign lands as a foreign reporter to perform his journalistic assignments. He should be mentally and physically prepared for all this, because when one leaves one's home and goes to a foreign land, one becomes highly homesick. He may also have to travel day and night in strange places to meet all sorts of people. Sometimes, a journalist may be given a courteous welcome, whereas at other times he may have to face harsh treatment.

While covering the war news, a journalist may have to endanger his life for the sake of his profession. A person who wants to enter the profession of a journalist should have a lot of guts and courage. He should be bold and courageous in the moment of a crisis, especially when covering riots, communal disturbances, workers demonstrations etc. He may also have to be present at the scene of a lathi charge, police firing, or teargas. He should have the stamina to undergo all these physical strains, stresses and risks. Like a soldier, he cannot back out from such dangerous situations involving physical risks, once he has been assigned the duty to cover such events. Many a time you must have read in the newspapers how journalists have to suffer injuries while discharging their duties. They even lose their lives while covering a battle, a communal riot or some police firing.

There is a lot of competition in the profession of a journalist and the newcomer has to work hard especially in the first few years to learn the basic things of his profession. The life of a journalist has many compensations like high rewards—when a person has established himself as a famous journalist and writer—incessant change, a career full of adventure, meeting very important persons like big businessmen, famous industrialists, ministers, Prime Ministers, Kings, Presidents and other very important persons. A journalist goes everywhere and sees both the good and bad things of life behind the scenes, but his life is not a bed of roses. On the other hand, it is full of constant struggle, because a journalist works in a highly competitive profession where only the fittest and the ablest survive. An incapable and inefficient person cannot survive in this profession for a long time

Patience Required : A journalist may not earn a very handsome salary in the very beginning of his career. When he starts his career, he may even have to work as an apprentice or as a junior for a few years to learn the rudiments of his trade. During this period, he will have to content himself with an income which may not be very high. Of course, when he has proved his worth and knows his work thoroughly, he will have ample chances of progress and promotion in his career and earn a handsome salary.

As we have already seen, journalism is a very competitive profession. The progress and success of a journalist depends solely on his worth and merit. He may get many chances to rise in his career, but it depends upon him how he makes the most of these chances which come in his way. Once he has established himself as a good journalist, he will start earning a very comfortable and high salary according to his worth. The famous journalists in this profession draw higher salaries with many fringe benefits.

It is a profession where only the proficient and the best have a chance to reach the top. You can find many top journalists and editors of today who joined as juniors and learnt the art of journalism through their hard work. Even today, there are many chances for the brilliant youngmen and women who have the ambition to join this profession, provided they have a strong will power to undergo the hard life, especially in the beginning of their career. No doubt, once a new entrant establishes himself as a good journalist, then life becomes a smooth sailing for him to a great extent. Learning all the techniques of the profession of journalism by going through the mill is the only sure and certain road to success.

Functional Aspects

Journalism like many other professions has also become quite organised now-a-days. In the foreign countries there are a large number of organisations and professional institutions which impart theoretical and practical training in journalism. In U.K. and U.S.A., there are very good arrangements for imparting training to those who want to join this profession

In India also many universities have started the course of journalism in their teaching curriculum. After completing this course the students are awarded the Diploma in Journalism. In the recent years, many professional institutions have also come into existence in India, which are running full time and part time evening courses in journalism. Some of these institutions are also running correspondence courses. These courses are becoming quite popular in our country.

In U.K. the training for journalism is organised by the National Council for the Training of the Journalists.

It was set up in 1952. The aims and purposes of the Council include the establishment of standards and qualifications for entry into journalism as well as the formation and administration of schemes for the training and education of journalists including press photographers. In 1956, an international centre for advanced training in journalism was also set up in Strasbourg under the auspices of UNESCO.

Although it can be said that there are certain men and women who are born journalists, yet in reality they are very few. Now-a-days all those desirous of joining this profession can be trained. If you read this booklet thoroughly, it will give you the basic knowledge regarding the profession of journalism. Of course, vast general knowledge, common sense, objectivity, logic, clear thinking and a flair for writing, are very important requirements for a successful journalist. These are the qualities which one must develop and acquire. Although methods and techniques of journalism media can be taught, yet it is necessary to have some practical experience.

Role of Education

There is no doubt that in the past there were no hard and fast rules regarding the educational or professional qualifications for a person who wanted to join the profession of journalism. In reality, journalism was an open profession for all. Anybody having the flair for writing and liking for this profession could join it, because ultimately his succeess depended upon his merit and capability. Even then, there were not many institutions in the past which imparted training in journalism.

In the opinion of certain authorities, journalism, like writing, should and will always remain an open profession for which no specific educational qualifications should be laid down. It is a fact that the famous writers of the world like Shakespeare and Rabindra Nath Tagore did not possess any university degree or for that matter any professional training in writing.

Similarly, many famous journalists and editors in the past did not possess very high educational or professional qualifications. Even some of the top journalists and editors of today neither possess very high educational qualifications nor any professional training. They have come to occupy the high positions in the journalistic profession due to their flair for writing and their hard work.

In fact, the two main qualifications of a journalist are that firstly he should be a good writer and secondly he, should have a 'nose for news'. Possession of academic educational qualifications like a B.A. or M.A. degree and professional training like a Diploma in Journalism are not a guarantee for a definite success in this profession. A university degree or a diploma in journalism may be desirable these days, but not absolutely necessary for achieving success in one's career.

However, some of the educational and other qualifications which a person who wants to join the profession of journalism should possess are mentioned below :

(i) A minimum basic educational qualification which may enable a person to express his ideas fluently in writing. Of course, now-a-days a minimum educational qualification of a B.A. degree is insisted upon by the management of most of the newspapers for the new entrants into the profession of journalism.

(ii) A Diploma in Journalism, which is desirable but not absolutely necessary. Some newspapers do insist on this qualification also.

(iii) Good knowledge of shorthand and typewriting.

(iv) A flair for writing.

(v) A good knowledge of grammar and the correct use of language.

(vi) An inquisitive mind and willingness to learn more and more concerning different fields of subjects.

(vii) A vast general knowledge about national and international affairs.

(viii) A person who wants to become a journalist should possess a vast vocabulary and love for learning new words, because the words are the tools with which he has to work.

(ix) Whatever may be your educational qualifications, if you are prepared to study hard, then there is no reason why you should not excel in the journalistic profession.

(x) You must develop the habit of reading, especially the important national and international newspapers and periodicals to increase your general knowledge.

(xi) You should try to possess some background knowledge of history, culture, civilization and other, interesting facts of life.

(xii) You should also try to pick up some of the basic knowledge of business, industry, commerce, banking etc. It will help you greatly in your profession.

(xiii) You must also have the curiosity to know about places, things and events happening around you. A knowledge of the political affairs of the country and the laws under which it is administered will also help you in your profession.

(xiv) You must possess the qualities of honesty, integrity and character. These are essential to win the faith of the people you come, across.

You should not be frightened by the long list of the qualifications mentioned above. Of course, the person who possesses all the above mentioned qualities, will be an ideal in any profession. Even if you possess the majority of the above qualities, the others you can develop by hard work and study. But you must have the basic qualifications like a minimum educational qualification, flair for writing accurately, spirit of learning and an aptitude for the profession of journalism.

There is no doubt that a young man or a woman who possesses a good educational qualification and a flair for writing, will not find it very difficult to become a good journalist, provided he has the liking for this profession. If you want to join this profession, start writing small articles or join some newspaper and try to learn the rudiments of this trade practically to become a successful journalist in due course of time. There is a lot of scope for the intelligent and hardworking young men and women in the field of journalism in our country.

9

NEWS PERCEPTION

A news is a report of a recent or current event or an information published in a newspaper or other periodicals. In its final analysis, news may be defined as any accurate fact or idea that will interest a large number of readers; and of two stories the accurate one that interests the greater number of people is a better news. In a news strangeness, abnormality, unexpectedness and nearness of an event, all add to the interest in the story but none of these is absolutely essential.

Similarly, freshness, enormity, and departure from the normal also add greatly to the value of a news, but even these are not absolutely essential. The only requirements are that the story should be accurate and contain facts or ideas interesting to a considerable number of readers. Thus, the news is an information about an event, some development plans, movement of important persons, announcement of Government policies etc.

The news, of course, should be meaningful and have some importance for its readers. But a news should be an information that is both important and meaningful for the people. There is no doubt that an information may have importance for some people while it may have no significance for others. In fact, to become a good news, an information should have importance for a considerable number of readers.

Although the factor of timeliness may not be absolutely essential, yet it does matter. A hot burning news is more eagerly awaited than a stale and old news. Immediacy of the news arouses the interest of the readers. Nevertheless, it does not mean that the past events can never become a good news. For example, if a new light is thrown on past happenings, even this may become a news. The quality of a news is in reality determined by many factors. Sometimes, proximity of an event may increase its importance for the readers. Similarly, stories of human interest and local problems may make a very good news.

Sometimes, the novelty or unique picture of an event may add to the importance of a news. Unusual events always make good news. The information factor in a news is also very important. Whatever adds to our knowledge about which we had no prior information makes a good news. The stories with human element are gaining much importance now-a-days due to their news value. These stories with human element arouse the emotions and sentiments of the readers and create an interest and sympathy in them for the human beings involved in these stories.

Which Type of News are Interesting ? : Newspapers now-a-days are also giving a lot of news in which their readers are particularly interested. Some newspapers even hold opinion polls to know in what columns their readers are more interested. The readers are also interested to read news about the day to day common problems which concern most of them. Because of this, a lot of news about water shortages, electricity breakdowns, inadequacy of transport, scarcity of essential commodities, rising prices etc. appear in the, newspapers quite often. The letters to the editor column is also a very good indicator and mirror of the problems and the interests of the readers.

The Requirements

There are four requisites of a successful news story. These are the power to estimate news value, the stories to write, the ability to work rapidly and the power to represent facts accurately and interestingly. Of course, recognition of these news values implies the need for a "news nose". Without it a reporter may not be able to achieve much success in his career. There are numerous examples of reporters who could not achieve success in their career because they lacked the quality to recognise news.

While writing a news, the reporter should remember the following points :

(i) The first essential of news writing is its accuracy.

(ii) Every reporter should remember that a newspaper's reputation for fairness and reliability rests upon an accurate presentation of the facts.

(iii) You should also keep in your mind, while writing about the facts, the number and class of people who would be interested in them as well as the need for printing them while they still have news value.

(iv) The geographical nearness of an event does add to its interest.

(v) The readers have a lot of interest in all sorts of contests.

(vi) News stories regarding the miseries of the people, helplessness of old people, children and animals also never fail to have an emotional appeal.

(vii) News concerning the well known local, national or

international personalities is also welcomed by the people.

(viii) Even the stories that touch upon the domestic problems faced by the people, business interests of the people and industrial unrest, also command the attention of the public.

There is no doubt that all the features mentioned above are quite important and any of them will contribute greatly to make a story news-worthy. But you should always remember that none of these is absolutely essential. The main essential pre-requisite is that the news should be based upon facts and it should present a new situation or problem or even a new face of an old situation or problem.

Concise News

A professor of journalism was telling his students that "news" had to have a mix of religion, royalty, sex and mystery. He then asked them to write a news report. One answer went thus: "My God!" said the Duchess, "I'm pregnant! whodunit?"

Ask any ten newspapermen what they understand by news and you are likely to get ten different answers. Everyone has heard of the familiar cliche: "When dog bites man, it's no news; when man 'bites dog it's news."

Think of other definitions. "North, East, West, South, what comes from there makes news."

"News is something revealed."

"News is something which somebody wants suppressed." "News is anything you didn't know yesterday."

"News is any event, idea or opinion that is timely, that interests or affects a large number of people in a community and that is capable of being understand by them "

"News is what the newspaper prints and radio

broadcasts." "News is a compilation of facts and events of current interest or importance to the readers of the newspaper printing it."

"Sex, money, crime-that is news."

"News is anything and everything interesting about life and materials in all their manifestation."

"What is new in news."

These are definitions actually provided by distinguished news papermen. They are not necessarily contradictory. News has no "geographic boundaries. News is always revealing. News is what interests popple. News is news.

No news interests all people. Without consciously realizing it, mast people read only part of the paper they buy. In others words their reading is highly selective. They read what *they* consider is news. This need not tally with the news editor's own understanding of what makes the front page. Too often the average reader's interest does not go beyond scandal, murder, crime of all sorts, and sex. Also the unusual (man bites dog), the incongruous and the unexpended (the cow jumps over the moon).

News Traits

A guide to advanced techniques in journalism prepared by the Editorial Study Centre of the Thomson Foundation lists 20 categories of what makes news.

Let us examine them:

Novelty: Man bites dog. Wife beats husband. Cripple scores goal. Something that could happen but had never happened before. Mini-skirts were news when they became a vogue; so did flared trousers. And in an earlier era bikinis were hot news indeed.

Personal Impact: What interests the average reader in his daily life. Bombay Dyeing paying a bonus. Raj Kapoor's son getting married. Stories about people like himself (or herself) which gives the reader a chance to identify with them.

Local Interest: A local bus crash with three dead can be more interesting than 60 dead in a plane crash on the others side of the world.

Money: The budget (national, state, municipal) is news; so are taxes, fall in commodities prices, salary increments and economic crises.

Crime: Especially murder which has a morbid appeal. The Abhyankar murders, the Billa-Ranga kidnapping case are of steady interest, even to those who profess that they don't read crime stories. More often than not, they do.

Sex: This is of perennial interest as can be gauged by the number of even the most respectable magazines that cater to this aspect of life. Also, the more sordid the sex, the greater the curiosity about it.

Conflict: Conflict between man and wife resulting in divorce cases, between nations resulting in war, between man and nature resulting in the failure of one or the conquest of the other brings out reader interest. Thousands climbed Mount Everest with Tensing and Hillary.

Religion: Even an agnostic is interested in the election of a Pope; a Cardinal found dead in a Paris prostitute's apartment made news in a big way. Maharshi Mahesh Yogi, Rajneesh they all make news because they appeal to our emotions.

Disaster and Tragedy: The *Titanic* sinks with all aboard. French expedition to *Annapurna* fails. Lal Bahadur Shastri dies on the morrow of a successful peace treaty. A volcano erupts bringing in its wake death and destruction. "It could have happened to me" feels the reader.

Humour: H.V. Kamath is inform in Parliament making

light hearted comments on his colleagues or even against himself. Raj Narain does some monkeying to catch attention. R.K. Laxman,draws a cartoon that daily draws a chuckle.

Human Interest: Ordeals suffered, happiness experienced, love's labour lost, stolen money recovered. A Prime Minister's daughter is arrested for drunkenness. A wolf boy is found in the jungles of Uttar Pradesh.

The Underdog: Charlie Chaplin's tramp in all variations in real life. The peasant who wins a case against a rapacious money lender. Stories illustrating *satyameva jayate.*

An example of a human interest story:

New Delhi, March 19 (PTI): A man in Pune went to buy meat worth Rs. 2. The butcher asked him if he had a bus ticket. The puzzled man asked why?

The butcher said the prices had gone up so high that he could wrap up meat worth Rs. 2 in a bus ticket.

The man produced the bus ticket and the meat was wrapped in it. By the time the man reached home, the meat had fallen through the punch hole the conductor had made in the ticket.

The Rajya Sabha heard this story from Congress-I member Vithal Gadgil, who narrated it during the discussion on the general budget in support of his contention that prices had shot up.

Or take this story:

Teheran, March 18 (Reuter): A woman received 100 lashes and a man 25 after being caught committing adultery in the Caspian Sea town of Amlash, newspapers reported today.

The woman fainted as the sentence was being carried out yesterday, the papers said, similar sentences have been ordered by Islamic tribunals in several towns since last month's revolution which toppled the Shah. Both the items were carried as box items in *The Hindustan Times.*

The second item carried the headline: Woman gets 100 lashes, man 25. And that, of course, was the reason why the news got a box.

Mystery: How did it happen? Where was the body? Who discovered it? Under what circumstances? Suspense can keep a story running for days. Remember the Billa-Ranga Murder Case. Or the Nagarwala story.

Health: Miracle drug, medical advice columns are always popular items. Any time there is a story of a cancer cure, it invariably finds place in the news columns. So do stories of *hatha yogis.*

Science: Space flights have triggered the most sluggish imaginations into demanding more information. John Glenn, Yuri Gagarin made the headlines. Winners of state prizes for scientific discoveries make stories. Nobel Prize winners, of course, are always good for top billing.

Entertainment: Show business makes news. Who is making what film? Why was a certain play banned? What is Amitabh Bachchan's newest role? What is Satyajit Ray currently busy with?" 'The world of entertainment always holds a fascination that is perennial as the stars and the heavens above.

Famous People: People, especially famous people, make news. Whether they are film stars, sports heroes, musical prodigies or men in high office, their doings never fail to catch the attention of the reader. Famous people are especially newsworthy if they fall from power, fall from grace or fall into evil times. Jackie Kennedy Onassis continues to draw attention, so do the Shah of Iran or Mrs. Indira Gandhi, Ravi Shankar, Sunil Gavaskar and Vinoba Bhave.

Weather: They say that in Britain, the weather is an almost neurotic interest. In India there is a sense of impending doom if the monsoon is delayed or fails.

Food: Next to weather, food and drink is of abiding interest. Shortage of food is news, so is a glut. Have the prices fallen? Are they going up? What about hoarding and black marketing?

Minorities: In every country there is invariably a minority community and their treatment or problems are of especial interest. Blacks in the United States, Harijans in India or Christians in Orissa-as minorities and groups, they are in the news most of the time.

Sudden News

Some news is predictable. Some can be anticipated. But all too often news is unpredictable. What is predictable should be marked in advance by the Chief Reporter for adequate coverage. Failure to do so is inexcusable. Parliamentary or legislative sessions, inquiries by various committees, trials, international conferences.

I all these would have been announced in advance. So would news conferences, fashion and trade exhibitions and the like. Everyone knows when Diwali comes around and a pre-Diwali story literally writes itself.

Dates of strikes are often made known days or weeks ahead. What is involved in the strike? How many workers will be out of work? What is the strike's likely duration? A strike is a rich news vein to exploit for the competent reporter. Some news can be anticipated, such as the completion of a waterworks, the extension of a roadway, the appointment of a cabinet minister, even the coming of the monsoon. Some of this involves intelligent guesswork based on knowledge of people and personalities, prior promises and research in the newspaper morgue.

The unpredictable news is what stumps most reporters, and it is in their ingenuity in handling such news lies their real talent. The murder of a politician or a president, the collapse of a building, the eruption of a long dead volcano, a truant hurricane that leaves a trail of destruction in its wake the sinking of a ship in mid-Pacific, the theft of a priceless painting from a famous museum, these are situations that are unpredictable and tax the strategies of the reporter's desk.

For every one of these unpredictable events there is a sequential chain of inquiries to be made that a competent reporter knows how to handle Information sources are easy to identify: official, such as the District Collector, the District Superintendent of Police and their respective offices, the local Janata (or Congress or Communist or any parallel) party office, the offices of relief organizations (Servants of India Society, Ramakrishna Mission, Church missions), the mamlatdar or petty revenue officials, the postmaster, the headmaster of the local school, the local lawyer.

In big cities there is a wider range of information sources available, both official and non-official. It is knowing how to collect the information, have it double checked for accuracy and writing it that distinguishes the competent from the incompetent, the smart from the dullard.

The Follow-up: News is not merely the reporting of one day's events. If that were so, there would be no need for a newspaper. Gossip could suffice. After all, if a plane crashes off Bombay's seas, the news gets known in no time, a daily or no daily. What is important for the reader is not merely the reporting of an event, but its follow-up.

On 9 August 1942, the All-India Congress Committee meeting at Gowalia Tank, Bombay, passed its famous Quit India resolution. It was the biggest event of the month, if not the year. But what followed was even more sensational. The Congress leaders had hardly gone to bed that night when they were picked up, one by one, by the police, herded into cars, driven to a train that was being kept ready for their arrival and taken to Poona. As much as the passing of the Quit India resolution was the report of the arrest of the leaders and their subsequent incarceration important.

There is therefore much truth in the comment that the follow-up is not only an essential part of an active newspaper's function but it often leads up to a more important story than the original. In fact, in this instant, the follow-up story never ceased to interest the reader until the country became free.

Follow-up implies continuity. This is not difficult in the case of major stories such as a cabinet shake-up, an aircrash or a shipwreck. In the case of the latter two, it can never always be easy to get the full story at first shot. Lists of passengers are usually incomplete and in order to keep faith with the readers it will be necessary to balance out what was, very likely, an incomplete story that first broke out. Readers would be interested to know who the survivors were, what happened to them and whether they have been adequately taken care of. There will also be interest in why the accident occurred and what is likely to be done to see that there will not be a repetition of it in the future. In fact a newspaper which follows up and positively investigates what had happened takes its rightful place in the community.

Newspaper's Importance

A newspaper's role is to reveal the why and wherefores (background) and not merely the whos and whens and whats. This implies that it keeps up with a story until everything falls in its place and for all practical purposes its significance has been understood and appreciated. A newspaper that fails to follow up a story merely prints a series of unrelated events, never projects life as a pattern. A newspaper's approach must be holistic, not frog monetary. In a good newspaper office the News Editor or the Chief Reporter or the Editor himself (depending on how large the staff is) will carefully go through every item in his own or a rival newspaper looking for possible follow-ups. One will invariably find them.

It is better to have those items clipped and pasted on to a sheet on which instructions could then be written. It is important that the sheets are "marked," which means putting down the name of the paper, the date on which it was published and the page number for future identification. It is usual to mark the clipping in red ink.

Those clippings that may not be of immediate use, but could provide information for a likely story in the weeks ahead should be put into a folder for future reference. In all large newspaper offices there is usually a clipping service that provides ready reference. Smaller offices that cannot afford such a service must maintain their own, no matter on how small a scale.

The Curtain-raiser: A curtain-raiser is a story on what is likely to happen and not a report on what has happened. It raises the curtain to show what is on the stage and how the drama will unfold itself. It is to a news event what an appetiser is to a meal it whets one's appetite to know what is going to come. A curtain raiser is based on past events and the reporter's understanding of what is likely to come on the strength of his information on what had happened in the past. Take this example:

Patna, April 21. A split in the Bihar Janata Party seems imminent judging by the letter die outgoing Chief Minister, Mr. Karpoori Thakur, is believed to have sent to the acting governor, Mr. K.B.N. Singh.

The letter says that Mr. Thakur and his 104 associates will not support the government headed by Mr. Ram Sunder Das if anyone having links with RSS is sworn in as a minister in his cabinet.

A sealed cover containing the letter was delivered to the

acting governor a few hours before the swearing-in of the two member cabinet headed by Mr. Das.

Mr. Thakur's letter to the governor at this stage has far-reaching implications. Mr. Thakur specifically states that until the RSS is cleared of the charge of its involvement in the Jamshedpur riots by a three-man panel suggested by him, no persons having links with the RSS should be included in the cabinet.

The letter was drafted in consultation with Mr. Raj Narain and Mr. S.N. Mishra who have been camping here for the past three days. According to knowledgeable circles in Mr. Thakur's camp, a split in the Janata Party is a foregone conclusion.

The group has decided to show its strength on the floor of the house at the June session of the Assembly if the party does not formally split before that.

This was the lead story in *The Times of India* (22 April 1979) by its Special Correspondent. It is evident that the correspondent had close links with the Janata Party and especially the Chief Minister Mr. Thakur. The first paragraph or "intro" suggests that the Bihar Janata Party may split and that the split is imminent. It bases the prediction on what the correspondent knows-in this case a letter sent by the outgoing Chief Minister to the Acting Governor of Bihar. The correspondent then moves on to dissect the likely results if the threat implied in the outgoing Chief Minister's letter is met. The only "hard" news in this story is the fact that Mr. Thakur has sent a letter to the Acting Governor. The correspondent had obviously been told about its contents. His "curtain-raiser" is thus based on what is known to move on to what is likely to happen.

A curtain-raiser is generally careful not to be too specific. It is couched in such terms as "The likelihood of" "Possibilities were raised" "it seems obvious that" "the question is expected to be raised" all of which suggesting the reporter's grasp of how a given situation may develop.

Sometimes the reporter would have been briefed by an official source on what is yet to come. Take this example from *The Economic Times:*

New Delhi, April 21: The Union Government proposes to undertake legislation to provide safety for workers in building and construction industry and to regulate the conditions of work of inter-state migrant workers to prevent their exploitation by contractors, according to the annual report of the Ministry of Labour for the year 1978-79.

The Ministry is planning amendments to the Mines Act, the Plantation Labour Act and the Employees Provident Funds and Miscellaneous Provisions Act.

In this instance, the Ministry of Labour's report would have been made available to all reporters who would have been briefed on what the Ministry proposes to do in the future.

A curtain-raiser, to be sure, is scheduled on the day a meeting is to take place so that it has an aura of freshness. When the curtain is raised, there must be someone on the stage for action to begin. *The Economic Times* story comes under the category or Predictive Coverage, *The Advance Story.*

The Local Follow-up: It is important for a reporter to read overseas journals and magazines to keep tag of events that would necessitate local follow-ups. Thus, when it became known that several hundred women in Europe had given birth to malformed children as a result of taking thalidomide during their stage or pregnancy, it is the reporter's task to find out whether authorities in India have been apprised of the birth of malformed children in any significant numbers, whether thalidomide or any other drug of a similar chemical composition is available in the market and who is doing the marketing. A report in *The Times of India* that suggested that severe illnesses had been encountered in Japan as a result of taking enterovioform resulted in inquiries made of doctors in India as to whether similar illnesses had been observed among their patients. The inquiry showed that Indians, for some reason, seemed better conditioned than the Japanese.

The Hidden Story: Reporters have often to plough through long and laborious speeches and reports that taxes their patience. But ploughing through them with care and thoroughness can be very rewarding. In the mid 1950's, Secretary of State John Foster Dulles made a lengthy speech to the UN General Assembly dealing with great issues of State, but tucked in somewhere half-way was the barest of hints that Goa was part of Portugal. Unless a reporter went through the entire speech which was several thousand word long it was likely that this reference to Goa would be missed and it was probably the intention of the US Administration that the reference-and its significance-would be missed by reporters but not by Lisbon for whom it was evidently meant. All western news agencies which covered Mr. Dulles' speech missed this point, either unknowingly or intentionally but the Press Trust of India's correspondent in the United Nations got on to it and made it his lead.

Understandably it was the lead story in all Indian newspapers since India was concerned about American support to Portugal on the Goa issue.

Jawaharlal Nehru once addressed an AICC session and covered a lot of ground in a lengthy speech. He wanted, however, that one policy statement should be highlighted in the press. He therefore asked the senior PTI correspondent covering the AICC session to come and see him. Nehru then,handed him a slip of paper on which he had written down the policy statement with the suggestion that the PTI lead with it. The next day, according to Mr. T.V. Parasuram, the correspondent in question, several delegates asked him whether Mr. Nehru had indeed said the things the PTI had attributed to him. Nehru, needless to say, had carefully wrapped up his controversial policy statement in a lot of rhetoric in much the same manner as Mr. Dulles had covered his policy, statement on Goa.

Almost any report, if carefully persued, can give excellent leads for stories. It is the reporter's duty to go through reports page by page and line by line. *The Times of India's* Washington correspondent, going through the *Congressional Record,* soon after the Bangladesh war was over, learnt that the Pakistani submarine *Ghazi* with ten torpedo tubes which had been sunk by Indian-action off Visakhapatnam had been an American submarine on Joan which had been in Pakistan's possession illegally, the loan period having been exceeded by 18 months. His story made the front page lead on 27 December 1971. Reading the voluminous *Record* systematically paid off.

The Other Side: Politicians are apt to give only their version of, an event which is only to be expected. Rival politicians inevitably will have *their* version of the story to give which provides the reporter with fresh copy to file. On occasions, the other side may provide even newsier information which the first side had wanted to suppress or otherwise keep out of the press. The other side is the simplest form of follow-up. A reporter is advised never to take the word of a politician, no matter how highly placed, as final. There is always another side to a story and not infrequently it could be the more exciting one.

Enlargements: More efforts are spent in hiding the truth while, giving answers to written questions in Parliament than most readers are aware of Reporters should read the written answers and the supplementaries-very carefully for possible leads. Some of the replies could conceal a good news story if developed. What is being sought to be concealed?

And for what reason? Who are the people who could provide the necessary background for an investigative report? The first thing for a reporter to do is to contact the Member of Parliament who had submitted the question and to see who his contacts are.

Quality of News

Four main factors determine the value of news: Timeliness, proximity, size and importance.

Timeliness: The reader wants his news to be new. That is why he buys his paper or listens to the broadcast. A newspaper that publishes stale news soon ceases to have any meaningful circulation. News coming out of the press must be really hot, in the sense of being not only exciting but new not till then known. The saying "stale as yesterday's news" is its own comment.

Proximity: The reader finds more interest in a minor event close at hand than in a more important event miles away-James Gordon Bennett Jr., when he first published his Paris edition of *The Herald'* gave his reporters this principle in the epigram. "A dead dog in the Rue de Louvre (the paper's address) is of more interest than a flood in China." This may be exaggerating a bit, but it makes the point nicely. But proximity is both geographical as well as emotional. The murder of an Indian diamond merchant in New York is news in Bombay, not only because the merchant happens to be an Indian but because he may be having friends in Bombay. The murder of the wife of an Indian official in the World Bank in a Washington suburb similarly made the headlines in Bombay papers, especially because the murderer happened to be the official's Indian domestic servant.

Size: The very small and the very large draw attention. If Mrs. Indira Gandhi addressed ten people at a wayside village it is unlikely to make news but if she called on Capt. M. M. Chopra and his wife following the murder of their two children Geeta and Sanjay, it is news. If Morarji Desai failed to get a sizeable audience at Ram Lila grounds it becomes news even as it becomes news if Mrs. Gandhi attracted large crowds when she was taken in procession through the streets of Old Delhi in 1979. Similarly, if a Tiger Moth crashes while a cadet is under training, the accident may be dismissed in a brief paragraph while the crash of a Boeing 747 carrying 400 passengers would make the headlines.

Importance: In the final analysis the question that a News Editor will ask is whether what has been submitted to him is really important. While this is subjective, it has direct bearing on the kind of audience that the newspaper has in mind. What sounds important to *Blitz* may not be important to *The Statesman,* and *vice versa.* In the context of the political situation prevailing in April 1979, a dinner meeting between Karnatak Chief Minister Devraj Urs, then a prominent Congress (I) leader and supporter of Mrs. Indira Gandhi with Chandrasekhar, president of the Janata Party assumes special meaning and significance and makes news. For that matter Mrs. Gandhi's call on Charan Singh when the latter was out of office following his dismissal from the Morarji Desai cabinet made news because of what it could mean in terms of a approchement between Mrs. Gandhi and Charan Singh.

10

NEWS PRESENTATION

Presenting News

Subs have to be particularly chary of words and phrases that sound correct but are not necessarily so. Thus “alleged thief” is correct. You don’t allege a person, but rather a crime or a condition, but in this instance the word “alleged” is used in the sense of “supposed” or “presumed” and can just pass muster.

Similarly be warned against confusing “allusion” with “reference,” An allusion is an oblique, indirect mention which leaves the task of identification to the reader or hearer. A reference is a direct naming or description of the thing. It is wise to steer clear of people who chair meetings. “Mr. B. G. Verghese chaired the meeting” could well be the precursor of “Ravi Shankar podiumed the orchestra” and Norman Vincent Peal pulpiting the congregation. Nouns, as Mr. Theodore Bernstein of the *New York Times* remarked, do become verbs, but not overnight.

Far too many Americanisms have of late been creeping into the English language. "Do you dig me, man?" may sound all right in an American novel introducing a black, but does not go well in an Indian dialogue in English, even Indian English.

Paroo Nihalani, R. K. Tongue and Priya Hosali have provided some fresh insights into what has generally come to be known as Indian English. In their interesting work *Indian and British English,* the authors do not use the words Indian English but rather the phrase Indian Variant of English (IVE) to distinguish Indian usage from British Standard (BS).

There are purists who insist that IVE should not be encouraged but this is increasingly becoming a matter of opinion. What is IVE and how does it differ from BS? Consider these examples:

Abode: "His former abode was in Mangalore."

In BS *abode* is somewhat archaic or limited to fixed phrases (mostly hackneyed) such as "my humble abode" or "an abode of vice." In everyday usage, a BS speaker would probably say "He used to live in Mangalore."

About: "We were discussing about politics."

Many IVE speakers insert the word "about" after such verbs as "conceive," "confess" or "describe." It is redundant.

Abscond: "The bus-driver was absconding since yesterday."

"The miscreant is still absconding."

In BS "abscond" is much less frequent than in IVE. The BS version of the above two sentences would be: "The bus-driver has been missing since yesterday" and "The criminal has not (yet) been caught" or "No arrest has yet been made."

After: "Can I come after ten minutes?"

The use of "after" in this manner is fairly widespread in IVE.

In BS one would ask "Can I come in ten minutes?"

Afterwards: "I'll see you afterwards."

In IVE this word is used as a synonym of "later" while in BS the speaker normally means that he will carry out the action after some (implied) event.

Channelized: "Students' energies should be suitably channelized."

In BS, students' energies would be suitably "channelled" or "canalized."

Hotel: "Let's have lunch at a non-vegetarian hotel."

The word "hotel" is used rather indiscriminately in IVE and means what in BS would be a restaurant, cafe or inn. In India, a hotel does not necessarily provide accommodation unless "boarding and lodging" is specified. Taj Mahal Hotel, at the Gateway of India provides tea and coffee all right (in addition to other things) but it is primarily a place where rooms and suites are let out. But Taj Mahal Hotel on Mohammad Ali Road in Bombay gives you only tea.

What should be permissible in modern Indian English or IVE are purely Indian words like *lakh, crore, chhota peg, burra sahib, lathi-charge,* and some 500 other words presently included in the Oxford Dictionary.

Brick and Mansion : Let it be said rightaway: a reporter is to a news organization what a brick is to a mansion. A newspaper is what its reporters make of it.

The reporter's job, to put it in a nutshell, is to gather news. If he is good at his job, he will work with speed, clarity and accuracy. On these three pillars is erected the whole of the reporter's function in journalism. Speed is the very essence of a reporter's job. Time, tide and news wait for nobody. News delayed is no news, unless no one has had access to it till then. The best reporter is still Narada of mythological fame: he was always right where the event was taking place.

Writing in *The Practice of Journalism,* Maurice Fagence, one of Lord Northcliffe's "bright young men" (he died in 1962 after 47 years in journalism, having, in his life-time, covered the Second World War and the war in Korea) had this to say about the reporter he needs the best qualities of a detective (as an investigator), of a psychologist (for handling and summing up people), and of a lawyer (for drawing logical inferences from fact). He has to develop certain thinking processes called for by his special skill. It affects his reading and his way of life. I would ask a beginner to try to comprehend the importance of his basic raw material-news. Without it rumour runs riot. Delay it and there is confusion, uncertainty and worse. In unskilled hands it is more dangerous than dynamite.

Winston Churchill was a reporter. So was Ernest Hemingway.

(He covered the Spanish Civil War). So, indeed, was John Gunther. While-not many Indians have made their mark as reporters (in India, the profession of journalism is of recent origin) the journalistic world is aware of some famous western names such as Herbert Matthews, Evelyn Waugh, Edward R. Murrow, Edgar Snow, Ian Morrison, Alan Moorehead or David Halberstam. American journalist and poet John Reed, author of the famous book *Ten Days That Shook the World* was correspondent for the radical publication *The Masses,* and achieved journalistic greatness with his unparalleled description of the November 1917 events in Petrograd.

While Indian newspapers in the 19th century had their reporters,not much is known about them. In Europe and America, however, reporters of that era had already become part of the national scene. In most instances, these reporters were temporary employees and when their assignments ended, they looked elsewhere for work. It was the American Civil War that finally made the reporter in the United States a full-time professional, a new vital part of American journalism. More than 125 correspondents-most of them special reporters for big-city journals-covered Union forces in the field. They reported with relentless intensity and I sensitivity the drama of the life-and-death struggle for keeping the nation intact. James Gordon Bennett of the *New York Herald* despatched more than fifty reporters to cover the heroism and horror of the Civil War. Among the more distinguished reporters of the day were Charles Carleton Coffin (1823-1896), Henry J. Villard (1835-1900), and Albert D. Richardson (1833-1869).

In Europe, the war in Crime a was covered for *The Times* by William Howard Russell. His dispatches from the Crime a marked the beginnings of war reportage. Russell concentrated on the pride and splendour of war, but another war correspondent concentrated (as Ernie Pyle, the American reporter was also to do during the Second World War) on compassion for the individual. This was Edwin Lawrence Godkin.

All these reporters wrote vividly. Consider this example from Reed's reportage of thy Second Congress of Soviets, as Lenin's turn came to speak. (Reed along with Philips Price and Arthur Ransome of the *London Daily News* were the only western correspondents allowed into the Bolshevik headquarters in the Smolny Institute, a girl's school):

Now Lenin, gripping the edge of the reading stand; letting his little winking eyes travel over the crowd as he stood there waiting, apparently oblivious to the long-rolling ovation, which lasted several minutes. When it finished, he said simply, 'We shall now proceed to construct the Socialist order!' Again that overwhelming roar. And later on: Suddenly, by common impulse, we found ourselves on our feet, mumbling together into the smooth lifting unison of the International. A grizzled old soldier was sobbing like a child. The immense sound rolled through the hall, burst windows and doors and soared into the quiet sky. 'The war is ended. The war is ended!' said a young workman near me, his face shining.

It was Reed who was to tell the world how, what we now know as the Soviet Union came into existence. It was brilliant reporting, at its very best.

Some of the great reporters of the late nineteenth and early twentieth centuries not only provided excellent copy, they also were to some extent responsible for making history. The disclosures or Januarius Aloysius MacGahan of Turkish atrocities against the Bulgarians helped lead to the Russo-Turkish War of 1877. James Creelman, along with MacGahan and the Italian Luigi Barzini was one of the few correspondents to protest the conduct of war and write with truth and compassion. His report of the Japanese massacre at Port Arthur in 1894 caused the Japanese to offer him a bribe to tone down his report, but he refused; American opinion was changed overnight. Barzini was so famous that newsboys had only to shout "Article by Barzini!" for his paper, *Corriere della Sera,* to sell out.

Ernest Hemingway, reporting from Spain for the North American Newspaper Alliance (NANA) became the most influential figure in the fight against fascism. And Wilfred Burchett of the London *Daily Express* broke the first eye-witness account of the aftermath of destruction at Hiroshima, a month after the bombing. His report was the first to describe radiation sickness which subsequently was to be the basis of anti-nuclear sentiment throughout the world.

It would be a mistake to think that all reporting is as exciting as has been made out above though, for a reporter, all news whether it is a local rose growers convention or a meeting of the municipal council—ought to be equally exciting. To him nothing human is and should be, alien.

What are the tools of the reporter's craft? Some brilliant journalists will tell a beginner that there aren't any. That, of course, is an exaggeration. First, there is a sound, general education. A poorly educated reporter may be good at covering a minor local event but evidently he will not be much good, at covering international affairs where he would need a profound knowledge of history, economics and politics. Again, a knowledge able police court reporter with wide contacts in both the worlds of crime and law and order may be an asset to a newspaper but he may find himself totally at sea covering the state legislature or national Parliament. In other words, in addition to a good educational grounding, a reporter needs expertise. A well-educated man, may be able to turn his talent to any field-James Reston of the *New York Times* started his career as a sports reporter and ended his career as a columnist whose every word was read with avid interest by diplomats in Washington and elsewhere. But a poorly educated reporter may find himself doing the crime beat for the rest of life. In the circumstances, a reporter ought to keep up with the world and never refuse to learn. It is a never-ending process. A reporter is a student throughout his career.

A good education implies knowledge of languages. In India, especially, where more than a dozen languages are spoken and written, a reporter with knowledge of the more important languages has an obvious advantage over others who are not multilingual.

During the pre-independence days, when meetings of the All India Congress Committee (AICC) meant so much for the national press, those reporters who understood Hindi and Urdu (the latter used by many UP leaders and also by Maulana Abul Kalam Azad) were in great demand. As English is increasingly being demoted, reporters will feel the necessity and importance of learning at least three languages, including English. An aspirant for a foreign posting, in addition, should know at least French to start with. If he knows Spanish, German, Arabic or Chinese he has an unchallengeable advantage over the rest. He need not wear his knowledge on his sleeve. Very often it is wiser not to exhibit one's knowledge too openly. Chinese diplomats pretend that they do not understand English. Two Indian diplomats in Washington once called on their Chinese counterparts who insisted in speaking to the Indians through an interpreter. One of the Indians knew Chinese very well, but pretended he did not know the language. After their meeting was over he could reproduce all the snide asides that the Chinese said during the conversation and, thereby get to know better the minds of the Chinese colleagues.

At the same time, talking to foreigners in their own language helps loosen their tongues. A foreigner, especially one not belonging to the Anglo-American world, would be flattered to hear a reporter speak to him in his own mother tongue, whether it be French, Spanish or Arabic. For that matter Jyoti Basu would probably be more forthcoming if a fellow Indian addressed him in Bengali and Karunanidhi would be less reluctant to voice his feelings if a reporter spoke to him in Tamil. That is only natural.

It is considered necessary-even important-that a reporter know how to type and how to write in short-hand even more relevant as a reporter's tool than typing. Some of the best-known British reporters like Hannen Swaffer, James Dunn and Henry Doig never used a typewriter in their lives. But increasingly short-hand is becoming relevant as a reporter's immediate tool without which he cannot truly be effective. To take down a speech as is needs short-hand, especially where coverage of Parliament or state legislatures is concerned. To report a speech *accurately* implies that a reporter has taken down his notes in shorthand. While it is held in some quarters that this can bog down a reporter needlessly in a lot of verbiage-and there is some truth in that-in the end he will learn to appreciate that short-hand will stand him in good stead on a great many occasions.

This is not to say that those without a knowledge of short hand do not make good reporters. But it is usually the key-word that may be challenged and here an accurate transcription will come in handy. Many reporters take down in long hand, putting down' key phrases and a *sense* of what has been said and trusting the rest to their memories. Memory is a poor servant and there aren't many reporters, anyway, who can recount a conversation in all the essential details. It is, however, necessary to add here that occasions may sometimes arise when note-taking may become either impossible or unwise, in which case, of course, put away your notebook, sharpen your memory and you can remember as soon as it is possible.

It is said of one of *The Hindu's* reporters that he could listen to a major speech by, say, C. Rajagopalachari, and reproduce it verbatim, without missing a word. For years, the paper's Chief Reporter, G. K. Vasudeva Aiyer, was a name to be reckoned with.

When Jawaharlal Nehru toured south India; he always asked for the services of another of *The Hindu's* Chief Reporter, A. K. Venkatesa Aiyar to accompany, him. Venkatesa Aiyar excelled in verbatim reporting, however fast or confusing and repetitive the speaker might be. Vasudeva Aiyer's name was a synonym for accuracy and fairness in reporting. And while *The Hindu* reporters no doubt occasionally relied on their memories, they were adept in short-hand.

What else would a reporter need? A standard size note-book, at least one pen and two, if not more, pencils. The note-book should be of standard size so that it can be stored conveniently over the years. It comes in sizes 20 cms by 10 cms and is generally ruled. Such a note-book can be conveniently kept in an inside pocket. A note-book should always be preserved, not because it contains words of wisdom but because no one can tell when a reporter is challenged. When challenged in a court of law, the wise reporter will be able to produce his note-book and say that what be reported had been actually said. If the notes are in short-hand, so much the better for their authenticity cannot be questioned as easily as they might if the notes are in long-hand. These days reporters have an additional tool available to them: the tape-recorded.

While there is still no substitute for a note-book, taped voice, if preserved, can hardly be challenged; the only drawback in taping a voice is that the reporter has to return to his office, and transcribe the tape laboriously before submitting his report. He has to reckon with the time factor. If he has plenty of time to do his report, as for instance in magazine reporting the tape-recorder is a marvellous acquisition.

A good reporter will also keep a file on everybody he knows or, ought to know, along with their correct addresses and telephone numbers, so that he can, at a moment's notice, get in touch with them for information, comment or reaction. Often, time is of the essence, and a reporter who does not have quick access to his news sources or contacts can lose out to his competitor. Most newspaper offices maintain a file of their own for ready reference, but reporters ought to supplement these with their own files. Loyal journalists make their personal lists available to their office..some will let colleagues have them on an exchange basis, but many are aware of competition and stay tight-fisted. A foreign correspondent is especially well-advised not only to have such lists in as extensive a manner as possible, but to keep on hand maps of cities and the location of important news sources, restaurants, hotels, police stations, telegraph offices and the like.

He also ought to maintain a 'forward diary'. A forward diary is-one in which you enter information of events to come. If a Minister makes a promise that a road or factory will be completed by such and such date, enter that date in your diary and check near the time. If the promise has not been kept, there is a readymade story of a promise broken.

A forward diary is also useful to write what is known as a 'curtain raiser'. You know, for instance, that a meeting of the All-India Congress Committee is due to meet on a particular date. A story outlining what issues are likely to come up for discussion at the meeting will definitely be welcome for publication on that very, date or a day or two earlier. A forward diary is a useful adjunct to memory, which can be tricky at times when dates are concerned. Never put all your trust in memory. Memory can err, but a forward diary, if accurately maintained, never does.

Going on an Assignment: There is no such thing as a 'routine' assignment, since even a routine assignment can turn out to be anything but routine. A bitter quarrel may develop at a meeting of the Municipal Council resulting in a member turning in his resignation; sensational developments may come up at the hearing of a trial court; the chance discovery of bodies of drowned men lying on the open shore near Sassoon Dock in Bombay led to the-suspicion that the *Ramdas* may have capsized in one of the greatest disasters in Bombay's seas. A reporter is always alert for developments. There is the story of the reporter who was sent to cover a society wedding. He returned empty handed. When the Chief questioned him he replied "There was no story. The bridegroom didn't turn up." It is not often that a reporter is sent on assignment fully briefed. It is his job to know where to go, how, quickly to go, whom to see, what to see and what to look for. When a reporter receives a spot news assignment, the first thing for him to do is to go to the *news-at once.* It is only on a feature assignment that he may have time to consult the library or check on background information.

Reporters learn from experience when and where to go for certain types of stories. For fires, accidents and disasters of other kinds, the scene of action, obviously, is the best source of news. Here time is of the essence. There is no point in going to the scene of accident long after the house has been reduced to ashes or the bodies have been removed to a morgue. For police news, however, it is not always certain that a visit to the scene or the crime will be the most useful way of picking up the threads of the story unless the principal news sources are there. However it is important that the scene of the crime is visited quickly to get an accurate description *at first hand* of where the murder was committed. This has to be supplemented with interviews with police officials who may not always be forthcoming. Inquiries with people who may have been around the scene of the crime-neighbours and others-would be of inestimable help in constructing a story. So would the views of friends of the deceased.

At political and diplomatic conferences the biggest news is often made far away from the speakers platform. It is important that the reporter maintain close contact with politicians and diplomats to know what is really going on. At the United Nations, for instance, reporters get most of their information from quiet telephone calls to briefing officers of respective embassies or still better from the ambassadors themselves who can sometimes be more cooperative. At international conferences in major capitals of the world, a reporter is well-advised to be present in the city at least a week in advance to familiarize himself with hotels, telegraph officials and offices, bus routes, taxi stands and fares so that, arriving there at the last minute, he does not have to waste time trying to gather information on allegedly minor but relevant things. At the conference of non-aligned countries held in Algiers, Indian correspondents who, because of financial stringency, could arrive only a day or two in advance, found that they had been billeted by the authorities some 25 miles away from the conference site with no means of transport available to them. In terms of coverage, that conference proved to be a disaster for them.

Every reporter quickly learns which are his best news sources and how to maintain cordial relations with them. Politicians like to be called even when there is no news and they have nothing to communicate except gossip. What they appreciate most is the sense of recognition that reporters give them. This can pay rich dividends when politicians who have been out of power get into the saddle again. Because Kuldip Nayar was a victim of the Emergency, he found it easy to maintain his links with Charan Singh who became a source of important news once he became a minister. Never spurn a politician, no matter how down he is. You lever can tell. He may be returned to power in the years ahead.

On assignment, the reporter should first ascertain where the news is, whom to contact, how to reach them and in the final analysis, how to relay the information gathered.

Example : Take floods in an out-of-the-way district. News has just been flashed that the floods have taken a heavy toll of life and property. The news obviously first originated from the District Collector.

How would a reporter go about getting the details?

First, check whether the newspaper or any other newspaper has a local stringer in the area. This is where the office file should come in handy. Does the stringer have a telephone? Can he be immediately contacted? If not, does he have a telegraphic address? Which is his nearest telegraph office? Second, check with the Information Officer of the government in the state capital. He could be an important source of information as all news from the districts would be monitored at headquarters. Get the District Collector's address and telephone number will he be available at a certain hour in his office? Will he be on tour? In his absence who is the next person who could be contacted? The District Superintendent of Police? How can *he* be contacted? Meanwhile, get some one to find out how quickly to go to the scene of the flood. Is there a plane service to a spot nearest the flooded area? An early train?

If not, would it be faster to hire a taxi? Are there any hotels in the area? What facilities would be available to spend the night? Depending on the severity of the floods and the damage they have wrought, the reporter would then rush to the spot while his colleagues would check on when such floods had last occurred, what damage those had wreaked etc. The reporter on the spot would file factual information. The background will be supplied by either his colleagues or the news editor who would have assigned a man to fill in on what the reporter would be missing.

Very often a major newsbreak will have to be dealt wish not by one reporter but by a posse of reporters. Take this example of the coverage of Krushchev's visit to New. York by the *New York Herald Tribune.*

Thursday, September 17, 1959.

Kelley: The column how Krushschev behaves, how the crowds react.

Miss Higgins: The diplomatic aspects State Dept. analysis of his talks.

Berck-silberfarb: Welcome in Penn Station baggage room. Kelley: Riding in the motorcade.

Barstow-fulbright: Among 7th Avenue route.

Lyle-bird: At Herald Square.

Parella: On Park Avenue.

Gleason: Waiting outside the Waldorf.

Loory: Outside the Commodore.

L. Barrett-bird: The Mayor's luncheon at the Waldorf.

Mrs. Crist: Mr. K. and his family.

Mrs. Crist and Mrs. Sheppard: Mrs. Wagner's lunch at the Waldorf

Ross: Economic Club dinner, Waldorf.

Gleason-loory: Inside Waldorf.

Endler-parella-finklestein: Outside Waldorf.

Barstow: Mr. K. goes to "The Music Man". Barrett-Silberfarb: To Hyde Park.

Consider how thorough the assignments are. Nothing is left to chance. The entire route of the Krushchev tour is covered by *different* reporters so that should anything happen to him en route, reaction from all areas can be quickly ascertained. But the general lead of the story was written by a senior correspondent, Bird, who had before him not only his own staffers' reports, but those of the agencies as well. This is thorough reporting at its best.

There are some rules that reporters ought to remember in the discharge, of their duties. One of them is: *never take anything for granted.*

Dining a critical vote at the United Nations General Assembly a young reporter noticed that a delegate who looked like a Chinese was raising his hand regularly to vote with the Soviet bloc. The reporter duly noted and wrote that Nationalist China's delegate had been supporting the Soviet Union, which would have been a shock *to* Chiang Kai-shek. Paul Ward, the Pulitzer prize winning reporter of the Baltimore *Sun* was sitting behind the young reporter but took the trouble to walk 100 yards to the Asian delegate's desk and check. He found that the Chinese-looking delegate was in fact a Burmese-which made an entirely different story. The young reporter found himself in trouble the next day. In this instance appearance proved most deceptive.

Another rule is: *ask-ask-ask!*

More stories have been written because a reporter had asked questions relevant to the issue than is normally realized. A reporter should never be shy of asking questions. Asking questions is his job. The reporter who breezes into a briefing officer's room and :asks gaily "what's new" is likely to be told "Nothing." In the first place, a reporter should have some idea of the story he is after; in the second place, he should know whom to ask. In the third place, he should formulate his questions in such a manner that he gets positive replies. Persistence is not a crime. A reporter should not be easily put off by a peremptory No. Politeness often helps. So does verbal communication of his sense of purpose and seriousness. To those who can maintain a smooth, even temper and a moderate manner in the face of anger and wrath go most of the rewards of the professional news gatherer.

A third rule is: *check and double-check!*

Beginners tend to accept the word of the suave politician for granted and many have got into trouble because they did not bother to check and double-check their stories. News sources are sometimes erratic; on occasions they may not be above deliberately misleading the reporter. The only recourse open to a reporter is to check what is passed on to him as a fact with other, even hostile, sources. During the 1946 riots of a communal nature, each community leader would inflate the number of people killed from his community for obvious reasons. Sometimes police officers would deliberately understate the numbers killed by police firing. A reporter is bound to give official figures but he is not bound to stick by them if his own impartial inquiries reveal that official, figures are grossly wrong.

Similarly, reporters, either out of sheer laziness, or because they are pressed for time, tend to accept second hand information that may prove to be wrong. It is better, in such circumstances, either to make it clear that what is purveyed is second hand information, or not to use the information at all. Do not pass the buck on to some body unnamed. A *Daily Mail* political correspondent who wrote that he had been told something "by an authority whose probity was not open to doubt" had his copy returned with a note from Northcliffe saying, "I am credibly informed that a well-known bystander has vouchsafed this to be a lie!"

It is often in the reporter's best interest to send the transcript or an interview to the person interviewed for the latter's Final approval. Often a politician will say things that he will later regret having said. If he is embarrassed after his statement has been published, it is more likely that he will flatly deny ever having said what he has been quoted as saying, and demand a retraction. Waving your note-book at him will do you no good. In the circumstances, the wiser course would be to send him a copy of your report for approval; have it initialled by the politician, or high official, if necessary. Accept his corrections or modifications in good spirits. He will appreciate your courtesy to him and you will remain in his good books for ever. The aim of a reporter is not to embarrass an official but help put across his views before the public. What has been said in anger may make good copy, but to report it, without giving the individual the right to retract his statement, is bad journalism.

It is customary where high officials are concerned, like Cabinet Ministers or heads of state, for them to ask for questions in writing; answers will then be provided also in writing after much, sober consideration. They do not often make sensational copy, but represent the views of a government; their relevance lies in the stamp of authority bestowed on them by the official concerned. Dr. Rajendra

Prasad, while president, once gave an interview to three Indian correspondents jointly. The three filed identical reports to their respective papers. In due course the reports came to the attention of Prime Minister Jawaharlal Nehru who took strong exception to what the President had said and let Dr. Prasad know. The President was also asked to retract his statement if that was possible. Whereupon he summoned the three unfortunate reporters and told them that he had never said what had been attributed to him. Had the reporters taken the trouble to have the President approve their copy, they could have stuck to their reports and refused to succumb to pressure. As it was, they were compelled to eat crow.

There are times, as during the state visit of a President when only one reporter is invited to be present at a state dinner. There is general agreement that the reporter concerned will share his information as to what happened on the occasion with other reporters concerned. This is known as pool reporting. The reporter present at the dinner is duty bound not to hide or suppress any information he is privy to but to share it fully and comprehensively with others. A pool reporter who tries to hold something back to his advantage breaks an unwritten law and deserves to be ostracized. Most reporters dislike pool reporting, but there are times whell they have to accept it as the best way out often, when there are many one-man bureaus working in a large city, the correspondents try to cover events by agreeing to share the information they get on a mutually acceptable basis. If a reporter has clear instructions from his office not to work with a pool, he must make this known to his colleagues and disengage himself from such activity and he will then be on his own.

Reporters on a crime beat tend to have informal arrangements among themselves on sharing information. Many newspapers are aware of this but turn a blind eye to such goings-on because through informal reporters cooperatives, it becomes possible to give maximum coverage with minimum manpower. It is not, however, the best way to cover news. Invariably, while one reporter writes from first-hand knowledge, the rest are purveyors of secondhand information.

It is easy for a reporter to report a speech made at a public meeting or in Parliament or a State Legislature. It is on record. The politician or parliamentarian of legislator can be quoted directly. Those who make news can be named. There is nothing to fear or hide. But there are times when he has to protect his sources and respect such confidences as he is willing to accept. There are clearly defined ground rules that a reporter breaks at his peril, in these matters.

The basic premise on which any reporter operates is that whatever told to him or learned by him is for publication and "on the record." But that is not always so. Everything said is not always on the record. There are many variations on the theme.

One is *attribution, but not for direct quotation.* In this case, the reporter is permitted to say who said what, but not in quotes.

The importance of quotation marks is that every word within quotation marks is directly attributed to the person making the statement. Quotation marks, in the circumstances, take special meaning. They have to be used with care.

The President of the United States may not be directly quoted; as a general rule, but what he said can be reported in indirect language. This is becoming increasingly redundant when presidential press conferences are televised and seen and heard by millions of people. The luxury of demanding that he be not directly quoted is not permitted to ordinary mortals but is conceded to top diplomats, judges and high military officials. Ambassadors will talk to reporters freely if they are not directly quoted. So win Generals, if they can get away with it.

Before World War II, the presence of a spokesman was unheard of Editors generally insisted that the sources of the news be named, whether or not they could be quoted directly. The blossoming of the spokesman is a post-war phenomenon, not often widely acclaimed. It is difficult to trace the origin of the practice. On the European continent and in Britain, reporters have always respected the desire of working-level government officials to remain anonymous. In the United States it is customary to identify the spokesman, as speaking on behalf of a particular department. Thus:

Mr. Charles Leach, spokesman for the State Department, said today.

This makes it official. When the State Department spokesmen are not in the picture and the reporter has got his story from a high official who does not wish to be personally identified, the reporter takes recourse to such expedients as-saying that "high government officials said today" or "authoritative sources said to day" and it is clearly understood that the sources indeed are official or authoritative. Woe betide the reporter who tries to attribute his own beliefs to official sources; he may well expect to be put on the mat by the department spokesman.

Mr. Henry Kissinger, former Secretary of State used to brief reporters travelling with him on the clear understanding that what he said would be attributed to a "high official." The more knowledgeable reader knew, without being told, that what had appeared in the papers was what Mr. Kissinger told reporters, but the :Secretary of State enjoyed the dubious advantage of being in a position to deny the reports if he felt that they were counterproductive. He could thus indulge in "kite-flying" that is to say in putting out ideas to see how the public would react to them. If the public reacted adversely, the Secretary of State could always deny being party to the published reports.

"Back grounding" is a device adopted by many officials to say a lot of things they otherwise would not dare to say. European foreign offices have used this device for many years and is an informal way of leaking damaging material to favoured correspondents. It was adapted for American use during World War II and Ernest K. Lindley of *Newsweek* magazine is generally credited with being the first to popularize it.

Finding that high officials could not talk to him on the record and being unwilling to talk to them off the record, Lindley apparently persuaded many to give him needed explanations of current and coming events under the strict understanding that he would not identify them as his sources. Current practice is for a briefing authority to say: "This is just background material for your personal use." A reporter is free to use it as long as he does not attribute it to anybody as if he is knowledgeable in regard to the issue being discussed.

Normally, the word "background" is used in connection with information, usually of a historic nature, that a reporter supplies to make his story contextually understandable. It is not necessarily top secret information that he is giving to his reader. But in present day journalism "backgrounding" assumes a sinister meaning. A spokesman of a government may pass on highly damaging information about another government to reporters with the passing comment: "Now, I can't be named as the authority for what I'm about to tell you, but I'll give it to you for your background."

The information, of course, is given to be used, but reporting it is *not* mandatory and a reporter need not print it if he sees no real reason to do so. Often, news editors and editors resent being made use of by scheming officials but it is the reporter's task to inform his superiors of the nature of his copy. Writing in the *New York Times,* James Reston had this to say about background reporting:

This is a remarkable rule, for it imposes upon the writer what can only be described as a compulsory form of plagiarism. That is to say, the official explains what he has been doing or is about to door is thinking about doing, on the specific understanding that the writers may publish what he says on their own authority without any attribution to him or his department or even to an "official source".

The reporters are permitted under these ground rules to say that the government is planning to do these things or thinking about doing them, or if they are inordinately cautious, they can dream up such phrases as 'there is one view in the government'. But they cannot give any authority for what they are told.

This has many advantages for both the official and the reporters. The official, if he is thinking about introducing a new policy but isn't quite sure how it will be received (officials are always in this state), can thus discover public reaction to his proposal without being identified with it. More important, he can explain some of the intricacies of his problems (including his difficulties with, other officials) and thus help win understanding and approval for what he proposes to do. Similarly the reporters stand to gain, for in such meeting they acquire an understanding of what is going on and are therefore better able to inform their readers. But the trouble is that, if there is a misunderstanding of what is said, or if what is said causes embarrassment to the Government, the White House can always repudiate the published stories and the reporters, who cannot disclose their source, are left without any plausible defence.

Normally, the reporter gets away with what he has written and the average reader stands in awe at the scribe who seems to know so much! At best it is a smart way of getting news and at worst it is dishonest journalism, depending on one's point of view. Very often the gimmick is used by unscrupulous officials to damage the reputation of other officials or departments but the tendency among reporters is to get along with such tactics in order not to be left out as informed men. In many western countries, the "background dinner" or "background breakfast" is fast becoming a source of much information to favoured reporters.

When a reporter is summoned to a meeting and is told that what is being communicated is off the record it is with the intention on the part of the purveyor of information to keep the reporter informed of what is happening or is about to happen so that he is not taken by surprise by the unfolding events. This is more honest than backgrounding.

It is a well-known axiom in journalism that in politics, diplomacy, science and crime-to mention only a few fields of major news-no reporter is every fully privileged to write all he knows.

Giving information to the press off the record serves the officials in the sense that they cannot be accused of withholding vital information from the public. The information is shared, so officials are free of future blame. Police officials often tell the reporters who it is that has been arrested on smuggling charges but the in formation is given off the record so that the arrested man's accomplices are not tipped off. This serves the public good.

Similarly, the names of juvenile criminals are held back on the ground that it may hurt future chances of the young offenders being rehabilitated. This, too, serves the public cause. But there are occasions when being part of an "off-the-record" briefing is not to the public good, in which event, the reporter concerned must refuse to be party to such a briefing. An off-the record briefing is one sure way of strangling the press and is often resorted to by high government officials. Some of the off the record confidences should not be given or, if offered, they should not be accepted. There is an old saying among newspapermen that anything known to more than two persons eventually will be known to everybody.

It is common practice, especially in western countries, for politicians and officials to provide reporters with advance copies of their speeches so that the latter have plenty of time to read them and report them accurately.

This is useful to the officials concerned in two ways: it ensures accurate reporting of a given speech, since the full text is provided in advance it also is a way of tempting a reporter to give greater space to the speech than is normally warranted. It is a temptation that a reporter must resist with all his professional zeal.

Usually an official will follow the advance copy to the letter, Sometimes, though, he may feel tempted to insert a paragraph that-could be meaningful in terms of news. The reporter who prepares his copy on the basis of the advance text provided to him may find, if he does not listen so the speech as it is made, that he has lost out to his competitor. In the circumstances, no reporter should absent himself from the arena where the speech is delivered.

In order to prevent reporters from "jumping the gun," most advance texts are accompanied by what is known as an "embargo."

The embargo clearly states when the text of the speech or the contents of a report, may be released. It is an unstated agreement that no reporter will break the embargo. The reporter, however, is free to use the copy available to him to gather reaction to it from other concerned people. An embargo which specifies the exact time is not difficult to observe. Newspapers which have received the advance copy set the report based on it in type, ready to be used. Sometimes, however, the hour of release is not specified and the reporter is expected to keep his patience until the speech is actually delivered.

Social Issues

A major problem arises when a politician does not say the things that have been released in the advance text. The late Mayor Fiorello H.E. LaGuardia of New York once issued an advance text bitterly criticizing Washington for not fully supporting an international relief programme proposed at the United Nations. In his actual speech, however, he dropped the attack and blandly told reporters that he was not accountable to them for what he did or did not say!

In a sense the advance copy is a handout-something handed out to a reporter to make his task easier. Often this ploy is used by government departments to provide reporters with copy favourable to the ministry concerned to prevent him from making too close an inquiry into the state of affairs, on the presumption, usually correct, that given enough material to chew on, the newsman will not proceed to make his own inquiries. Public relations people also use the ploy to publicize extravagant claims for various organizations; news editors are wary of such efforts on the part of PR men to con their reporters. The news releases put out by them may not necessarily be untruthful, but a trained reporter will be able to separate the grain of truth from the mass of verbiage. Handouts should be accepted for what they are worth but the reporter will go beyond them to write his own copy. If he doesn't, it is the duty of the news editor to pull him up.

What has been said about subs and editors in regard to accepting gifts and "junkets"—free trips either within the country or abroad-is equally, even more so, applicable to reporters frequently they are more susceptible to the wiles of PR men than are editors who at least are better paid. Reporters are better off staying at home and playing with their children than accepting invitations to cocktail parties. Reporters covering the diplomatic circuit suffer cocktail parties as an occupational hazard. It is, however, untrue to say that reporters get news at such parties. More often than not they don't.

A diplomat who opens his mouth after a few drinks will soon find himself transferred to a desk job back home. A cocktail party may be an occasion to make new friends in congenial surroundings, but that is about all. An editor or a reporter who accepts junkets without the knowledge of his superiors may find very soon that he has lost credibility with his colleagues. In any event a reporter ought to inform his superiors of any offer made to him, as a matter of principle, so that they know who is up to what game. The reporter who gains a reputation for incorruptibility will find that a positive asset in his discharge of his duties. In the end this is more valuable than a bottle of scotch or a free trip to the United States or France.

A truly great reporter is the most important man in the office. The public comes to respect him and honour him-as his own office should. There is the story of Tom Marlowe, the first and greatest of *Daily Mail* editors and his news editor, Tom Clarke. One day, one of Clarke's star reporters returned with a really top story. Marlowe, on hearing of-it, asked Clarke to send the reporter or to see him. Clarke replied: "When one of my reporters is doing the story of the day, he is the most important man in the office. With all respect, sir, I suggest that you come upstairs to see him." And Marlowe did.

In his book *The Professional Journalist,* John Hohenberg says it all when he sums up the qualities of a good reporter thus:

> He is diligent without being a busybody, penetrating without being offensive, persuasive without being a confidence man, perceptive without being a reader of tea leaves, thoughtful without being pedantic, skeptical without being a confirmed cynic, thorough without being a stenographer, careful without being hesitant; determined without being argumentative, well-mannered without being a doormat. He does much more than report the news. Journalism would not be his profession if it were a mere recording network for events. He is a primary force in our daily life, a force that transmits, explains, and sometimes originates a world-wide flow of current events and ideas. He exerts a vast and incalculable influence over the people within range of his communication. He is no demigod. He is reporter on your daily newspaper.

Before we go any further it may be useful to acquaint ourselves with some of the jargon used in a newspaper office to know, better what is being said. The terms are in common usage.

ABC: Audit Bureau of Circulation which has the unenviable-task of certifying audited statistics on the circulation of a publication. This is a highly respected watchdog body.

Ad.: An advertisement.

Add: Additions of any kind to a news story. If copy sent down to the printing has to be supplemented by additional material, this is done by marking the new copy with the connotation "add to"

Agate: 5½ point type. As a unit of advertising, 14 agate lines equal one column per inch.

AM's: Morning papers.

Angle: An approach to a story, the slant given by the reporter.

AP: Associated Press.

Art: Any newspaper illustration or art work.

Assignment: Duty given to a reporter.

Bank: Also called a *deck;* the part of a headline that usually follows the top or the cross line, often both.

Banner: A headline stretching across all the columns on the top of the front page, not to be confused with a *binder* which is a headline across the top of an *inside* page. A banner is also known as a *streamer.*

Beat: The exclusive territory assigned to a reporter or a series of places visited by a reporter to gather news. Police courts, the Municipal Council, the Docks are examples of beats.

BI: Reference to setting of copy in black or bold faces, which is heavier and darker than regular type.

Body: Part of a story that follows the lead. Also the name of the type in which regular newspaper reading matter is set.

Box: Matter enclosed in a border to make a box. Many modern-boxes have only top and bottom borders. Those put in the middle-of a related story are called Drop-ins.

Black and White: Not a brand of Scotch favoured by newsmen but reproduction of photographs and illustrations in black or white paper.

Bleed: When an illustration of photograph runs (bleeds) into the edge of the page. Instruction given to printer to follow this direction.

Blurb: Publicity material.

Boil Down: Reduce or summarize a story to manageable proportions.

Border: Line rules used to form box in display.

Break: As in news break, when something news happens.

Bulletin: Brief despatch containing major news. Usually no more than 40 to 50 words.

Byline: Signature on a story, which tells who is it by.

Caps: Capital letters.

C and lc: Capital and lower case.

Caption: Descriptive material accompanying pictures and photographs.

Caseroom: The area where the printer works.

Centre Spread: The two pages in the centre fold of a newspaper.

Chase: Metal page form into which type is locked.

Cheescake: photograph in which the female form is more than, ordinarily revealed for male admiration if not approbation.

Clean Copy: Copy without errors, well-edited.

Clipping: Items clipped from newspapers for reference.

Copy: Universally known as the term for material written by journalists.

Copy Desk: Where copy is edited, cut and headlined. Not to be confused with the proof room where typographical errors are caught in proof.

Copy Editors: sub-editors.

Copyholder: In proofreading, one holds proof of type matter and makes corrections while his partner holds the copy (hence the term) and reads it out loudly so corrections can be made.

Correspondent: A reporter who is out of town on duty, who corresponds with his head office.

Cover: As in covering an event, that is, reporting it in full.

Credit Line: To name the source of a picture, illustration, photograph; giving credit to the person responsible. A credit line is to a photograph what a byline is to a story.

Crop: cutting out non-essential parts of a photograph to sharpen the visual impact.

Cross-heading: A headline in small type within set matter to highlight what follows.

Cub: An untrained newsman, a beginner, usually a reporter.

Cut: An engraving; also removing portions of copy in order to tighten it.

Date line: The place from which a news story is sent and the date, as in United Nations, New York, August 15.

D/C: double column.

Deadline: The last minute to ready copy for an edition. Closing time.

Desk: The sub-editor's desk.

Dope: Usually 'inside' information, as in: "What's the dope on this story?" In the United States, dope story is also called a *think piece,* or soft news based on reliable opinion, which seek to develop trends.

Drop: Used to indicate that a letter should be in larger type; it is the first letter in the first paragraph of a story and is set thus for purposes of effective display.

Drop Headline: Headline in which the first line begins on the-left and the others below it are away on the right of the alignment of its beginning.

Dummy: A drawing usually freehand, outlining the position of news stories and cuts on a page, along with advertisements and illustrations.

Ears: Boxes on either side of the nameplate on page 1 of a-newspaper that usually carry advertisements in India. In the West-they may carry the day's weather and the name of the edition.

Edition: Remake or revision of some of the pages of a news paper, as in City Edition, Dak edition, also total run for anyone issue of a paper.

Editorial: The editor's opinion or comment on events. It is invariably assigned a permanent position on the editorial page.

Em: A measurement of column width based on the square of M in a type usually 12 points (one sixth of an inch).

En: Half an em, also called *a nut* in the United States to avoid phonetic confusion.

Embargo: Mandatory deadline for the release of a story.

Exclusive: A story that no other newspaper has for that day; a scoop.

File: The act of despatching copy to or from a news centre.

Filler: Small items used to fill out columns where needed and where copy cannot be leaded out.

Flush: Set copy without para indenting.

Flash: A rarely used message of a few words describing a momentous event. It consists mostly of the place of filingless than half a dozen words of text, the signature of the sender and the time sent.

Fold: Line at which newspaper is folded.

Follow-up: Further developments in a story. To chase details of an earlier report.

Feature: A story of interest beyond and more than the news. Also to give special prominence to a story.

Font: Type of one size and style.

Forme: A page of type locked and ready for the press. See *chase.*

Galley: Narrow and shallow tray of metal in which set matter is put in column width.

Galley Proof: Proof of set matter put in a galley.

Glossy: Shiny print (of photograph).

Half Stick: Matter (usually plate) in half column size.

Handout: Generic term for written publicity.

H.O.: Short for Hold Over. Or Hold for release. Reference to typeset copy that could be used later.

Human Interest: Story about human or emotional appeal, but not necessarily hard news.

Indent: Start matter at some distance away from the margin.

Insert: New matter added in body of story already sent for setting.

Italics: Type face with characters slanted to the right, as contrasted to Roman, or upright, characters.

Jump: Continuation of a story to another page.

Jump Line: The continuation line giving the succeeding or preceding page numbers.

Kill: Elimination of news material at any stage in the processing. When used the instruction is mandatory.

Layout: Arrangement of illustrations, a page plan.

Lead: Beginning of a story, which may be a sentence, a paragraph or several paragraphs depending on the complications involved; also, the main story on page one. A tip that may give a new story. Also (pronounced 'led') thin metal strips used to space out lines and paragraphs of set matter.

Leg-man: A reporter who gathers but does not write the news; one who runs around in the pursuit of news.

Lino: Lino-type; a machine for setting type.

Late News: News that arrives too late to make the front page (or last page to go down to press) but is accommodated in the Stop Press column.

Leader: Editorial.

Libel: Any defamatory statement expressed in writing, printing or other visible form.

Lockup: Deadline in the composing room for getting all page formes off the floor and into the stereotype department.

Logotype: Also called a *logo,* usually by printers. A single matrix containing two or more letters used together such as AP, UPI. It is also another name for the flag, nameplate.

Lower Case: Small letters.

Make-up: Assembling the newspaper in the composing room, art of putting set copy to make a page, artistically and effectively.

Mask: Cover picture over areas not needed.

Masthead: Statement, usually on the editorial page, giving information on the newspaper's ownership, place of publication etc. Sometimes confused with the nameplate.

Matrix: Or Mat. The hard cardboard or paper-mach impression of page or advertisement upon which metal will be cast. Also called a *flong.*

Mono: Monotype. A machine for cutting type.

Morgue: News library; also known as reference section.

Must: When this term is used on copy, it indicates that the story must be used. Only editors in authority can designate musts.

Name Plate: Paper's name given on top of front page.

Obit: Short for Obituary. An announcement of a death with biographical details appropriate in length to the news importance of the subject.

Overnight: Also called overnite or overniter, a story filed by a reporter or turned out by a rewrite man for the first edition of an afternoon! newspaper of the following day.

Overse: Type left over from an edition. Usually wasted; in tightly-knit news department cause for editorial.

Page Proof: Proof of the page taken on paper by hand machine.

Pica: 12 point type, also a lineal measurement of 12 points. Also called an *em.*

Pix: Picture.

Play: The display given to a story or a picture. Most editors talk of playing a story, rather than playing it up or down.

Plate: A page of type cast in metal fitted in press for printing.

Point: Basic printing measurement, roughly equivalent to one seventy second of an inch. 72 point type roughly measures an inch in height.

PM's Afternoon papers.

Proof Reader: One who reads proofs to make corrections in setting and sends it back for revision.

Puff: Publicity material, usually quickly thrown into the waste paper basket.

Pull: Proof, because proof is pulled (as by a roller over paper) from type.

Put to Bed: When all pages have been locked up and the press is ready to print.

Quotes: Quotation marks. What has been said by an individual in his own words.

Rewrite Man: A writer (usually a sub) for a newspaper or agency whose work consist in part of re-doing stories and in part of writing original copy for the reporters who turn in notes by telephone. A good man who seldom gets thanks for his efforts.

Retainer: Amount paid to retain use of correspondent who may not necessarily be filing copy all the time.

Reverse: Instruction that picture plate should be made in reverse, the right coming on the left and *vice versa,* for lay-out purposes.

Revise: Redo copy incorporating corrections.

Run: A reporter's beat

Running Story: A chronological story of an event topped by successive leads as the news changes.

Runover: Another name for a jump.

Round-up: A comprehensive story which may combine reports on the same subject from several sources.

Routing: Removing metal not needed and unwanted from non printing areas of a plate.

Run-on: Linking passage together to make them go in the same paragraph. To set a long list into one paragraph.

Rush: Instruction to have copy set quickly as when important late news breaks.

Sic: Single column.

Schedule: List of assignments.

Scoop: An exclusive story for a newspaper for which a reporter lives laborious life.

See Copy: Instruction to proofreader to see original copy and don't try to improve upon it.

Short: A short item, a filler.

Shoulder: Usually for top line of headline which is set in smaller type on one side (left) while the rest of the headline is set as usual.

Slug: Each story has a name, which is caned a slug. The slug must be included with each page number. A story on President Carter may be slugged as Carter-1, Carter-2 etc. until the last page is marked Carter-last.

Space: Empty space between type lines.

Space-out: Instruction to printer to put more space between parts of set matter.

Spread: An elaborate lay-out. Any story that takes a headline big enough to be used at the top of an inside page.

Standing Matter: Matter set and ready for use, often the left over from a previous edition.

Stat: Used to indicate that matter originally cut should be used.

Let it stay.

Stone: The platform or table on which the printer makes the page

Stringer: Correspondent of a newspaper who is not on the regular payroll but is paid for copy used.

Stick: About two inches of type.

Syndicate: An organization that sells articles and features on behalf of a writer. An agency.

Tailpiece: Usually paragraph with finishing touches, a joke at the end, something added on to enliven a column.

Tip: A small bit of information that could lead to a news story.

Top: Reference to a story that should go in a single column at the top of a page.

Take: A page of copy, which may contain as little as one paragraph. There could be several 'takes' to a story.

Trim: To cut a story down to its essentials.

Turn: A lengthy story that does not all go on page one and has to be placed in an inside page with another headline, when it is said to "turn."

Typebook: A book showing various families of type which a press has for use.

W.f. Wrong font, or wrong face that may have accidentally crept in type set in one particular face.

Yellow Journalism: Publication specializing in stories that are sensational or grossly exaggerated and dealing generally with sex, crime and gossip.

Wire Service: News agency.

The vision of the communication system has changed for future. Only in the last five to ten years, as computers and video display terminals have flooded into scientific laboratories and percolated more slowly into printing houses, has the dream more much nearer to reality, at least in scientific communication. Traditional methods of scientific publication still flourish and more journals are born than die every year (see Ulrich's International periodicals directory from one edition to the next), but now every conference of editors or publishers pays much uneasy attention to the changes looming ahead and those already on us.

With one computer terminal available for every 15 professionals, 'computer pervasion of the -research process is Virtually complete' in the USA, as Baker et al have pointed out. In Europe and other parts of the world the computer explosion is perhaps 10 or 20 years behind the point it has reached in the USA. Nevertheless on both sides of the Atlantic the age of electronics, is already affecting the scientific information system in certain ways, and other possibilities are being investigated now or arc forecast for the future. These technological innovations may soon drastically alter the way scientists work and communicate with each other. One confident prediction, for example, is that in 15 years' time electronic journals will be cheaper than the conventional kind printed on paper.

Computer's Role

The present uses of computers in scholarly publishing include making printing faster, and sometimes cheaper, easing distribution, by maintaining and updating subscription lists and printing addresses; keeping records and organizing the refereeing system; and possibly helping with the copy-editing of manuscripts and preparing them for publication. Other technical advances have led or will soon lead to new forms of publication. I shall mention these developments first, then refer to the computer-based processes already in use or under investigation, and end with some comments on professionalism in editing and on the outlook for editing and editors.

The term microform (or micrographics) covers both microfiche and microfilm. Microfiches are sets of reduced transparencies of typescript or printed pages, with 80 to 100 pages mounted together. Ordinary microfiches are reduced by a ratio of 24. There are as utrafiches, reduced by a ratio of 150, allowing 3000 or more pages to be concentrated on a fiche the size of a postcard. A microfiche reader is used to project an enlarged copy of one page at a time onto a screen. Paper copies can be made from the microfiche on reader printers or separate printer. Microfiche versions of journals or books are ideal for libraries that are short of space, provided that the publication which they have condensed is likely to be needed only occasionally, for reference: it is no pleasure to browse through microfiche or scan many articles in succession on a microfiche reader.

Microfilm, which is less convenient for the user than microfiche, is useful for archival purposes, and many journals now provide microfilm versions when each volume is complete. Users apparently do not like microform journals much yet, but societies whose journals have a very small circulation may find microform the best (or only) way to keep their journals going, especially if authors cooperate in providing good clean typescripts and illustrations, since production and mailing costs are much lower than for-paper journals. A few journals are in fact successfully published in microfiche or microfilm alone (e.g. the American Journal of Computational Linguistics). Microforms and journal publishing have recently been surveyed by Campbell and Ashby, who conclude that the trend towards the use of microfiche in journal publishing will continue and will 'aid the development of journals as more powerful vehicles for the distribution and storage in accessible form of research material and ideas.'

Microfiche is also exploited in the experimental synoptic journals now being published in Europe and the USA. One way of publishing synoptics is to issue the journal in two forms: a full form in microfiche, made either from typeset or camera-ready copy and perhaps also available in miniprint (see below) for use in libraries and other reference centres; and a synoptic form, probably typeset, in which the author summarizes the full paper in some fixed fraction of its length or a fixed number of pages (ranging from two to six). Alternatively the synoptic form alone might be published, with copies of the full original typescript available on demand from a data store. In both systems subscribers to the synoptic journal can buy microfiche, reprographic or miniprint copies of full papers if they want more detail. In the method used by the Journal of Chemical Research (S) and (M), the synopsis is accepted for publication only after the full paper has been through the complete editorial selection process

This system could have a retrograde effect on both science itself and the editorial process. If people read synopses without obtaining full details of the work that interests them, they nay acquire the habit of accepting statements without examining the evidence. Likewise, refereeing for seldom-consulted archive may prove so unrewarding that standards in this activity too will deteriorate. And copy-editing should probably not even be attempted for the archival form, provided that the manuscript is comprehensible to readers. It is inauspicious that, in the first trials conducted by the chemical societies of the UK, France and Germany, only one out of 310 papers summarized in the synopsis part of the journal was requested in the complete version.

The Disadvantages : A drawback of synoptics is that authors have to prepare three versions of their papers-the full text, an abstract and a synoptic. The guidelines for authors preparing synopses should be very carefully thought out and more detailed instructions than usual should be given about the presentation of typescripts.

Miniprint, which is just legible to the naked eye, is used either for complete articles or for extensive data that can usefully be printed immediately after an article. It may either be typeset in very small type of be reduced from typed pages supplied by the author. Readers need either very good sight or a magnifying glass. Use of miniprint reduces paper and mailing costs, and significant savings can be made.

The selective dissemination of articles has been discussed, tested and, to a certain extent, practised. Subscribers either order articles from regularly supplied lists of titles available, or arrange for articles that match their 'interest profits' to be sent to them direct. The profiles are based on index terms chosen by the subscribers as reflecting their interests. They are spared from receiving material they do not want. This system may be suitable for societies or publishers dealing with several different fields, but its cost-effectiveness is still in doubt. And as readers and authors are often unskilled at finding accurate key-words, even when given a thesaurus from which to select them, the system also has intellectual drawbacks.

On-demand publication sometimes refers to arrangements like those provide by selective dissemination systems, by which readers can obtain printouts of journal articles as wanted. It also refers to a service offered by a few publishers by which photo duplicates of books or typescripts can be provided on request. Copies are not cheap, and the system is not economical if more than 250 copies of a book are likely to be ordered.

Although electronic journals produced and stored in a computer and read on a video screen sound an expensive proposition, a University of Toronto study predicts that from the middle or late 1990s onwards they will become cheaper than the conventional kind; and a study in Norway predicts that 1990 will see the start of the 'paperless society' there. The Arpanet communication system which links computers in the USA and Europe already allows scientists to exchange 'information even more easily than by mail or telephone, and at least one newsletter (the Sigart Newsletter) was being produced through the system two or three years ago. Arpanet has also proved useful for transmitting manuscripts to referees and for other editorial tasks. This and similar interactive systems allow co-workers thousands of miles apart to communicate effectively when they draft joint papers, and editors can work with referees and other advisers through these systems. Audio cassettes, gramophone records, video cassettes and televised information systems are other types of process into which editors may find themselves venturing. Those are also video disks which can hold many books or journals on a disk the size of an ordinary long-playing record.

The savings that can be made in composition costs when authors provide camera-ready copy have been mentioned several times in this book. Camera-ready copy can be prepared more easily with word processors than with conventional typewriters. Word processors record typed characters on a magnetic card, disk or cassette and allow the typist to correct, insert or delete material without retyping the rest of the manuscript.

The more expensive word processors have video screens which display what has been type and allow for changes and corrections to be made on the spot. When the copy is perfect, the tape or other magnetic record is fed into the same or a separate machine, which types the whole page or chapter flawlessly and at high speed. Some word processors can be used to control photo-composers, and various instructions can be incorporated to control the typeface, type size, format, right-margin justification, italicization, and so on; words can even be flagged for indexing later.

Another refinement is to have the original copy typed in an optical character recognition (OCR) typeface which a scanner can translate directly into a magnetic tape or other recording. The tape can be used to produce any number of copies of an article for the editor, referees, author(s) and copy editor to work on, and instructions for change from any of them can be incorporated into a corrected tape which can be used to control photo-composition. When scanners and OCR typefaces come into wider use, copy editors should be spared some of their more humdrum tasks, such as proof-reading.

The existence of a magnetic tape or other record mean that even before a book or journal is printed, the tide, bibliographic details, key terms and abstract of a chapter or article can be fed to abstracting and current-awareness services without further keyboarding, with its almost inevitable errors. This is unquestionably an advantage in time, money and accuracy.

The use of computers and scanners in editorial procedures

forms part of the concept of Editorial (or Electronic) Processing Centres (EPCs), much discussed since it, was first put forward in 1972. In an EPC several learned societies would shake an automated system, providing enough work to make the system financially worth-while. Four levels of automation are envisaged. In all of them authors would submit manuscripts typed in an OCR typeface to the Centre, where the manuscripts would be scanned and entered into a computer system.

Printouts-preferably the kind without typesetting instructions embedded in the text-would go to the editor and later to the referees. Comments would be typed in OCR type for recording via the scanner, with printouts being provided at any stage as needed. The computer would be programmed. For copy-editing, with printouts going to authors before publication. If authors approved of the changes they could simply telephone the Centre and the message would be typed into the computer. If they disapproved of the changes or had more alterations to make, the manuscripts would be recycled through the EPC to the editor. Final versions of manuscripts would be transferred from the computer to a magnetic tape which the printer would use to control photo-typesetting. Again, date for abstracting and indexing services would be available as by-products.

The computer could also handle the various 'housekeeping chores assigning manuscript numbers; providing lists of referees with their specialities matched to the key terms given in the title or assigned by the editor together with information about referees' past performance and present work load for the journal; typing letters to referees; automatically producing reminders to referees, the editor or authors when manuscripts become overdue at any stage; and, after acceptance, providing deadline reminders to copy editors, printer and authors. Computers should not, however, be used to chum out letters to authors from the editor; no software program yet devised can cope satisfactorily with the countless different circumstances an editor should discuss individually with authors. As well as editorial activities, an EPC-computer system should he able to hand the maintenance and upkeep of subscription lists for the societies taking part, sending invoices and reminders out as necessary.

Studies of the EPC concept funded by the National Science Foundation in the USA have indicated that the system is technically feasible and economically viable but at the moment is showing no signs of becoming an operational reality. Its a system of this kind feasible in countries other than the USA? Woodward has described a modified version more suitable for European and other countries where full-scale EPCs would be too expensive or are not needed. In the Cooperative Publishing Office (CPO) proposed by Woodward, editors and referees would work on authors, typescripts until final edited versions had been accepted and approved. At that stage manuscripts would be retyped in OCR type in the publishing office.

Copies would go to authors for checking, and the corrected version would be scanned and stored until needed for a journal issue. Material for secondary services would also be typed by the CPO for input to the computer system, and reminders and other letters could be sent out as from an EPC. Woodward calculated that at 1976 prices in the UK the initial investment in a CPO would be about f: 150 000. With the capital sum discounted over five years, the operating costs would be about the same as conventional costs; at 20000 pages a year the CPO should save about 9% of the conventional publishing, printing and distribution costs.

EPCs and CPOs were intended to solve some of the temporal and financial problems of publishing for learned societies, but commercial publishers who invest in scanners or editing terminals are in effect already running editorial processing centres themselves. Learned socialites may find it more satisfactory to have their journals published commercially than to collaborate with other societies in setting up an EPC or a CPO. For the societies they are supposed to help, the greatest drawback to EPOs or CPOs would be the initial capital costs and the extra salaries of people employed to run them. At present some of the costs of copy-editing, improvement of illustrations, and correspondence of all kinds may disappear into institutional over heads. The rest of the work is done by the editor in trains or planes, in the lunch-break, or after the children have gone to bed. Learned societies benefit from this freely donated time, and as long as dedicated people are prepared to do the work, the societies will want to encourage them.

Many scientists edit journals and books either in their 4 spare' time, as just mentioned, or in a small part of their working lives. Yet editing is clearly no job for an amateur. Editing should of course be in the hands of scholars active in the fields covered by the publications for which they are responsible, but this often means that the editors are professional scientists first and editors some way afterwards.

Editors can help themselves in several ways. One is to read appropriate journals, among them Scholarly Publishing, IEEE Transactions on Professional Communication, the Journal of Technical Writing and Communication, the Journal of Research Communications Studies and others, as well as the books and articles on editorial practice and policy referred to in this book. One book that is particularly valuable on technical and other innovations is Capital Systems Group's improving the dissemination of scientific and technical information, a loose leaf publication that is updated from time to time. A similar publication produced in the UK is also helpful. DeBakey's book, The scientific journal is essential reading, and Gtunewald's guidelines provide a succinct account of the work of editors. The Editerra editor's handbook has (or will have) three useful sections (publishing and printing; editing; standards and style) that will interest editors in all disciplines.

Another way to improve one's professionalism as an editor is to join an association of editors (some of these, such as CBE and Editerra/ELSE, have useful newsletters). The number of associations covering different disciplines and different geographical areas in increasing and the First International conference of Scientific Editors, held in Jerusalem in 1977, has given birth to IFSEA-the International Federation of Scientific Editors' Associations as well so to a volume of proceedings. A third solution-where funds are available-is for editors to share their responsibilities with one or more scientifically trained assistants, either part-time or full-time. Assistant editors, like any professionals, should master all the details of editorial work, keep up to date with developments, and themselves make innovations.

Although assistant editors of large-circulation journals in the UK are usually scientifically trained, in the USA it is quite common for editors to send accepted papers direct to scientifically untrained copy editors, who deal with the technical editing work but do very little rewriting. As this did not seem very satisfactory, Woodford attempted to introduce a system for training 'executive editors' for biochemical journals in the USA.

Those who took the course had advanced degrees and research experience in the biosciences. They were trained to assist chief editors by working in detail on publishable typescripts before their acceptance for publication. The philosophy on which the training was based was that a scientific paper is in most cases more intelligible, useful and enduring if it is the product of cooperation between the author and an executive editor: the author originates the ideas and does the work but is not necessarily good at getting it onto paper, while the executive editor, though not an expert on the subject matter, understands it and is also an experienced communicator. Clearly, there must be mutual respect in such cooperation, and both partners must be willing to learn.,

Authors are not always willing to learn from copy-editors who are not scientists, but executive editors are more acceptable on several counts. First, with their scientific training executive editors are less likely to make misguided changes that arise from a lack of understanding of the subject; and if these editors do misinterpret a passages, the authors should realize that other well-informed readers may do the same. Secondly, sub-editing of manuscripts submitted to journals can be done before the manuscripts are finally accepted, at a time when authors are more amenable to guidance. Thirdly, rank pulling is impossible because the executive editor has high scientific status. Experienced copy editors can overcome the inherent disadvantages of their position, especially if editors back them up firmly, but they often start at a disadvantage.

For these reasons it seems sensible for a part-time chief editor with a heavy work load to persuade the sponsoring organization to employ a professional assistant editor with scientific training in the appropriate field(s).

Finding and paying for suitable copy editors may be nearly as difficult as finding executive editors. Neither a first degree in science nor one in English (for English-language journals) is any guarantee that a person without previous experience will turn out to have the necessary qualities of patience, attention to detail, and eye for spelling and typographical errors, a sound knowledge of grammar and a feeling for language, together with the sense not to antagonize authors and the wit to know when to stop comma-catching and let the book or journal get to press.

In a few large organizations copy editors receive some formal training, but many of them learn as they work. When employers can afford to break their copy editors in gently, proof-reading and reference-checking are the best jobs for them to tackle first text editing should be left until they have experience of all the other copy-editing procedures. Editors can speed up the learning process by getting new copy-editors to read Judith Butcher's book on Copy-editing , as well as Writing scientific papers in English and any relevant disciplinary or national style manuals that are recommended to authors (Nordic biomedical manuscripts, 'Dorothy Mizoguchi's book for Japanese authors, and others), since style manuals and guidelines for authors show copy editors what to look for in typescripts. (Copy editors should read this book too, of course.)

Whether or not they are blessed with help from executive editors or copy-editors, journal editors who take a professional attitude to editing can subject themselves and their journals to regular review and self-assessment. One mechanism for doing this is to discuss the objectives of the journal with readers, using the editorial pages as a sounding-board in the way mentioned earlier. Examples can be found in the Journal of Medical Education, in which a new direction for the journal was announced in 1971; in Biochemical Biophysical Acta, in which a change in editorial policy on the acceptance rate was justified on the grounds that there had been an unmanageable logarithmic growth in the number of papers submitted; and in the New England Journal of Medicine, whose editor confessed that several innovations by the journal had not succeeded, and suggested some reasons for the failures (Ingelfinger's articles, incidentally, is a goldmine for the innovative editor). These three editorials are all examples of editors discussing their policies and procedures with their customers-thinking aloud and using the scientific method of hypothesis, testing of hypothesis, and deduction.

A second procedure for self-assessment is to use the Journal Citation Reports published by the Institute for

Scientific Information. The number of times journal, as opposed to an individual paper, is cited is a fair indication of the impact-positive or negative-it is having on the scientific community. If the impact factor (average number of citations per article during the first few years after publication of each issue) of the journal, falls over the years, something is certainly wrong; the editor has to discover what it is.

At present, only the full-time editors of certain large-circulation journals are accorded the status they deserve, while scientific editing in general confers little prestige on its exponents. As editors become more proficient the status of editing will rise, together with the general standard of the publications for which they are ultimately responsible. This is a highly desirable state of affairs at which to aim-but it depends partly on the continued existence of books and journals in a world where communication systems are advancing and changing very rapidly indeed.

In practice, what changes are we about to see in the scientific communication system? Will scientific articles in future always flicker at us from video screens? Are we really heading for a paperless world devoid of the pleasures of browsing? Are editors to be replace by electronics?

The answer to all three questions is 'No', or at least 'Not for a long time yet'. In 20 or 30 years electronic journals will probably be widely used but it seem likely that journals printed on paper will exist aide by side with the electronic species. Words on paper are still the most efficient and acceptable way of transmitting archival information or any material that readers have to study for any length of time. Until scientists everywhere have instant access to computer terminals, books and journals will remain the most acceptable and attractive means of packaging that information. And because the costs of entering material into computer systems an storing it are high, editors will still be needed for electronic journals for the same reasons as they are needed for paper ones-to control the quality and form of what goes into the system.

Even though this view of the future for editors and publishers is an optimistic one, a concerted effort is needed now to improve the state of the art of scientific publication. Costs need to be brought down or prevented from rising exorbitant, and ways should be found of drastically shrinking the publication flag for books and journals without diminishing the quality of the information offered to readers. Above all, production and distribution should be made vastly more efficient. It is many years since it became possible for newspapers to he composed in one city and for facsimile versions to be produced in other cities, hundreds of miles away with more communications satellites circling the world, and with decreasing computer costa and ever-improving production methods, how long will it be before books and journals can be economically photocomposed in one continent and reproduced as bound copies, in any number needed, anywhere in that continent or another? The electronic era will show its achievements in this way just as surely as it already does in allowing access to one or more pages at a time on a screen.

Although many of us will be happy to look at material for which we are in a hurry on a video screen or microfiche reader before deciding whether to obtain hard copy versions, most of us—whether we are reading for pleasure or to obtain general background information-will also want to go on reading books or journals in their conventional form, however unconventional the production method nay he, Even when terminals sprout in every office or laboratory, 'Who wants to go to bed with a floppy disk-or with a microform projector? All the indications are that paper publications, and their editors, will coexist happily, and for long time to come, with whatever electronic and other innovations may spread into the world of scientific publishing.

Technological Aspects

The history of typography has shown that the type which is easy to read is better than any fancy type and the Italian humanist lettering now called Roman ousted Coxton's Germamic Gothic in England and everywhere else because people found it easier to read.

Various Kinds

Types bear many eighteenth century names of pioneers who cut type. William Caslon of London cut his famous type in 1720. John Baskerville of Birmingham and Giambattista Bodoni who made his fame from 1786 in the printing office of the Duke of Parma. But these types were originally designed as small-sized types for books. When the type manufacturers had to meet the demand for display faces for posters, shops, advertisement and newspapers, they produced strengthened versions of the book faces and later wholly new designs of their own.

Though there is today a vast range of display type, a newspaper must select from a limited range. Speed of production requires that headline type in general use in the newspaper shall come as metal from a key boarded machines of linotype and intertype or the semi-mechanized Ludlow system, or as film set characters from these and other manufacturers. An attractive hand set type from a founder can only be used for larger sizes at wide measure when hand-setting will be as fast as machine because type setter will be setting just a few characters.

In hot-metal process the Ludlow system of slug casting from handset matrices is most popular for headlines as the key board machines do not set above 36 pt in upper and lower case. There is no need to leave extra-white between letters and words. It normally spoils the visual impact of the headline. Spacing in the headline should always be judged visually. If it looks wrong it is wrong without any doubt. Use of underscoring, bucket, hood or curtain and box should be avoided in headline particularly when it is spread over single or double column. It indicates failure to choose right type size and only therefore one needs column rules to separate this headline from the rest.

While using reverse block one should always choose an open bold face without fine serifs Open sans or a slab serif is ideal.

Full point is not used in headlines. The last word is the end of a thought and therefore no need to put full stop. When two thoughts are joined together in a deck (though one should avoid this) they should be separated by colon. The use of semicolon should be avoided for simplicity and typographic neatness for easy reading. Exclamation and question marks should be rarely used. Comma should be used to separate clauses and sometimes used to indicate the omission of 'and'. While using comma care should be taken to ensure right meaning. Quotation marks are used to indicate external authority for a statement and also to indicate doubt about an assertion.

New Technology of Type Setting: For many years the only kind of type setting was that done by hand and therefore the production of newspapers was necessarily slow. The invention and adoption of line-casting typesetting machines 'linotypes' enabled publishers to greatly speed up the production of newspapers. The Linotype continued to be the most widely used technique of setting type until about 1966 when a number of typesetting inventions began to be accepted and adopted by many newspapers throughout the world.

The type is now set photographically and with the aid of computers and some related inventions revolutionised the speed of newspaper production. The video display terminal (VDT) allows the reporter to not only type his original story and a have the words show up on a video display screen but he can also correct and edit that story without touching a piece of paper and operate the phototypesetter on a push of button. The optical character reader (OCR) enables the reporter to type his story on a special electric typewriter, edit it on the same machine and then feed his written story to the OCR to 'read' the words on the paper and operate the phototypesetter subsequently.

Handset and machine-set type were best adopted to letter-press printing which consists of printing from raised letters, directly on paper. Phototypesetting is better with offset printing method in which after a printing plate is coated with ink and water it first prints on a rubber sheet (called a blanket) and then from the blanket onto paper.

Photoprints, when used with offset, are pasted directly on a page format along with screened pictures. Then the entire page is photographed as a single entity, converted into a negative and finally into a printing plate. The basic phototype setting technique consists of placing a film negative of each letter in a sentence in front of a light source and then shining light through the negative onto light-sensitive photographic paper. The result is a picture of letters assembled into lines. Once enough lines have been set photographically they can be pasted on to a page form photographed and converted into a printing plate.

The first generation of phototypesetters were really a modification of hot typesetting machines where each letter of the alphabet was first made in the form of a mold (called a mat). Hot lead was poured into the molds thereby producing a line of metal type. These mat were modified by replacing the molds with a film negative of each letter. After the first line was set, the photographic paper would be advanced ready to receive a new line of letters. Thus, the first generation phototypesetters were really photo-mechanical in nature and therefore relatively slow. The fastest could set twenty lines a minute depending upon the versatility of the operator. The second generation of phototypesetters could set type faster and the method of photographing the letters was different. At least four different modes of negatives were developed by various competitors. All the letters of the alphabet, numbers and punctuation marks were prepared on a single film negative surface such as a disc, a drum, a film strip or a rectangular grid. It was possible to move these letters more quickly than older machines. This generation increased the speed of setting to about 150 lines a minute.

The third generation phototypesetting machine are almost totally electronic. They use a cathode ray tube (CRT) as a scanning device and throw light through a lens and then through each of the letters in a sentence on the negative surface. A photoelectric cell behind the negative picks up the light and delivers it to another cathode ray tube which eventually prints the letters originally scanned on photographic paper. This third generation typesetter can set upto 500 lines a minute.

The fourth generation typesetter has also emerged. The distinguished feature of this typesetter is that it uses laser beam in the setting process and has no photographic negative to shine light through. Instead a laser beam generates letters from a memory control, electronically through a series of strokes and build letters somewhat like that of CRT machine but without a master negative. Fonts of type are stored in the memory unit of this machine and can be called forth by pressing a button. This machine can set 1000 lines per minute. It is also possible to generate line art and halftones in the laser typesetters. This will enable the user to make up all of the elements of a page on a video display tube. When the page is made up, it may be printed on photographic paper ready for conversion to an offset printing plate.

Most photosetters installed in newspaper plants are operated in conjunction with either a VDT or an OCR in addition to a computer. Assembly of these various operating machines wired to each other is called a system.

In this system the reporter types copy on VDT key board. He then corrects and edits it. When he is satisfied he sends the story to computer for storage. Other stories are also in storage. Sub-editor or chief sub can retrieve it from the storage for checking and can do editing using the VDT. He can also write headlines, specifying the kind of type, size and width and returns the story to computer for storage. If he feels he should edit it fully or rewrite it he can have it printed on paper at 360 lines a minute speed. Then he can edit it on paper and later on VDT and return it to computer for storage.

When the news editor is reading to dummy page, he can ask computer to print all sluglines on VDT. and decide what stories he wants. After this decision he calls up each story on VDT, determines its length and begins to dummy the page. After this he presses a button and sends body copy and headlines to be set on a phototypesetter which delivers a photoprint. Story now goes to the printer for paste up.

Importance of Photography

Good pictures speak for themselves. While making selection of news pictures the prime consideration should be context in which the picture is being used. The picture should have information related to the story with which it is to be used.

A good news photograph should reflect the feelings and responses of the people photographed. Even routine events yield good photographs if the people are caught by the camera in action and their feelings and emotions are expressed on the faces. Animation is one of the prime quality of a good news photograph.

Photograph should reflect the mood of the moment. Even

selecting from file pictures care should be taken to select a photograph which depicts the right mood. When a person is sacked a picture depicting him in a happy mood will be a misfit. Like words pictures also have meaning. There are occasions when symbolism could be effective to impact meaning. Sometimes comparison provide meaning to pictures.

Looking at certain photographs one is surprised what little eyes can see when the event is taking place. Action photographs particularly come in this category. In sports events and cultural events action photographs depicting the climax of a movement if captured by camera becomes an exciting picture.

A photographer must reach on a scheduled event a few minutes before the time and look for key moment while shooting. Camera is very much similar to the notebook of a trained reporter. It should catch the key moments of the event that are most relevant to the news event. News photographer should have news sense and it should be sharpened by selection of his most newsy pictures by the photo-editor.

Only a photographer with a keen news sense will be able to catch decisive moments of history with is camera. In every event there is sequence of action of which only a few moments are at the climax and only one of them is really decisive. Nearer the photograph is to that moment the better news photograph it is.

The photograph once selected has to be edited for size, shape and story content. The basic determining factor is the story content because it determines the size and shape of the photograph or whether the photograph should be used at all.

It is debated whether a photograph should be cropped. Many photographers of international repute argue that a good photograph should never undergo cropping. But it may be true of only excellent news photographs capturing decisive moments. Most of the photographs can be improved by cropping. While cropping the emphasis should be on the story and what is in the picture. One may remove irrelevant portion of a picture and emphasis could be added to the relevant portion of the picture. Shape of picture is also decided by the story content.

While determining the size of a picture emphasis should be on legibility and impact. It is pointless to give a photograph if it is printed so small that the relevant detail is lost. Legibility determines the minimum size of the picture and maximum has to determined by the availability of space, competition from other news pictures or stories. It should also be seen whether giving a bigger size justifies the expense of space by increase in the impact. Space should be used with discrimination to ensure that the photograph which really needs it should get it.

Cropping is a creative job. Looking at the above factors one has to identify the key image in the photograph and enlarge it to give maximum information or impact. The words with the picture should match. The reader must be told what, where, when and why of the photograph. If explanation improves the understanding the key factor it should be given.

It is essential to realise that newspaper design is part of journalism. It is not decoration ut communication. Newspaper communicates news and ideas and design is an integral part of the process.

A sub-editor begins with a blank sheet of newsprint and wants to communicate several ideas and the day's news. It is the function of newspaper design to present that mosaic in an organised and comprehensive way by using text type, display type, photograph, line work, white space and a sequence of pages in the most fitting combination.

Drafting of a News

Newspaper design has to care for the audience too. Researchers find out the readership habits and give, it due consideration. For example, the broadsheet format of a serious newspaper will not suit a metropolitan evening daily which is produced for commuters on crowded trains or buses. Ideal format for such a newspaper will be tabloid for ease in handling. Front and back page of such a newspaper should have the widest possible range of appeal. There are other considerations of utility. A family newspaper should not publish women's column on sports page or on the other side of sports page. Magazine sections are separate from news sections of the newspaper. Such elementary consideration form the framework of newspaper design.

There is an important role in newspapers for artists and designers but they must be closely involved with journalists and journalism. They must share the idea of communication and the audience. A designer should not think that a day's news can fit in his preconceived patterns.

The design cannot be left to the artist alone. If he produces something which is more useful in communication of an idea it should be used. Any refinement which interferes with function should not be allowed. There should be a balance between form and function where function is the priority. There is need for continuous dialogue between journalist, designer and the researcher to achieve a better balance between the form and function of newspaper design.

Editorial content can be divided into two groups:

(i) *Unpredictable :* Spot news in words and pictures which can be divided into local, national, foreign, and so on.

(ii) *Predictable:* Stock-market prices, weather forecast, TV and radio programmes, film, art criticism, letters to editor, editorial, crossword puzzles, bridge column, etc.

Predictable content should be in predictable positions. Television and radio programmes, share prices, weather, etc., should be anchored in the same place day after day.

When the unpredictable news is organised in departments foreign, sport, business, etc., these should appear in approximately the same position in the newspaper every day. The space will vary according to the news and the size of the paper but the page should not be changed from day to day. Page sequence should be logical and consideration of reader habits should determine it. For example, right hand side pages particularly at the beginning of the newspaper get more reader attention so they should have material in which maximum readership is interested.

The Front Page: It is the most important page of a newspaper. It induces the reader to pick up the paper and read it. It establishes the identify and character of the paper and also introduces freshness by its display and content. According to function visualised for the front page it could be:

Signal and Text Front Page: It is typical modern front page where a selection of the most important news items is signaled by headlining and positioning on a clear scale of priorities and supported with text. Less important items go to inside pages. Most broadsheet newspaper follow this style with exceptions like Punjab Kesari, Jagbani, Akali Patrika. Efforts should be made to give the full text of an item on the front page. If the text does turn to another page it may be because of more items that deserve the signal treatment on front page.

Poster Front Page: It contains all the important news items on front page-just one or two paragraphs of each indicating the page on which details appear. Even as late as 1965 designers recommended this type for *The Times*, London. However, it was not accepted.

Many newspapers use variations and combinations of the two styles. Part of front page of signal and text front page can be used everyday to encapsulate the main news (and features) presented inside. The Times of India used this combination type front page.

Punjab Kesari, Jagbani and Akali Patrika give features on front page. Front page has normally nothing to do with news in these newspapers. This kind of front page has established in Punjab and it was regarded that change in this style may lead to fall in circulation. However, Ajit has changed from feature front page to signal-and-text front page an the circulation actually did not go down but increased.

Page Layout: Make-up or layout of the page is determined by the format of the page-the number of columns in which the page is divided

Eight columns of 11 or 11½ picas each is the standard for broadsheets partly dictated by advertising standards of 11 picas. Layouts can vary in this format and number of display positions are available if the nature of newspaper is serious.

However there are nine or ten column papers. This format provides excess of display portion. It is difficult to manage typography and make such a page attractive. Readability of such papers is poor.

There is a A6 column format also. The standard 11 pica measure is retained for six columns and the seventh column is equal to 1½ column and the remaining half column is distributed as white space in the gutters. Many papers use this format which is attractive and .convenient and also provides variety.

Six-column is regarded 'optimum format' because it takes optimum text line for easy reading (about 15 picas). However, the display positions are less than the eight column pages. In this format long stories can be handled with extra ease.

Five column format is also used by some papers. Some papers use this 14.6 picas grid for editorials or long analytical articles requiring long text.

For tabloids five and four column layouts are convenient and widely used. However, this format may vary from page to page and even on the same page. The varying format is most justified when it signals a distinct change of content. For example, editorial comment from general news content.

The column grid is part of basic format of the paper and is more or less a fixed element of newspaper design. Layout or make up occurs in this format.

Layout means arrangement of headlines, text, artwork and white space on a page or pages.

Layout could be static or dynamic. If one can predict the layout of tomorrow's page today because it has been similar with minor variations day after day the layout is called static. In such layout one can predict that the first lead story will be on say left hand side. There will be pictures and then there will be the second lead. There will be a third major story below the picture. The Times of India and Statesman provide good examples of such layout.

But layout is dynamic when no body can predict what it will be-the lead may be on left or right and if there is a striking picture headlines will be submerged to make room for it. Here designer is attempting to respond dynamically to the news. The Telegraph and Jansatta are god examples.

Layout, whether static or dynamic, could be modular or irregular. Modular layout breaks the page into series of rectangles-headline and related text form a four sided rectangular unit.

Irregular layout breaks the page into series of interlocking shapes. Most or all headlines themselves are irregular in shape and most or all headline-text units on a page form irregular shapes.

Vertical layout gives the simplest page organisation. Headlines are set in the width of basic single-column grid and the text runs single column. This oldest layout style has limited range of news value expression. Though it is visually depressing, maximum number of stories can be given above the fold. When headlines side by side are the same size and style the result if called 'tombstoning'. This is a major problem of vertical layout. It can be overcome with alteration of colour along horizontal line. Colour here means blocks, greys and white and with modern display type adjacent heads can be varied to express different news values or tone. The headings can be set left in the white to avoid clash of headlines.

Another way is to vary the width of the headline grid. For example, a two column head is used to express more important news. The width of text setting can also vary to avoid monotony of tombstoning.

Horizontal Layout: This is another simple layout but with more capacity for emphasis. It is modular with text squared up under multi-columns heads to create a horizontal unit. Page is then made up of a series of these units lying flat on each other.

In this layout a long story seems shorter. Complete stories can be read with page folded at the natural midpage fold and without the reader having to shuffle the paper up and down, headlines are separated from each other by text and thus each headline retains its emphasis. In horizontal layout full use of the width of the page is possible for display. However, there are only a few stories above the midfold which can be seen at retail outlets.

Quadrant Layout: It envisages the page as four separate sections divided by a line at the fold and a line down the middle of the page. Each unit has a strong display item consisting of either multi-column headlines and picture or panel. This formula reminds that there is more to a page than its top half. But this formula if followed with geometric rigidity may lead to display of news item disproportionate to news value.

Diagonal Layout: Here the designer places headlines along two imaginary diagonal lines, which divide the page and cross each other. It reminds that headlines can be distributed anywhere on the paper. But it is difficult to coordinate display with the news values.

France Layout: The columns one and eight on an eight column paper should be solid text so that beneath the paper's title and eight-column banner heads the frame, the content of the page. It is more a gimmick than a formula for layout. After all, newspaper page is not a picture to be framed and put on the wall.

Brace Layout: In brace layout headlines are arranged in steps so that the one higher in the page is supported by another running parallel. In such a layout the headlines compete for attention with each other and lose emphasis. It also forces text away from the headlines. Headlines can actually stand on their own. They do not need each other's support as is provided in this type of layout.

Circus Layout: In circus layout emphasis is on variety contrasts and movement but not on order or news value. There are many points of attraction, not necessarily related to news values. The reader is to be distracted and entertained. The mast head of the paper may appear in any position above the fold.

Symmetrical Layout: This layout attempts to produce an equal balance of eight around an axis, classically the optical centre of the page. Each side of the optical centre should be a mirror image of the other. Optical centre, the pivotal point, is a point one-third of the distance from the top where the horizontal forces are in equilibrium with the vertical forces and is the point of perfect balance.

Symmetrical layout need not be static. The essence of axial symmetry is balance at the centre and this can be achieved in dynamic layout.

Symmetrical layout has a powerful appeal for serious papers as it appears to organise the heterogeneous content rationally and satisfies the human mind's natural demand for -balance. It is of little use to the newspapers that thrive on excitement. Even in serious newspapers the symmetrical balance threatens display in relation to news values. It is also difficult to produce a perfectly symmetrical page, particularly a newspage. Further, perfect balance may be boring also.

Asymmetrical Layout: This layout is dynamic and excludes any axial symmetry, any predetermined point of balance. Here 'artistic balance' or 'informal balance' is achieved by a balance of unequal forces at unequal distances from the centre.

Asymmetrical layouts have a balance which is subtle. It enables the page to satisfy our natural desire for order, organisation and balance while providing emphasis and movement. Balance is there but it is not a mechanical balance and it does not force the news to conform to set pattern. This assists functional relationship of content and display.

The newspaper design and layout must be functional. There should be organisation and rational coordination of heterogeneous material but the news values should get priority in deciding the display. It should give emphasis to the most important news to attract the reader. There should be order, but the prime importance should be given to news values.

11

EDITORIAL JOB

Every journalist unless he is happy to remain a worker for the rest of his life-carries the dream of being an editor. Who is a newspaper editor?

He is not, as is commonly believed the man who writes the editorials. He is the man, who conducts a newspaper. Usually at the bottom of the last page of every paper, is what is known as the Imprint Line. The Imprint Line is mandatory and pins responsibility on what goes into print on the men who bring out a daily. Consider this Imprint Line:

Printed and published for the Proprietors, Bennett, Coleman & Co. Ltd., by *T.P. Pithavala* at *the Times of India Press,* Dr. D.N. Road, Bombay 400 001. Editor: Girilal Jain. Resident Editor: K.C. Khanna. General Manager: Dr. Ram S. Tarneja.... Everything is clearly stated.

If a newspaper in any way contravenes the law, the men responsible-the editor and the printer and publisher-can easily be identified and located and will have to obey the court's summons. The editor's chair in the circumstances, is not necessarily a comfortable one. The man who occupies it does not have an easy job. He bears a heavy responsibility and often has been called upon to pay a heavy price in the discharge of that responsibility.

Ability of an Editor

There is no one way applicable to all aspirants. Anyone who has the money to set up shop as an editor can become one. There are no rules and regulations, no memberships to be filled, no examination to pass. A mere declaration suffices.

Editors in the formative stage of the Indian Press were men imbued with a sense of mission. Robert Knight who made *The Times of India* into a great institution early in its career came to his job with experience in civil life and the running of public institutions. *The Pioneer* was started by Sir George Allen, a businessman of Kanpur and his son C.T. Allen. Of the three enterprising brothers Hemanta Kumar Ghosh, Sisir Kumar Ghosh and Motilal Ghosh who started the *Amrit Bazar Patrika,* the first two were working as employees in the Income Tax Department. S. Kasturi Ranga Iyengar who bought *The Hindu* in 1905 was a lawyer.

But there were others, men like Arthur Moore, Kalinath Ray, A.D. Mani, Benjamin Horniman, S. Sadanand and Prank Moraes who came to their jobs the hard way. Devdas Gandhi got his experience assisting his father in the running of *Young India.* Sadanand also had his apprenticeship with the same paper. Prank Moraes first worked as-an assistant editor with *The Times of India* from 1938 to 1946 during which, for a three-year period he also doubled as a war correspondent. He became deputy editor in 1949 and a full editor only in 1950. Kotamaraju Rama Rao, who became the crusading editor of *National Herald,* had his apprenticeship as a reporter under T.L. Vaswani of the *New Times* of Hyderabad, Sind. M. Chalapathi Rao worked as an assistant editor first at the *National Herald* and later at *The Hindustan Times* before he became editor of *Herald*. Pothan Joseph worked for a string of papers like the *Voice of India*, the *Indian Daily Mail* and *The Hindustan Times* interspersing his editorial career with a few executive assignments such as that of the Principal Information Officer of the Government of India. These distinguished men give the lie to the belief that editors are born and not made.

An editorship is not a bed of roses and has never been. Easy as his life may seem he works under all manner of pressures and not all-necessarily coming from the management. Because his is the final responsibility in bringing out the paper he has to bear the brunt of the wrath whether of advertisers or of existing governments', During the Emergency (1975-77) in India, it was the editor who had to shoulder the burden of official wrath.

Editors in India have been under pressure for decades, in fact from the very beginning of the British rule in the country. The Vernacular Press Act was passed in 1878 in order to control the *Amrit Bazar Patrika,* then published in Bengali as well as in English-the *Patrika* being bilingual. To get out of the clutches of the Act, its publishers changed over completely to English beginning 21 March 1878.

The *Patrika* has a long history of editorial daring and competence. At one time, the Government of Bengal recommended the deportation of one of the paper's earliest editors, Motilal Ghosh. On another occasion, the paper had to face prosecution in connection with the famous Barisal Conspiracy Case. Ghosh fought the charges and succeeded in getting the case dismissed. In 1932, the *Patrika* was penalized and a security of Rs 6,000 was demanded from it.

Another paper to fall foul of the government was the *Free Press Journal.* So powerful were the writings of its editor-publisher S. Sadanand that he had to forfeit the then phenomenal figure or Rs 70,000 as security. Indian editors were not the only ones to face the British government's wrath. E.G. Horniman of the *Bombay Chronicle* frequently clashed with officialdom and, at one time, the paper's printer and publisher were asked to deposit Rs 3,000 as security which was later forfeited. The history of Indian journalism is full of such instance of editors, fighting valiantly to protect the honour and integrity of the free press.

Many editors have also fallen foul of the owners of newspapers, though, in one instance, when C.Y. Chintamani differed from his paper's Board of Directors and offered to resign, it was the offending member of the Board, Pandit Madan Mohan Malaviya who decided to quit instead.

Individual Matters

No two editors are alike. The only common denominator that can be ascribed to them is their humanity, their concern for people, their interest in new. A delicate problem for every editor is the extent to which he can, and should, delegate authority. In a large paper an editor would have from two to six, sometimes as many as eight assistant editors. Each would have specialized in a particular field of activity such as foreign affairs, national affairs, law, finance, defence, agriculture or whatever. No editor can possibly be an expert in all fields and even if he happens to be an immensely knowledgeable man, he just would not have the time to keep up with new developments.

It is amazing how much a writer has to put in by way of reading. It could be new books on the subject, documents pertaining to it or upcoming literature dealing with the issue. No editor is expected to be a know-all. It is an editor's task to know who, among his colleagues, is best equipped to write on an event and to assign the task to him. By this the editor is not surrendering his responsibility, he is exercising it wisely. A good editor should know how best to tap the available talent in his office.

It is common in most editorial offices for the editor to have a morning conference with his staff. Often it-is done around the coffee table where assistant editors can sit informally and not only discuss the day's newspaper but engage in a post-mortem of the news. Depending on what the day's most important issues are, there will be a discussion of some of them at the end of which the editor would lay down his own views and give guidelines. If the editorial staff is fairly homogenous there would be no difficulty in arriving at a consensus as to what editorial line should be taken on any given subject. Often, if the assistant editors have worked over a long period with the editor, they would know instinctively as to what angle would be projected. In any event it is the editor who lays down the policy and the subject of the editorials. Who will write what is also discussed and decided on at this conference.

An editor of a party paper will have no difficulty in the matter of policy as it would have been laid down for him. It would be his task to argue the party case as well as he can; he has a brief. An ideal paper, of course, would be one where its owners would let the editor make his own decisions and argue on the merits of a subject. In that event he would have to be as honest and objective as he can possibly be, placing, as he should, the public interest before anything else. He will know that life is not a bed of roses. He must expect to be subjected to all forms of persuasion, not all of them scrupulous, including flattery, bribery, even physical threats, not to mention behind-the-scene wire-pulling.

Though an editor is once removed from the actual

production of a paper, it is in his power to decide what should be published and what shouldn't. In a sense he has to play God. This is a tremendous responsibility and cannot be ducked. It is an insensitive man and consequently a poor editor who has on occasion tortured himself over taking a decision that could possibly have harmed many people. The editors of *The New York Times* have admitted publicly their regret that they did not publish information about the US government's plans to abet the invasion of Cuba. If the paper had published the news, they have argued, the country may well have been saved the embarrassment of the Bay of Pigs fiasco.

Most editors may not be called upon to take momentous decisions, yet editing a paper is one long struggle against time, during: which decisions, one way or the other have to be taken. This is both the charm and frustration of being an editor Responsibility ends with him.

Editors have different methods of dealing with the problem of leader writing. Some dictate and then make the final corrections. Some do their own typing. Some others write laboriously in long hand. Some finish their writing by the end of the evening and place a phone call before retiring to bed to see that events have not-overtaken the editorial. Some others refuse to put down a word on paper until midnight.

Need of Interest

The important thing for an editor is always to be keenly aware of the needs of the public and to be able to feel its pulse. It is to him that the reader will look to, interpret yesterday's news. An editor-and certainly a good editor-will offer leadership to the country as only he can. But for that, he will have to offer leadership to his staff, in the first instance. What often makes a news paper great is the right combination of inspiration, emphasis design, control, tone and selectivity. It is the editor who will have to see that through his personal leadership, this combination is achieved. It is not-and cannot bean easy task.

An editor will soon learn-if he has not by the time-he has become one-that his time is not always his own. In the office he will have to be in constant, if not continuous, touch with his colleagues. Outside the office he will be in demand as a public speaker,-as a guest at dinners and parties. These are chores that may not always be pleasant for him and more often than not are tiring and time consuming. And yet only by listening to friends and foes in various situations can an editor come to know what the public thinks. Dinners may be hard on the waistline but it is during the after-dinner coffee that an important politician may want to unburden himself to an editor to seek his reaction. An editor must make himself available to those who have something important and worthwhile to say. This may not be very conducive to a settled married life, but it is an occupational hazard that editors have to face. A major problem confronting the "ideal" editor-the editor who 'puts public' interest before everything else is the extent to which he should extend cooperation to the government.

It is not the job of the editor to give uncritical support to whatever administration is in power. Neither can it be said that his should be an unrestrained attack. Some journalists pretend that no one but the editor and proof reader read editorials. Such a view is extremely misleading. Whatever the situation be elsewhere in the world, in India there is ample evidence to show that editorials are read with interest. Editors often are more influential than they are prone to tell themselves. It may be that editorial influence is more over policy makers than over the public at large. The fact remains that editorials ("leaders") cannot be dismissed out of hand as mere space fillers.

An interesting comment has been made on the subject by James Reston of the *New York Times.* Speaking about the influence or the American Press on the American foreign policy, Mr. Reston pointed out that in his view this is usually exaggerated. "Its influence" he said, "is exercised primarily through the Congress, which confuses press opinion with public opinion. No doubt the press has great influence on American foreign policy when things are *obviously* going badly. It has very little influence, however, when things are going badly but the impending disaster is not obvious and the government is saying, as it usually does, that all is well or soon will be if everybody only has faith and confidence."

This is largely true. When things are going reasonably well, the tendency for the public is to accept government statements; the public frequently wants to be assured and is willing to believe or, at the very least, to suspend judgement. The crunch comes when things go badly and then it is to the critical editor that the public will turn. This was amply shown when, soon after the Emergency in India was lifted, the sales of newspapers suddenly soared to phenomenal heights. The public was turning to the editors to tell it the whole story unvarnished. The circulation of *The Indian Express,* for instance, showed a remarkable rise in the immediate post-Emergency months.

The important thing for an editor is, to be intellectually honest. He does not always have to be right; in the nature of things he cannot be so. But as long as he is honest and is seen to be honest, his responsibility to his profession ceases there. Nothing more can be expected of an editor and nothing more should.

The problem of honesty is more complicated than one thinks. What, for instance, should an editor's attitude be towards Mrs. Indira Gandhi at a time when the Janata Government is at sixes and sevens? Should the editor refuse to support her as a possible leader of an alternate government on the grounds that her role during the Emergency disqualifies her to receive any support any time or should he take the stand that as a leader of proven stature and stamina, Mrs. Gandhi deserves support at a time of national instability? It is here that an editor whose credibility is beyond challenge can get respectful attention from his reading public. In other words, for an editor, credibility is all.

Regular Connection

It is important for an editor to be in constant touch with government officials from ministers downward. Senior editors get easy audience with ministers, since it pays the ministers themselves to nave their policies and views understood in the right perspective by the opinion-makers. The editor who lives in an ivory tower is becoming increasingly rare, if ever such a species existed. He cannot afford to be too far from the madding crowd. The crowd is and should be his business.

Almost all editors to a person, complain of the heavy schedule that they have to put up with. Consider this average day put in by one editor who usually is up around 6.30 in the morning and, goes for a half hour early morning walk. Then as he has his tea, he reads the morning papers, especially his competitors. If, as frequently happens, an item of interest has been missed by his paper, he will make a note of it for later discussion with his staff. He is in his office by 10 a.m.

10.00-10.45 a.m.: Staff meeting. This is the time devoted to dissecting the day's performance with assistant editors and assigning writing work to them.

10.45-11.30 a.m.: The editor meets the News Editor, the Chief Reporter and the Chief of his News Bureau. The discussion will relate to why some stories were missed, or why some were not adequately displayed or why some others should not have been displayed. The *post mortem* over, the discussion will deal with upcoming stories and how to cover them.

11. 30-12 noon: Individual assistant editors will stray in to discuss specific ideas and to get editorial approval for them.

12 noon-2.00 p.m.: The editor will do whatever writing he plans to do for the next day's paper, taking a 15-minute break for a quick lunch.

2.00-4.00 p.m.: This is the time to look into copy submitted to him by his assistant editors, to select articles and special features to go for the next day's editorial page.

4.00-5.00 p.m.: This is Visitor's Hour when public citizens, usually those who have previously made appointments call on the Editor with complaints, suggestions or plain gossip.

5.00-6.00 p.m.: Time to look quickly into New Delhi and provincial papers and also at foreign papers and dispose off work with-the Bureau.

At 6.00 p.m. the editor leaves for his home where he will wash, change and relax.

8.30 p.m.: Dinner engagement. This is not an everyday affair but is sufficiently frequent to be taken as part of the day's work. Before going out, however, the editor usually calls the office and tell where he may be found in an emergency. Usually he himself calls the news-editor to check on late news breaks.

11.00 p.m.: Back home and one more late night call to the office to check certain details. Mostly arrangements are made to send him the final proofs of the editorial page so that should last minute changes become necessary they can be quickly incorporated.

This does not permit much time to engage in sports or hobbies. A major complaint of editors is that they do not get the time needed to refurbish their minds. "I am living on my capital" is how Mr. Girilal Jain expressed his frustration. According to him, in 15 months he had taken only four days off and had seen only two films, which is probably a good average for most editors.

There are editors and editors. What makes for a truly great editor? According to Mr. M. Chalapathi Rau, C.Y. Chintamani was one. The following article written by Mr. Rau for *Swarajya* gives us a clear picture of why he thought so.

"Chintamani was a journalist, mostly an editor, with a pontiff's air but without pontiff's pomp. An editor of his period, enjoying considerable reputation, a legislator and political leader, possessing a muscular, vigourous style, he had a right to pontificate, and he pontificated giving a further lease of life to the leading article, before journalism made news techniques dominate the newspaper.

My acquaintance with Chintamani was brief but interesting my irreverence about eminence coinciding with the climax of career. It was my ambition not to be a journalist and neither the Spenders, nor the Chintamanis attracted me much. But style did, style as an extension of personality and not merely as an assembly of words, even if it was proper words in proper places or the best words in the best order.

With my interest in politics, I was reading in Madras with great interest the leading articles in a weekly edition of the *Leader* published from Allahabad. By then, I was forgetting Mill on Liberty and Morley on Compromise and was a convert to the Congress. So I could not but read the *Leader* critically. But an admiration for the argumentativeness, the consistency of outlook and the vigorous syntax of the main leading articles developed.

As an admirer of the orators who could rouse emotions one could not admire Chintamani, a speaker of cold logic, though with warm interjections, when I first heard him in Bombay. Then I heard him in Waltair in 1936 or so when he delivered his lectures which later became his book *Politics Since the Indian Mutiny,* abroad survey with many personalities, sketches and amusing anecdotes.

Dr. S. Radhakrishnan presided. I remember Radhakrishnan making caustic references to the Liberals and Chintamani reacting to them vigorously. I was among the few who listened to his Table-Talk as he sat at his brother's place in an easy chair-and pontificated off the record. He had no doubt about anything. Sastri had intellectual honesty but no intellectual courage. Sapru had intellectual courage but no intellectual honesty. Sivaswamy Iyer, who had both intellectual honesty and intellectual courage was India's most accurate thinker, and came only after Gandhi and Malaviya as a great man. Gandhi, of course, was one of the greatest men the world had known but he had done immense mischief in politics.

I had no prejudice against Chintamani but my irreverence extended to him. There was much talk of what people called his phenomenal memory. I held even then that memory was selective. If one remembered certain things, one did not remember other things. Chintamani was reputed to remember all the Congress Presidential addresses, the list of all the Popes, the birthdays of famous Indians, when and where he had met Gokhale or Malaviya first and so on. He also remembered British constitutional debates on India or the debates in Indian legislatures. And many other things. But I was afraid he did not remember many other things because he did not care for them or did not care to remember them.

He did not seem to care much for foreign affairs though India had no foreign policy of its own then as an appendage of an empire. He could elaborate some historical parallels and narrrate vividly some historical anecdotes. But in general he showed no sense of history. My point is not that he was not sufficiently educated but that he concentrated on a few things and did not care for much else.

The Leader was read mainly for its leading articles and Chintamani was admired, even adored, for most of them. He wrote on all important Indian political subjects, leaving South Africa and other matters to his assistants and whenever he wrote, the world knew that he wrote. There was first his vast knowledge of Indian political subjects, there was then no mistaking the conviction with which he wrote, there was finally the force and vigour with which he wrote. To the Liberals, his was the voice of the Mesosiah.... He had read all the best biographies and auto biographies in the English language and remembered them. He did not forget what this Secretary of State or that had said or what this Viceroy had done. The unflagging energy with which he wrote sustained the readers' interest, even when he wrote two columns. My irreverence disappeared whenever I read leading articles written by him.

Above all there was character in whatever he wrote or did. This enhanced his intellectual and moral stature. He would be no turncoat, no Titus Oates. Chintamani had resigned his ministership on a matter of principle, somewhat rare in our history before Independence, and after Independence. The people in D.P. could not forget it. He enjoyed life. He was kind to young people. He was a fine conversationalist.... I found he did not know enough of economics, did not understand what the Gold Standard was. Chintamani had his personal predilections believed in the other world and spirits and while I was hearing, it, he surprised me by saying that Gokhale's spirit had dictated an editorial to him. He wrote even on the transfer of Superintendents of Police and his obituary editorials ended with 'May his soul rest in peace'. When Chief Justice Thorn died, he wrote that 'the summons had come to his Lordship from above' which roused my amusement.

The more I have known of Indian journalism, however, the more reverent I have become about him. As a leader-writer, he was a rare type. Other leader-writers who have given me equal pleasure were Kalinath Ray of the *Tribune* with his logic chopping and N. Raghunathan of *The Hindu*, who at his best reminded me of the leading articles of the old *Times Literary Supplement.* Chintamani was a personality; he had character. He was a great editor".

Consider here the qualities that Chalapathi Rau admired in Chintamani: knowledge, ability, good memory, vast knowledge of Indian politics, adherence to principles at any cost, unflagging energy, courage of convictions; style, character. And an overriding ego.

Editors, to be sure, have egos that seem to go with the job. An ideal editor, of course, will have opinions (or what is an editor for?) but will not be opinionated. Some of the great editors of our times have been men with strong opinions, men like Sadanand, "Stalin" Srinivasan, S. Natarajan, Frank Moraes or C. Narasimhan. They lent to the papers they edited their strength of conviction. An editor without an opinion is like a river without water. He will go nowhere.

Chintamani confessed a lack of expertise in economics. No editor, it is fair to say, can possibly be knowledgeable in all subjects but it is expected of him to have a lively curiosity and an abiding interest in what makes the world go. Today's editor, besides, must be more than a leader-writer; to be an effective editor he will have to know something of making layouts, or cropping a picture or reviewing a film; in other words, it would not hurt to be a jack-of-all-trades while being master of a few.

In the twenties, thirties and well into the forties and fifties, a paper could still sell on the personality of the editor, though it is pertinent to remember that newspaper circulation was in the mid 50,000s for most papers and a circulation figure of 100,000 was considered something of a distant dream. But editors of that era were well-known to their readers and they carried something of an aura about them. Editors today are less well-known; editorials are read but they are disembodied views rather than the live thoughts of a man passionately committed to truth. Newspapers no more sell on the strength of editorials no matter how well they are written or argued or presented.

There was a time when writing in the *Indian Express* Frank Moraes placed his views on the front page. That did not perceptibly increase the circulation of the *Express.* If a paper is to sell it must take into account popular tastes whether in politics, economics, sports or films. That this is increasingly being recognized can be noticed from the fact that the *Express,* again, is devoting a page for features, an innovation in Indian journalism.

Knowing Public

We may take a brief *detour* to examine a subject that editors are continuously called upon to face, the public mind.

As all editors know, the public is not as well informed as it should be and it often does not even care. Editors are seldom known.

M.V. Kamath who has edited *The Illustrated Weekly of India* has had letters addressed to him in the name of H.V. Kamath, an older man and distinguished Member of Parliament whose name has long registered in the reader's sub-conscience. A Carnegie Endowment survey once established that many Americans believed and this in a country with a powerful communication media-erroneously that the NATO Treaty was negotiated through the United Nations. And the *New York Times* disclosed that nearly one third of the Americans surveyed by its reporters did not know that Berlin was located in communist East Germany. Social scientists can document such findings also in India at all levels of public intelligence.

If this be the case what is the public that the editor is addressing himself to? If public knowledge is limited should he, as one writer has facetiously suggested, put out papers that look like Mother Goose rhyme-books and write for readers with an intelligence, quotient just slightly above that of a moron? The fact of the matter is that in India, at least, there is a substantial section of the public that is highly sophisticated. This is borne out by the letters that editors get every day, some of which are witty, provocative and often throwing new light on old problems.

Role of Editorial

An editor enjoys immense powers such as are not often realized even in editorial sanctum sanctora. He can make or mar reputations. This is difficult to prove statistically. It has been said that even if the average mind could be plumbed for its reaction to any given editorial, no standard could be devised to project its long-term effect. The effect of the written word, by its nature, is incalculable. We know, for example, that newspapers down the years have been suppressed and the only conclusion that we can draw from that fact is that governments have always been conscious of the power of the press.

Obviously not every editor is powerful. And the size of a paper's circulation is no guidepost to an editor's influence. The circulation of *Harijan* that Mahatma Gandhi edited was not much to speak about. It never really ever touched even the 50,000 mark. And yet, in terms of moving the governments, it was probably the most powerful paper in its time, certainly as long as Mahatma Gandhi was actively engaged in editing it. But it was the Mahatma who made the *Harijan.* These days, too often, it is the newspapers who make the editors.

Nevertheless, editors have certain responsibilities commensurate with their powers. These are *(a)* to the state, *(b)* to their proprietors, *(c)* to their readers, and *(d)* to their own conscience, and not necessarily in that order. An editor without a conscience needs to be watched. He could be an enemy of the people. Unscrupulous editors may one day get their due, but they can do irretrievable damage to a nation's psyche, while they are in circulation.

The problem of an editor's responsibility to the state has never quite been defined though, when efforts have been made by governments to muzzle the press, it has been loudly articulated. During the Second World War, Arthur Moore of *The Statesman* was sought to be muzzled and the Viceroy even suggested that he be repatriated to England, on security grounds. In times of war, of course, governments will clamp down censorship on the press, but it is the peace-time relationship between the government and the press that call for examination.

When senior correspondents asked Mr. V.K. Krishna Menon-after the Goa take-over was completed-why they had not been given prior intimation of the "invasion," Mr. Menon blandly replied. "How was I to know that you would not leak the information to foreign embassies?" Mr. Menon is not alone in the kind of thinking that goes into government press relations.

On 2 October 1962, toward the end of the Cuban crisis week, Arthur Sylvester, Assistant Secretary of Defence for Public Affairs (and a former Washington correspondent of the *Newyork News)* called a press conference. It was a tense session. Newspapermen charged the US government with withholding the facts regarding the Cuban crisis and giving out misleading and even untruthful information. Sylvester responded:

> I can't think of a comparable situation, but in the kind of world we live in, the generation of news by actions taken by the government becomes one weapon in a strained situation. The results, in my opinion, justify the methods we use. News generated by actions of the government as to content and timing are part of the arsenal of weaponry that a President has in application of military force and related forces to the solution of political problems, or to the applications of international political pressures.

Sylvester and his State Department counterpart, Robert Manning (who was later to become editor of the *Atlantic Monthly),* signed orders requiring the military and civilian officers talking to the press report to whom they talked and what was discussed. (The State Department order was rescinded a month later but the Defence Department order was in force for full five years). The memorandum for Defence personnel said:

Subject : Procedures for handling media representatives.

The subject of each interview and telephone conversation with a media representative will be reported to the appropriate public information office before the close of business that day. A report need to be made if a representative of the public information office is present at the interview.

In such a situation how should an editor handle his job? Sylvester had suggested, by way of justification of the government's handling of information that there is a need to "speak in one voice to your adversary." Commenting on that-and laying down what an ideal editor should do in the circumstances, the *New York Times* said in an editorial on 31 October, 1962: "To attempt to manage the news so that a free press should speak 'in one voice to your adversary' could be for more dangerous to the cause of freedom than the free play of dissent, than the fullest possible publication of the facts."

Another and a yet more fitting answer was given by the chairman of the House subcommittee on Information of the Committee on Government Operations, John E Moss. He said: "Government pronouncements during a conflict of wills obviously have an effect upon the outcome of the conflict, but to imply that the entire government information process is part of the manouvers in international relations is to ignore the working of our democratic system."

That, of course, is not how the US Administration saw it. President Kennedy, for example, thought that by not using the information about the presence of Russian missiles in Cuba which the *New York Times* possessed, the paper had made "far-more effective our later actions and thereby contributed greatly to our national security."

There will always be two opinions as to what the true relationship between the government and the press should be and it will be argued that the circumstances in the end will dictate what such a relation should be. By and large it has been suggested that relationship is best which is adversary in nature. The press which means the editor-is better off to be on guard where the government is concerned than to work in cahoots with any administration.

Tough Job

The relationship between an editor and the proprietor is an even thornier one than that between an editor and the government. Where the proprietor is himself the editor-as it used to be in the *Free Press Journal* when Sadanand was alive-the problem obviously does not arise. But there were times when Sadanand employed separate editors and with his kind of temperament, conflicts between him and them were routine. On one occasion Sadanand without so much as consulting his then editor S. Natarajan, changed editorial policy overnight. Natarajan thereupon did what any self-respecting editor should do, resigned on the spot.

Pothan Joseph who, in his time, had served many masters and was willing to argue any case has been reported to have said that, an editor, like a lawyer, should have no compunction to posit the owner's point of view. Joseph himself at different times edited *The Hindustan Times* (a paper that strongly supported the Congress) and the *Dawn* (mouthpiece of the Muslim League). Pothan Joseph found nothing wrong in this.

Some old-fashioned editors have held the view that an editor is responsible solely to his conscience and to his readers and that any proprietorial interference in the discharge of his duties is an assault on the freedom of the press that should be resisted. Theoretically such a position is unassailable. In practice, however, many editors have learned that he who pays the piper calls the tune. An editor is well advised prior to his accepting his appointment to see that he is on the same wave-length as that of his employer. That is the best way to save later embarrassment and agony. Most editors are hired on contract and an editor who claims special privileges for himself on grounds of editorial independence may soon find that editorial independence and job security do not always go hand in hand.

News Editors

The news editor is a very important functionary in the organisation of a newspaper. He is the real backbone of the newspaper. The news editor is responsible for doing the most important work in the publication of a newspaper. In certain ways, he can be called the number two man in a newspaper organisation. He is solely responsible for the news coverage activities of the newspaper. It is his duty to see that the news service of his paper is always up to the mark and ahead of its rivals. The news editor deputes the reporting staff for news collecting activities. He also directs the work of the sub-editors. He is the final arbiter to whom all questions affecting the news columns are referred, and ultimately he decides the fate of every report and paragraph. However, much of this responsibility in actual working may be delegated to his subordinates. In the western countries, sometimes, the news-editor performs the functions of a general supervisor, because his work is divided among other employees of the newspaper like copy testers, planners etc. Generally, his time is occupied with administrative work.

Mere Control : He merely controls the activities of his assistants and makes the most important decisions. The rest of the work he leaves to his subordinates. But in India the position is quite different. In our country, the news editor has to deal with many aspects of collecting the news and making use of it. He is responsible for all the news stories that appear in a newspaper. In fact, he performs many functions which were previously performed by a district editor, copy tester and a planner of news coverage. The news editor not only acts as a senior journalist guiding other journalists, but he also has to deal with the administration of the staff under his control. He is responsible for alloting duties, giving assignments and making leave arrangements for them. The news editor is generally a very experienced person. He knows all the ins and outs of his job.

In a newspaper the news is received from various sources like reporters, correspondents, national and international news services etc. The news is continuously received on the teleprinter which is installed in the newspaper office. It is the news editor who plans how to use the news which is continuously arriving in the newspaper's office from various sources. He prepares the dummy for the next day's paper in which the space to be occupied by advertisements appearing in the newspaper is indicated. In fact, on the basis of this dummy, the next day's newspaper is planned by the news editor. For special reports he obtains photographs to be published in the paper. He tries to be in touch with all the events and news which are taking place or the reports which are trickling in.

He also discusses the coverage of news and events with the chief reporter as well as the editor of the newspaper. The timings of the city edition and dak edition are also decided by him. He tries to coordinate with the printer and the production side for bringing out the newspaper in time. He gives instructions to the chief sub-editor regarding the use of important reports and news items. Although the chief sub-editor is the ultimate in-charge of the actual shape the edition will take, yet the news editor always tries to know as to what is happening. It is the duty of news editor to build up the news service of the paper on a sound footing. No doubt, in the fast moving world of today this is not an easy task. He has to keep in touch with his paper's local reporters, correspondents, foreign as well as the numerous national and international news agencies for collecting the latest news regarding the important happenings. He may have to meet many callers as well as attend to immense correspondence reaching his office.

The Responsibility : The news editor has also to make arrangements to cover the unexpected occurrences hurriedly. To meet the rush of work and unexpected situations, things may have to be done in a hurry, yet in a systematic and proper manner. The unexpected is always happening in a newspaper office. It may be report regarding a big air crash or a railway accident, a mining disaster or a huge fire, a gruesome murder or a cyclone involving loss of many lives. Whichever of these occurrences it may be, the same has to be dealt with promptly and appropriately, no matter what hour of the night or day the news arrives in the newspaper office. A good news editor evolves cohesion and order, even out of a chaotic situation due to his cool direction.

The successful news editor possesses a highly trained news sense. He has the knack of anticipating events intelligently. A good news editor is a man of tireless and boundless energy. He should have a lot of driving force to direct his staff, sparing neither them nor himself, when a big story is about to break, or when the reputation of his paper is at stake. Above all, he should be able to make quick and accurate decisions in a crisis and remain cool and calm under all circumstances.

Role of Sub-editor

The sub-editor plays a very important role in the publication of a newspaper. He is a very important member of the newspaper's staff. The quality and style of a newspaper greatly depend on the good work done by the sub-editor. It is the sub-editor who prepares the copy for the printer.

Although the editor of the newspaper exercises the supreme direction and legal responsibility, yet it is the sub-editor who performs most of the functions of the editor, as far as the production of a paper is concerned. In a way, we can say that if the editor is the top stone, then the sub-editor is the key stone of the arch. In ordinary matters the sub-editor has undisputed control over every article and paragraph that reaches the newspaper's office. As far as the difficult and important articles of news publicity are concerned, he may be guided by the editor. The functions of an editor have become very vague now-a-days. His control is now merged into the side of the paper from which side he may exercise both a journalistic and commercial influence. An editor may hardly write much for the newspaper. In fact, it is the sub-editor who does most of the editing work in a newspaper. If the functions of the editor have now become a little less, as far as the production of a paper is concerned, then the functions of the sub-editor have definitely increased greatly.

The sub-editor is mainly responsible for the manner in which a journal or a newspaper is made-up, sent for printing and offered to the public. There is no doubt that the sub-editor must be a man of high ability and judgement. He must know thoroughly the news value of every matter which comes into his notice. He should have the ability to see the importance of even a small paragraph and the competence to reduce a lengthy paragraph to its deserving size. A sub-editor may not generally do much of original writing like an editor, but he should be an expert in revising the news articles as well as supervising the work of those who do the writing work. Thus, a sub-editor must possess the capability either to reduce or to expand a subject matter as per the needs of his paper.

All sorts of news go on trickling into the sub-editorial department all the time. It is just like a raw material out of which a sub-editor produces a finished product (the news to be published in the newspaper). The sub-editor has the power of life or death over all the newspaper's material that reaches him. Thus, the responsibility of the sub-editor is really enormous. A newspaper receives its copy from a variety of sources like reporters, correspondents, telephones, news agency reports and verbal communications. All this information is filtered by the sub-editor. The sub-editor is actually responsible, more than any other person for what the paper looks like and stands for, to the readers.

There are many ways in which a sub-editor can leave the impression of his personality on the newspaper. The format of a paper is in reality determined by the sub-editor. The sub-editor has the nose for selecting the right type of news. It is the task of the sub-editor to decide as to what is going in for tomorrows's newspaper and in what form. In fact, the sub-editor with a wide experience in his work, is the most suitable person to become the editor in due course of time.

There is always a big pile of news reports and other communications lying on the table of the sub-editor. He is also pressurised by the printing department for the copy. He has to attend to his functions in a very quick manner, using his best judgement as to the relative urgency, importance and the desirability of printing a particular news or article.

Wonderful Job : The sub-editor has to separate the grain from the chaff out of the great number of news material lying on his table. He should have an eye for accuracy. He must check the facts of a story and look out for the errors, if any. If there are certain facts which are missing, he must ask these from the reporters. The sub-editor has to read every story and sometimes contrive to make it interesting and news-worthy. Mainly, we can say that a newspaper receives the news from two sources, one from the paper's own correspondents and the other from the various news agencies. Generally, out of these two sources preference is always given to the news brought by the paper's own correspondents, because a good report under the headline 'from our special correspondent' indicates the initiative and enterprise and adds to the prestige of a newspaper.

Sometimes, a newspaper may receive a number of versions of a particular story from different sources. The paper's correspondent may give a different story where as the news agencies may give their own accounts. The sub-editor has to put all these conflicting accounts into one coherent and wholesome story. If the reports contradict or conflict with each other, then he has to believe the story put in by the newspaper's own correspondent. It is thus the responsibility of the sub-editor to make the story clear. He should see to it that the news story is based upon facts, it is as complete as possible and is clear from every angle for easy understanding.

A sub-editor checks the news stories one by one. He goes through every single piece of the copy. Then he adds a catch-line, if the reporter has not already provided a suitable one. He also writes a suitable headline for the story. This is a very important and difficult duty of the sub-editor. After this, he edits the story, cutting the unnecessary matter and trimming the length to the right size according to the space where it has to be printed. He checks the spellings of names and places so that these are not printed wrongly. A sub-editor also has to correct errors of grammar, capitalization, punctuation and abbreviations. He cannot afford to allow even the most minor error in the newspaper.

If a sub-editor feels that the intention of the writer of a story is not clear or the message of the story is very vague, then he can refer the copy back to the reporter and ask him to rewrite the story. Sometimes, he may have to refer to books like 'who's who', encyclopaedias, telephone and civic directories, almanacs etc., to confirm the facts of a story. He may even have to telephone the source of the news item to seek any clarification regarding which a doubt creeps up in his mind.

The sub-editor has to take into consideration the policy of his paper before allowing a news item to be published. He has to breathe life into some dead matter lying before him so that the story is made lively. Sometimes, he tones down a story which is too lively. He may also trim down a story, if it is too dangerous, to make it safe. He has also to decide the suitability of the news stories and articles on the merits of their news value to the particular paper. He has to reject a superfluous article and prune another to its justified size. He is always on the look out to print a news story which is a scoop, well ahead of his rivals.

After deciding the main contents of his newspaper, he has to use his utmost skill in their make-up and display. This is just like the window dressing of a shop which is fully stocked. And it is a very important function of the sub-editor. He has to be careful that in the final rush no mistake creeps into the print and no paragraph gets mixed up or overlooked. The maximum attention a sub-editor has to pay is to the layout of captions and the main news page. Balance and proportion are the qualities which should be aimed at before anything else.

The principal test of sub-editorial capacity in the art of make up is, of course, the appearance of the main news page. It is the page which the majority of the readers read first of all. Some very busy readers only read this page and no more—they simply turn the other pages. Although the eye may be arrested by the heading of the principal news, yet the total effect of the whole page should not be crudely sensational. In fact, the make-up of the first page should be in such a way that a reader is helped to find at a glance how the world has behaved during the last twenty-four hours. There is no doubt that the make-up of a newspaper is the reflection of the sub-editor's appreciation of news value. Sometimes, the value and significance of a news feature is largely neutralised by an ineffective handling of make-up.

Extra Knowledge : Side by side with the presentation of the news, a sub-editor should also know something about the gathering of news and arrangement of regular features. He should be fully acquainted with the reporters and correspondents employed by his newspaper as well as with the regular contributors who write special features from time to time, which are published in his newspaper. The sub-editor should also know the principal news-agencies which supply news stories to his paper. In fact, now-a-days more and more news is supplied to the newspapers by one or the other national or international news agencies.

The sub-editor should also be acquainted with the important photographers and photographic agencies which supply photographs of important events and news items to his newspaper. In fact, now-a-days every big newspaper has its own staff photographers, who cover the special functions and events for their newspaper. By knowing these sources of news as photographs, a sub-editor can contact them in case of any contingency without any difficulty.

Of course, many of the troubles of the sub-editor will be lessened, if the correspondents and other contributors take a little more pain to make their copy readable. If the reporters and writers try to follow the style in which their writings are presented finally in the newspaper, then they can greatly save a good deal of unnecessary work and worry on the part of the sub-editorial department. Sometimes, a contributor or a correspondent may even have a complaint against the sub-editor for the way in which his article has been cut down by the sub-editor, who may not be sufficiently acquainted with the importance of the material. Every sub-editor should be careful in the use of scissors and the blue pencils, so as not to give any cause for complaint later on to the conscientious writers.

There is no doubt that ultimately the public is the best judge of the work of a sub-editor. The good work done by him in the selection of the news and views will be much liked by the readers of his newspaper, whereas any fall in its standard may result in a reduction in its circulation. It is, therefore, the duty of every good sub-editor to do his best to put as much exclusive news in his newspaper as possible and as early as possible.

12

NEWS MAKING

Here, we discuss newspaper reporting and the main components of a news report-the body and the lead. The news items that appear in newspapers are also called news stories. In literature stories may not have their basis in actual events, but a news story is always based on facts. History is also based on facts but it deals with things of the past while news stories are on current events. Further, a news story is normally written in inverted pyramid style, that is, the most important facts come first followed by other facts in order of significance.

The inverted pyramid style has developed in journalism over the years. It helps the readers who don't have enough time to read the whole story. It also helps sub-editors who can easily discard as much of the story from the tail without affecting its readability.

London, May 1 (PTI)-The British Government today rejected the plea of Sikh separatists for recognition of Khalistan which they had proclaimed in Amritsar three days ago.

A foreign office spokesman said the unity and territorial integrity of India were central to peace and to the well-being of the whole region, when asked about reports that the separatists had appealed to Britain and certain other countries to recognise 'Khalistan'.

Past elections in Punjab had demonstrated that the people did not support secession. Therefore, the question of recognising 'Khalistan' did not arise, he added.

No UK Recognition for Khalistan which appears in bold type is the head line. It is put at the head of the story and gives an idea to the newspaper reader about the subject of the story.

London, May 1 is the date line. It tells the reader the place and the date of the news story. (P.T.I.) is credit line. The newspaper has published this story which was supplied by news agency Press Trust of India and by putting "(P.T.I.)" the paper acknowledges the source of the story and this gives the credit to the news agency.

Sometimes the name of the reporter or correspondent appears below the headline with a By or From. For example, "From V.S. Karnic" or "By Kanwar Sandhu". It is termed by line. The first paragraph of the story is called intro or lead. In the above example, "The British Government today rejected the plea of Sikh separatists for recognition of 'Khalistan', which they had proclaimed in Amritsar three days ago," is the intro.

The rest of the story is called body of the story. Intro gives the most important information which is contained in the story and therefore it is the most crucial part. It should contain highest quantum of news value. A good intro is prerequisite of a good story. The proverb-Well begun is half done-goes very well in this case, you really do half of the work on a news story if you write a good intro. They body of the story will automatically follow in the inverted pyramid style.

Basic elements of a news story can be found by asking and trying to find answers to six basic questions popularly known as he five Ws and one H. The five Ws are-What? When? Where? Who? and Why? and the H is How?

There was a time when journalists were supposed to answer all the questions in the intro. But slowly it was discovered that it resulted in over-crowding of the opening para, loss of clarity which at times confused and irritated the reader.

There is no hard and fast rule about these Ws and H and their inclusion in the intro or lead. A story may not have answers to all of them but all these questions should be asked to identify the basic elements of a news story. Then, according to news value, the most important element should come in the intro.

An intro may be in reply to one or more or all of these questions, but there should be no compromise on clarity of expression. If a reader has to look over a sentence a second time to understand it, then it cannot make a good intro or lead.

The Growth

A test for elements of news and their proper order could be provided with four letters from 'news' as keys:

N for news worthiness-does the story contain news values?

E for emphasis-does the intro contain the most important and interesting fact?

W for the five Ws and the H-do their answers exist in the story?

S for sources of information-does the story identify or imply the source where it is necessary?

Newsmen deal with a very wide range of subjects and

everybody has his own way of presenting things. Therefore, there are innumerable ways of writing intros and leads. This variety is obvious to everybody who reads newspapers carefully as the same news story is presented in different ways in different newspapers, while the same paper presents different stories in different ways. Any two reporters doing the same story will write it differently and this explains the variety.

There are various ways to classify intros or leads depending on different criteria. Based on the number of incidents involved, the intro could be simple or complex.

(i) *Simple Lead Involves a Single Incident :* Even if the event may have several different incidents, the intro takes account of a single incident. Simple lead is very common in newspapers and should normally be favoured as it is easy to write it clearly. For a complex event like police action in the Golden Temple Indian Express, Chandigarh, gave a simple lead:

Express News Service

Chandigarh, April 30. The Punjab Police and paramilitary forces entered the Golden Temple complex at Amritsar this after-noon to clear it of "terrorists, separatists and anti-national elements.

(ii) *Complex Lead Involves more than One Incident in the Intro :* It is normally used when similar or related incidents are clubbed together in one story. One has to be careful with this kind of intro as it is normally long and a times confusing. Various incidents of violence in Punjab have been clubbed in this complex lead (Indian Express, Chandigarh):

Express News Service

Chandigarh, April 30. Three persons were killed and two others injured by suspected terrorists during the last 24 hours while a petrol pump and two liquor vends were looted in

Faridkot district. Among the killed is a brother of a Deputy Superintendent of Punjab Police.

Two armed terrorists gunned down Rajiv Kumar a dispenser at Pakhoke village near Taran Taran and injured seriously Daljit Kumar. Both were travelling in a tonga. They were made to get down and shot at. Jaspal Singh, a brother of Mr Sukhdev Singh, a DSP posted at Batala, was also killed by the terrorists.

According to a report from Moga, four car-borne armed persons today looted a petrol pump, and two liquor vends at three different places in Faridkot.

It appears from the intro (the first paragraph) that all the incidents took place in Faridkot district while the second and third paragraphs make it clear that three different districts were involved. Taran Taran is in Amritsar district while Batala is in Gurdaspur district. A little more care was needed to avoid this mistake. In the following example care has been taken to avoid a similar mistake:

Substantive Clause Intro

New Delhi, April 10 (PTI). Despite adverse agro-climate factors, foodgrains production in 1985-86 was likely to touch 150 million tonnes, the Agriculture Minister Mr. Bata Singh disclosed today.

Conditional Clause Intro

New Delhi, May 2. The Minister of state for agriculture, Mr Yogender Makwana, has assured the Rajya Sabha that the government would take prompt action if charges of bunglings against any of the NAFED officials were found to be true.

Present Participle Intro

United Nations, April 30 (UNI). Calling the United Nations' current financial crisis "Yet another" challenge to multi-lateralism India has asked members to defeat those trying to weaken the world body.

Past Participle Intro

Cherrapunjee, April 27 (UNI). A large number of people here were disappointed today as President Zail Singh cancelled his Cherrapunjee visit due to inclement weather.

Prepositional Phrase Intro

Dhaka, March 11 (UNI). In the backdrop of the political imbroglio in Bangladesh, the leaders of the two major Opposition alliances held an unexpected parley last Sunday at an undisclosed venue to discuss the launching of a movement to make the government of President H.M. Ershad concede to Opposition demands to ensure free and fair elections.

Intros or leads can also be classified according to the elements of the news (five Ws and H) that dominate in the lead:

Who Lead

Hoshiarpur, May 3 (UNI). The Punjab police chief, Mr. J.F. Ribeiro on Saturday said maintenance of law and order in the state was not an easy task.

What Lead

Bombay, April 27 (UNI). M.V. Jhansi Ki Rani, a 76,600 dwt bulk carrier owned by the Shipping Corporation of India (SCI) ran aground at Fredrick Reef, some 500 km off the Australian east coast around 2 p.m. yesterday, a delayed report reaching the SCI's headquarters in Bombay said. No casualties were reported.

Where Lead

Sonepat, May 3. Rail traffic on Sonepat-Delhi junction

of Northern Railway remained disrupted for about five hours following the derailment of two bogies of a goods train near Ganara railway station, about 1.6 km from here early this morning.

When Lead

Ahmedabad, April 10 (PTI). Since Vedic times, ancient Indian astronomers observed and carefully studied rare celestial phenomena, including comets, according to Mr Parmanand Desai, executive director of the Vedhshala (astronomical observatory) in suburban Naranpura here.

A close study of some of the not so well-known Sanskrit works cast new light on comets, the "old faithful visitors" to the solar system he said.

How Lead

Jayaprakash Pattan (Pune) April 29 (UNI). Janta Party's national council meetings plunged into turmoil this afternoon when Swami Agnivesh staked his claim for party presidentship after Mr Chandra Shekhar was unanimously re-elected.

As the confusion in the Ashoka Mehta Shamiana-the venue of the meet-came to an end, election returning officer Bapu Kaldate, owned up his mistake in declaring that he had received only the nomination of Mr Chandra Shekhar and announced that the election would now take place tomorrow morning.

Another classification is possible on the basis of variety of presentation in the intro.

This intro is of moderate length, from twenty-five to thirty-five words, and tries to arrest the reader's attention by presenting the unexpected but not of world rocking importance.

Express News Service

Ludhiana, April 29. As many as 27 persons were killed and another 26 were injured when two Punjab Roadways buses collided head on the Ludhiana-Malerkotla road near Gopalpura village this morning.

This lead is brief and goes right to the point and presents news with high concentration of news value.

Express News Service

New Delhi, April 29. Six cases of AIDS disease (Acquired Immuno Deficiency Syndrome) have been detected in Tamil Nadu. Punch: Milder than the astonisher or cartridge, its length is somewhere between cartridge lead and the astonisher lead. It is useful for presentation of news that is not inherently exciting or sensational.

Lusaka, April 28 (Zana-pool). Woman are under represented in and misused by the mass media, a study on women in the media has shown.

Historical or literary-allusion lead: It draws some character event in history or literature in relation to an event or person in the news.

It fits with unusual or routine stories that need an informal tone as well as with those that deal with matter of universal interest.

New Delhi, May (UNI). What accounts for the phenomenal rise of the marwaris in the industrial field?

Geographical factors and the social set up have been responsible for drawing the best from the community, says a recent study. This study on Industrial Entrepreneurship of the Shekhawati Marwaris, was made by Dr. D.K. Tanket of the department of business administration in the University of Rajasthan.

Marwaris, particularly those from the Shekhawati region of Rajasthan, are 'unsurpassed by any other community in the world, Dr Tanket says. The region at one time accounted for 60 per cent of investment in the private sector.

The dry climate of the region compels the people to wage a continuous struggle against the vagaries of nature. Entrepreneurship springs out of adversity, the study says.

Direct Quotation: When the lead is using a direct quotation it should be short and eye-catching.

Bombay, April 20. "1 have no other friends except those that are strictly political," said Mr Pranab Mukherjee to Mr Pritish Nandy in an interview in the Illustrated Weekly of India issue April 27-May 3).

Indirect Quotation: Instead of using the speaker's actual words, the reporter can say what the speaker said in his own words. Credit must be given to the speaker in the intro. Compared to direct quotation more information can be given in this variety of intro.

S.S. Barnala over the telephone this morning and congratulated him for the prompt action taken in flushing out terrorists and other anti-national elements from the Golden Temple complex in Amritsar.

Contrast Lead: It attracts readers' attention by comparing extremes. Here is an interesting example:

Express News Service

Jammu, January 22. The "darbar move" of the secretariat and other government offices has been in vogue in Jammu and Kashmir from the times of the Maharajas.

Mr. G.M. Shah has now introduced the "darbar move" of the detenus as well. That is how a state government employee at Kud put it to ENS on Tuesday. He was referring to the winter "move" of the detenus from the tourist bungalow at Kud to some warmer place.

Direct Address Lead: It speaks directly to the reader or an interesting subject or one with a universal appeal.

Dallas, April 27 (Reuter). Living in Dallas may be hazardous to your marriage. A new book of statistics about 785 international cities, reveals that Dallas is he divorce capital of the world with 84 divorces per 1,000 people.

Descriptive Lead: Also known as situation or picture lead, it tries to paint a word picture of an interesting person place or thing to help create mood for the story.

Lucknow, April 10 (PTI). One could hardly see any crossing or eye catching spot or an electric or telegraph pole in "Kumbh Mela" are at Haridwar, where something or the other was not written in the form of a banner or a hoarding or a poster concerning what one could do to improve prospects of child survival and development, as part of a campaign launched by UNICEF.

Parody Lead: It attempts to play on words, using widely known proverbs, quotations, song titles, currently popular sayings book titles and other expressions to help establish immediate identify with the reader and to bring a bit of sparkle to what otherwise might have been a outline story.

Bangalore, May 2 (UNI). Comet Halley has said 'au revoir' after more than eight months of its tryst with the solar system.

Prof. K.R. Sivaraman of the Indian Institute of Astrophysics (IIA), coordinator for the country's Halley observation programme, told UNI that the comet was now moving away from the solar system.

One-two-three\one-two-three-four lead: This kind of intro is rarely used now. But it is useful in giving the salient points of an important programme or putting important budget provisions. In this kind of intro a general statement is followed by various important points with numbers (1), (2), (3), (4) or letters (a), (b), (c), (d), and so on.

Staccato Intro: It consist of short clipped words, phrases, sentences, sometimes separated by dots or dashes. It is casually disruptive and should not be used if the facts of the story do not justify it.

Mid night an old Yamuna Bridge ... a scream ... a shot ... a splash ... a second shot ... a splash.

This morning Delhi police recovered bodies of a couple... Miscellaneous freak lead: This type of intro has a novel approach in sentence structure and presentation, in order to catch the reader's attention.

Express News Service

Nagpur, October 27. It's Kapil Dev, of course. All the idle speculation on the choice of a captain for next month's visits to Sharjah and Australia after the setbacks in Sri Lanka were set at rest by the selectors, here, this afternoon. And it took them only five minutes to decide to retain Kapil Dev for the job.

The formal announcement of the unanimous choice of Chandu Borde (Chairman). Hanumant Singh, Kripal Singh, Amber Roy and Manmohan Sood was made by the Indian board secretary Ranbir Singh Mahindra. And it surprised nobody.

Chairman Borde said that no other name was discussed." There was no difference of opinion any rumours of dissensions on the issue are false."

Many of the above leads actually summarise the story and therefore they can be described as summary leads.

With interpretative news stories becoming more and more prominent in journalism interpretative leads are also becoming common in newspapers.

Interpretative leads normally do not quote any body and begin with a statement from the writer of the story. The interpretative lead gives the assessment of the reporter or special correspondent based on facts of the situation. Here is an example:

Express News Service

Washington, May 4. The future of India's entire national television network and its two way telephone system is under enormous strain. For the launch of Insat 1-C the only back up satellite for insat I-B (itself the only satellite to handle this enormous Indian workload for the last 30 months) is now postponed indefinitely.

India has abandoned all plans to launch insat 1-C through the US space programme following the unexpected explosion of the US space rocket Delta over the Atlantic on Sunday night...

Thus we see that all sorts of composition can be used in an intro. Its contents must have highest news value in the story. It must be easy to read and understand.

Things of Importance

After the intro is written the body of the story will follow in the logical order of inverted pyramid style.

Mention of the source in the lead is inescapable, when the news point is controversial or, in any case, not indisputable. But where the fact is unchallengeable, the opening paragraph may give the straight news, bearing the source for mention in the next.

In such cases, one should avoid starting the next paragraph with: "This was announced (or stated) here today by Such a sentence just after lead arrests the momentum of the story. The second paragraph can go straight to the next important point of the story, bringing in the source in an easy manner, so that the story is kept moving smoothly.

In the body of the story choice of apt words is essential to ensure precision and better readability. The body should be concise and shorn of all verbiage. It should take notice of all material points concerning the news event, elaborate or background them where necessary, but should not be burdened with dispensable details.

The Expression

The language of news story should be simple and familiar to be understood by the average reader. Simple and direct sentences are more effective than long, involved ones. The simple style is also easy to translate if copy is used in some sister publication in a different language. In multi-language societies like India this is a significant advantage.

It is not enough to collect news. It must be put across. Meaning must be unmistakable and it should be succinct. Readers do not have time and newspapers do not have space for elaborate reiteration. Every word should be understood by the ordinary man, and every sentence must be clear. There must be no abstractions.

Some people are proud of writing long sentences with many dependent clauses, with subjunctive and conditional, with exclamations, and interjection, quotations, allusions, metaphors, long images, Latin terminology, subtlety and conceits. They presume that the reader has enough time and has old classical education and has not to work for his living.

One must always keep in mind that a sentence is more likely to be clear if it is short, communicates one thought or closely related ideas. The length of sentences with too many ideas is not the cause of the disease but it is often a clear symptom where the ideas in a sentence are complex they cannot intelligible be presented in subsidiary clauses separated by a mere comma. A full stop in such cases proves a great help to clarity.

The prefixing of a subsidiary clause with one or more ideas in advance of the main idea often produces a long confusing sentence. Opening a sentence with a subsidiary clause has special difficulties for the reader if the two ideas go in different directions. The sentence carrying the most important thought should be given immediate identity of its own.

This does not mean that newspapers should use only simple sentences. Economy of space as well as rhythm requires all kinds of sentences to be used. For example, it may be wasteful to introduce a complete subject and predicate for each idea. A subordinate clause in a complex sentence can express better precisely and economically than a series of simple sentences or compound sentences joined by 'and', etc. The crux of the matter is-have something to say and say it as clearly as you can.

Unfamiliar words and jargon (expressions peculiar to various fields of special knowledge) should be avoided as far as possible. The choice of words should be simple and elegant. Unfamiliar words should be explained in simple language.

Latin and Greek expressions appear in law, medicine, biology, etc., and some of these expressions have become part of the English vocabulary through usage. If these are readily understood, they may be used without any explanation, but if the Latin or Greek expressions have a popular English equivalent that should be preferred.

In other cases these expressions if used, should be accompanied by an interpretation or an explanation for the benefit of the lay reader. Mere fashionable use of foreign expressions should be avoided, profanities or obscene or vulgar language should be totally eschewed. They should be cut out even from direct quotations. Slang, though not in such bad taste as obscenities, should also be avoided, even in portions quoted. Colloquialism in also best avoided except in quoted texts.

Preference should be given to the active voice sentences in the passive voice have a deadening effect. Vigorous, economic writing requires a preference for sentences in the active voice. One should always prefer "The directors will meet next week" to "A meeting will he held by directors next week."

Official reports are full of the passive: it was felt necessary, in the circumstances it was considered advisable etc. In official sense the language is polluted by viscous verbiage, meaning is clouded by vague abstraction, euphemism, conceals identity and heavy words weigh the mind down. It does not rain, in officialise, but precipitation is experienced. However, in certain circumstances the passive voice is useful, especially where he deed is more important than the doer. "A general strike has been called for tomorrow by... to protest against is better than: "The... has called a general strike for tomorrow in protest against..." All names in the copy should be properly identified as far as possible. Where the subject of a copy has multiple identification, that is, if he or she can be identified in more than one ways, the most pertinent among them-as a rule the office or position of consequence he or she currently holds-should be mentioned in the first instance, the , others being suitably mentioned in later parts of the copy. Where the subject does not hold any office currently, he or- she would of necessity have to be identified by the former office.

Adjectives and epithets retain their significance only when used in proper context and sparingly, chosen carefully and used aptly. They add colour to a news story and improve its quality. On the other hand, they can mar a story when used needlessly. Further, in view of objectivity no adjective or any other expression that smacks of bias, involves a value judgement should be used. Language should be used carefully to avoid any value judgement when it is not intended. For example, while reporting police firing one can say. "They police had to open fire,.." or "...was forced to open fire". The correct way to give a factual narration is, "The police opened fire". But when a minister or an official states that the police had to open fire, it may be reported as such with attribution.

Quotations should not be over used and must be restricted to more telling portions. Sometimes a couple of words within quotation marks are more effective than a whole sentence. It should be remembered that excessive use of quotations can spoil a copy. In reporting statements or speeches the safest verb is "said". There is no harm if it appears repeatedly in a copy. In appropriate circumstances, an occasional charge from "said" should be considered.

Verbs that substitute "said" are : observed, remarked, stated, averred, declared, affirmed, pointed out, told, informed, opined, confined, admitted, accepted, conferred, alleged, denied, rejected, repudiated, refuted, argued, contended, disclosed, revealed.

"Remarked" may be used with any ordinary statement, but "observed" and "stated" may be used only where there is really an observation or a statement. They are not to be treated as normal variants of "said."

"Averred" is legalistic in use and it is better to steer clear of it. "I declared" is acceptable subject to the condition that the person making the concerned declaration is competent to do so. "Declared" must be backed by the strength of authority, not in an absolute sense but in relation to the concerned statement.

"Affirmed" has an element of "firmness" in it and is stronger than "said". "Asserted" is stronger still. The use of these verbs, if at all, should be restricted.

"Opined" sounds pedantic and therefore should not be used except as part of a quoted passage.

"Told" and "informed" cannot stand by themselves "Told" or "informed" whom? "Told newsmen or a conference or informed parliament would be correct, but not, "Mr ... told that..."

"Pointed out" may be used only in relation to a universally accepted proposition or an incontrovertible fact, and not in relation to a matter on which views differ, or are likely to differ. Since it is not always easy to determine what is a universally accepted proposition, the use of "pointed out" is best avoided.

"Accepted," "refuted" and "confessed" should too be avoided. "Admitted" is admissible in the coverage of court proceedings.

The words "denied", "rejected", and "repudiated" may be selected on the basis of how strong a denial or contradiction is "argued" and "contended" should be used when a serious contention is involved and not when a mere opinion is expressed.

"Alleged" can be used with reference to a statement which contains an allegation or a charge. "Revealed" should be avoided altogether. "Disclosed" can be used when the person has the competence to make the disclosure.

Sentences should assert. The reader does not want to be told what is not he should be told what is. As a general rule newsmen should strive to express even a negative thing in a positive form. For example, "The project was not successful", should be written as "the project failed'. Likewise, "They did not pay attention to the complaint", should be written as, "They ignored the complaint".

No sentence should contain unnecessary words and no paragraph should have any superfluous sentence. There should be the right words in the right order. Adjectives and adverbs should be used only when they add to precision and economy of a sentence.

Redundancies or meaningless modifiers should find no place in news copy. No word should have a parasite consuming space and debasing language. An accident is either unique or it is not. It cannot be "rather unique". It is like being "rather pregnant". In "widow of the late Mr..." words "the late" are redundant since "widow" presupposes that the husband is no more. One should not write "at 9 a.m. in the morning". It should be either " a.m." or "morning".

Repetition is always needless, at times it becomes irritating. A peculiar journalistic problem is repetition of source. It has crept into Indian journalism through Associated Press (AP) news agency copy. Once the report has identified the source of the information there is no need to keep parading it. Only if identity is in doubt should it be repeated.

The grammar of the language applies to newsmen as it applies to others. On finer points of usage the style book of the newspaper or news agency should be adhered to. Many newspapers have not developed style books. They can make use of Press Trust of India Style Book with modifications to suit their specific requirements.

Bibliography

Alva, Joachim : *Men and Supermen of Hindustan,* Mackeray & Co., Bombay, 1943.

Anthony, Smith : *The Newspaper—An International History,* Thames and Hudson, London, 1979.

Baehr, H. : *Systems & Concepts,* Pergamon, London, 1980.

Bannerjee, D.N. : *India's Nation Builders,* Headley Brothers, London, 1919.

Bard, F. E. : *An Introduction of Journalism,* MacMillan Co., New York, 1991.

Bastian, George C. and Leland D. C. : *Editing the Day's News,* MacMillan Co., New York, 1997.

Bhatnagar, V. : *Development Dynamics of Press and Journalism,* Printwell, Jaipur, 1996.

———————: *Role of Press in Women's Development Issues,* Printwell, Jaipur, 1996.

Brewer, J.M. : *Journalism as Guidance,* MacMillan Co., New York, 1998.

Chakravarty, S. : *Press and Pliant Governors,* Kanishka Publishers, New Delhi, 1997.

Chauhan, S.S. : *Principles and Techniques of Journalism,* Vikas Publishing House, New Delhi, 1982.

Chauhan, Swati and Navin, C. : *Hand Book of Journalism Style and Substance,* Kanishka Publishers, New Delhi, 1999.

Czitrom, D. J. : *Media and the American Mind,* University of North Corolina Press, Chapel Hill, 1998.

Dan, Steinbock : *The Practice of Journalism : In the America Media and Entertainment Industries,* Quorum, London, 1995.

Das, Gupta : *Desabandu Chittaranjan Das,* Publications Division, Government of India, New Delhi, 1960.

Edwards, Michael : *History of Journalism in India,* Sidgwick & Jackson, London, 1967.

Elizabeth, Grey : *The Story of Journalism,* Longmans Young Books, London, 1968.

Emery, Edwin : *Media Technique with Youth,* Prentice-Hall, New Jersey, 1997.

Emest, C. Hynds : *American Newspaper in 1980s*, Hastings House, New York, 1980.

Gapta, Narayani : *Between Two Empires,* Oxford University Press, Delhi, 1994,

Gerbner, G. : *Mass Media Policies in Changing Atmosphere,* Wiley, New York, 1992.

Glendevon, John : *The Viceroy at Bay—Lord Linlithgow in India,* Collins, London, 1971.

Gowher, Rizvi : *Linlithgow in India,* Royal Historical Society, London, 1978.

Gupta, V.S. : *Media and Development,* Har Anand, New Delhi, 1994.

Heimrath, H. : *Indian Nationalism and Hindu Social Reforms,* Oxford University Press, New York, 1964.

Hugh, Tinker : *The Ordeal of Love, C.F. Andrews in India,* Oxford University Press, New York, 1979.

James, Cameron : *An Indian Summer,* MacMillan, London, 1974.

James, Currant : *Newspaper History: From the 17th Century to the Present Day,* Constable, London, 1978.

James, S. : *The Developing Areas of the Journalism,* Princeton University Press, Princeton, 1992.

Jamnadas, Dwarakadas : *Political Memoirs,* United Asia Publications, Bombay, 1991.

Jan, R. H. : *Print Media Communication,* Anmol Publications Pvt. Ltd., New Delhi, 1999.

Jasra, A. S. : *Information Technology in Journalism,* A.&M. Publishers, Delhi, 2002.

Jefferson, T. : *Policing the Crisis,* MacMillan, London, 1997.

Jhingan, M.L. : *The Economics of Development and Planning,* Konark Publishers, New Delhi, 1994.

Joshi,Uma : *Understanding Development Communication,* Dominant Books, New Delhi, 2001.

Kivlin, J. E. and Sen, L.K. : *Communication in India : Experiments in Introducing Change,* NICD, Hyderabad, 1969.

Klapper, J.T : *The Effects of Journalism,* Free Press, Glencoe, Illinois, 1960.

Krishnamurthi, Nadig : *Indian Journalism,* University of Mysore, Mysore, 1966

Malcolm, Muggeridge : *Chronicles of Wasted Time,* Collins, London, 1973.

Marin : *Servant of India: Diaries of Sir James Dunlop Smith,* Gilbert Longmans, London, 1966.

Mary, Lutyens : *The Lyttons in India,* John Murray, London, 1979.

Masani, R.P. : *Dadabhai Naroji,* Publications Division, Government of India, New Delhi. 1960.

Mehrotra, S.R. : *India and the Commonwealth* (1885-1929), George Allen and Unwin, London, 1965.

Melkote, S.R. : *Communication for Development in the third World : Theory and Practice,* Sage, New Delhi, 1991.

Menon, M. and Gandhi P. : *New Information Order,* Kanishka Publishers, New Delhi, 2001.

Michael, E. : *The Press and America,* Prentice Hall, Englewood Cliffs, 1978.

Michael, Maclagan : *Clemency Canning,* MacMillan, London, 1962

Moraes, Frank : *Witness to an Era,* Vikas Publishing House, Delhi, 1977.

Naiarajan, S. : *A History of the Press in India,* Asia Publishing House, Bombay, 1962.

Naipaul, V.S. : *India—A Wounded Civilization,* Andre Deutsch, London, 1981.

Nanda, B.R. : *Gokhale—Indian Moderates and British Raj,* Oxford University Press, London, 1977.

Nehru, J.L. : *Discovery of India,* Asia Publishing House, Bombay, 1961.

Page, C.M., and Iver, R.M. : *Society and Media,* MacMillan, London, 1950.

Panickkar, K.M. : *In Two Chinas: Memoirs of a Diplomat,* Allen & Unwin, London, 1955.

Prasad, Rajendra : *An Autobiography,* Asia Publishing House, Bombay, 1957.

Rama, Rao : *The Pen as My Sword,* Bharatiya Vidya Bhavan, Bombay, 1965.

Rao, Seshagiri : *Studies in History of Telugu Journalism,* Narla Shastiyabdapuri Celebrations Committee, Delhi, 1968.

Rastogi, T. N. : *Encyclopaedia of Professional Journalism,* Anmol Publications Pvt. Ltd., New Delhi, 2001.

Rau, Chalapati : *The Romance of the Newspaper,* National Council Educational Research and Training, Delhi, 1975.

Rayudu, C. S. : *Principles of Public Relations,* Himalaya Publishing House, Delhi, 1996

Rider, L. : *Elementary of Broadcasting,* McGraw- Hill Book Co., New York, 1993.Rider, L. : *Elementary of Broadcasting,* McGraw- Hill Book Co., New York, 1993.

Robert, Payne : *The Life and Death of Mahatma Gandhi,* the Bodley Head, London, 1969.

Rudyard, Kipling and Bonamy, Dobree : *Realist and Fabulist,* Oxford University Press, London, 1967.

Sahni, J.N. : *The Lid Off,* Deep Publications, Agra, 1977.

Sastri, Srinivasa : *Life and Times of Sir Pherozeshah Mehta,* Bharatiya Vidya Bhavan Bombay, 1975.

Steven, A. B. and John, T. M. : *Communication in Small Groups,* Longman, New York, 1997.

Stevenson, R.L. : *Communication Development and Third World,* Longman, Maryland, 1988.

Valentine, Chirol : *Indian Unrest,* MacMillan, London, 1910.

Ved, Mehta : *Protrait of India,* Weidenfeld and Nicholson, London, 1968.

Vigneshwara : *Our New Rulers,* B.G. Paul & Co., Madras, 1961.

————————: *The Avadi Socialists,* B.G. Paul & Co., Madras, 1964.

Waldrop, A. G. : *Communication and Media* , Rinehart & Co., New York, 1996.

William, Digby : *India for the Indians and for England,* Talbot Brothers, London,1885.

Wolpert, A. : *Morley and India,* University of California Press, Berkeley, Los Angeles, 1967.

Woodruff, Philip : *The Men who Ruled India,* Jonathan Cape, London, 1953.

Zaina, A. M. : *Personality Assessment,* Methuen Co. Ltd., London, 1999.

Zaller, J. R. : *Outline of Journalism,* Cambridge, New York, 2001.

INDEX

A

Advertisement, 13, 35, 279, 285, 303.

Agency, 25, 26, 27, 28, 29, 30, 89, 287, 288, 289, 340, 346, 362.

All India Radio, 19, 21, 40, 45.

Article, 44, 97, 99, 100, 102, 104, 113, 114, 115, 116, 118, 127, 170, 190, 221, 258, 292, 294, 301, 327, 339, 341, 342, 344.

Association, 98, 125, 135, 144, 145, 298.

Audience, 6, 11, 12, 13, 14, 15, 21, 43, 49, 58, 60, 67, 77, 78, 79, 86, 87, 88, 89, 90, 92, 93, 94, 95, 140, 141, 144, 198, 201, 207, 212, 213, 214, 252, 310, 325.

Author, 187, 256, 291, 292, 294, 298.

B

BBC, 19, 79, 196.

British, 5, 18, 28, 30, 44, 72, 75, 113, 117, 122, 134, 135, 196, 254, 260, 319, 320, 328, 345, 346.

C

Cable, 3, 79, 96, 144, 162, 164, 197, 198.

Camera, 9, 11, 108, 145, 291, 293, 307, 308.

Channel, 24, 60, 79, 140, 144, 163, 164, 207, 210.

Chief Editor, 28, 299.

Commission, 5, 19, 40, 98, 107, 113, 115, 124, 130, 131, 132, 133, 134,

135, 136, 137, 139, 185, 204.

Communication, 2, 3, 4, 6, 7, 8, 10, 11, 12, 13, 14, 15, 16, 17, 22, 23, 24, 25, 33, 34, 35, 41, 43, 44, 46, 47, 49, 50, 53, 54, 55, 56, 57, 58, 59, 60, 61, 62, 65, 66, 67, 68, 69, 70, 71, 72, 73, 74, 78, 79, 80, 81, 83, 88, 92, 95, 139, 140, 141, 142, 143, 144, 145, 146, 147, 148, 149, 150, 151, 152, 153, 154, 155, 156, 157, 158, 159, 160, 161, 162, 163, 164, 165, 166, 167, 170, 173, 176, 179, 181, 194, 197, 200, 201, 204, 206, 210, 224, 268, 279, 289, 293, 297, 301, 309, 310, 331.

Community, 4, 23, 55, 58, 59, 70, 71, 72, 84, 85, 105, 146, 151, 152, 153, 161, 173, 174, 190, 206, 238, 243, 245, 268, 301, 352.

Conference, 18, 110, 135, 145, 177, 178, 264, 265, 289, 298, 321, 333, 360.

Copy Editor, 294.

D

Dawn, 47, 336.

Director, 10, 32, 33, 41, 109, 135, 188, 222, 351.

E

Edition, 34, 122, 251, 282, 283, 286, 288, 289, 327, 338.

Editor, 15, 28, 31, 33, 36, 41, 42, 99, 100, 101, 102, 103, 104, 108, 109, 110, 120, 137, 139, 143, 175, 176, 188, 190, 192, 210, 215, 217, 220, 221, 225, 237, 245, 252, 266, 277, 278, 294, 295, 296, 297, 298, 299, 300, 301, 307, 308, 309, 310, 317, 318, 319, 320, 321, 322, 323, 324, 325, 326, 327, 330, 332, 333, 334, 335, 336, 337, 338, 339, 340, 341, 342, 343, 344.

Editorial, 28, 33, 34, 137, 143, 176, 177, 216, 223, 224, 225, 283, 285, 286, 291, 293, 294, 295, 296, 297, 298, 300, 310, 313, 317,

319, 321, 322, 323, 326, 329, 332, 334, 336, 340, 343, 344.

Education, 9, 25, 33, 54, 59, 72, 76, 77, 78, 182, 197, 231, 217, 218, 224, 225, 230, 259, 300, 357.

Emergency, 28, 36, 37, 40, 41,46, 107, 265, 319, 324, 325, 326.

Europe, 202, 248, 256, 257, 289, 291, 293.

Express News Service, 348, 352, 353, 355, 356.

F

Film, 2, 8, 9, 10, 11, 15, 22, 77, 78, 90, 165, 205, 225, 242, 303, 305, 306, 310, 330.

Foreign News Agencies, 30.

Foundation, 153, 239, 296.

France, 28, 30, 113, 116, 147, 278, 292, 315.

Front Page, 120, 239, 250, 280, 285, 311, 312, 331.

G

Germany, 45, 52, 116, 147, 292, 332.

Government, 4, 10, 18, 19, 20, 23, 27, 28, 29, 30, 36, 37, 40, 41, 42, 44, 45, 46, 53, 54, 56, 72, 76, 95, 106, 107, 108, 110, 111, 112, 125, 133, 139, 146, 147, 172, 175, 176, 177, 180, 181, 185, 198, 202, 204, 206, 207, 223, 235, 246, 248, 265, 269, 272, 273, 274, 276, 277, 319, 320, 323, 324, 325, 333, 334, 335, 345, 346, 349, 350, 353.

Growth, 10, 18, 28, 44, 59, 73, 75, 80, 147, 300, 347.

Guide, 36, 155, 196, 239.

H

Hindustan Times, 241, 319, 336.

Human, 3, 16, 39, 40, 44, 47, 48, 51, 54, 59, 66, 70, 71, 77, 83, 97, 100, 117, 122, 127, 137, 140, 141, 142, 146, 147, 148, 149, 150, 151, 152, 153, 154, 155, 160, 164, 171, 172, 174, 178, 179, 180, 236, 241, 258, 284, 316.

I

Importance, 4, 15, 33, 59, 61, 92, 124, 150, 169, 178, 206, 216, 223, 235, 236, 239, 245, 251, 252,

256, 259, 271, 286, 307, 316, 340, 341, 344, 351, 356.

Important News, 262, 265, 311, 314, 316.

India, 1, 2, 3, 4, 5, 6, 7, 17, 18, 19, 20, 21, 22, 23, 27, 28, 30, 32, 35, 36, 37, 40, 41, 42, 43, 44, 45, 46, 47, 48, 50, 53, 54, 55, 56, 57, 58, 59, 60, 61, 62, 65, 66, 68, 71, 72, 73, 74, 75, 76, 78, 80, 81, 97, 99, 100, 101, 103, 104, 106, 109, 111, 112, 113, 115, 137, 147, 161, 178, 198, 199, 200, 203, 216, 219, 220, 221, 222, 230, 242, 243, 244, 245, 247, 248, 249, 255, 256, 259, 261, 263, 283, 312, 313, 317, 318, 319, 323, 324, 328, 331, 332, 337, 346, 350, 353, 356, 357, 362.

India Today, 100, 101, 109.

Indian Express, 2, 35, 36, 41, 109, 222, 324, 331, 348.

Indian News, 30.

Indian Press, 1, 2, 18, 30, 41, 318.

Industry, 5, 22, 33, 47, 75, 77, 79, 91, 130, 133, 137, 146, 172, 192, 195, 210, 233, 248.

Information, 2, 3, 4, 8, 9, 11, 13, 14, 15, 17, 20, 21, 25, 29, 35, 37, 38, 39, 40, 47, 49, 51, 52, 55, 56, 58, 65, 73, 75, 76, 77, 81, 88, 89, 90, 96, 98, 100, 102, 110, 116, 118, 119, 120, 121, 122, 123, 125, 126, 127, 131, 138, 139, 140, 141, 144, 145, 147, 150, 151, 153, 156, 161, 162, 163, 164, 165, 170, 173, 179, 180, 183, 184, 185, 186, 189, 190, 191, 194, 195, 196, 199, 200, 201, 202, 204, 210, 224, 235, 236, 242, 244, 246, 250, 262, 263, 264, 265, 266, 269, 270, 271, 273, 275, 282, 285, 288, 289, 293, 295, 297, 301, 302, 307, 309, 319, 322, 333, 334, 335, 340, 346, 347, 353, 362.

Internet, 150, 161, 162, 196, 197.

J

Job, 17, 40, 42, 47, 53, 195, 209, 211, 215, 217, 219, 226, 255, 263, 268, 278, 297, 309, 317, 318, 323, 330, 334, 335, 336, 337, 341, 355.

Journal, 33, 99, 100, 175, 176, 215, 216, 217, 219, 220, 291, 292, 293, 294, 295, 296, 297, 299, 300, 301, 335, 340.

Journalism, 1, 4, 5, 6, 17, 33, 34, 35, 38, 100, 118, 120, 147, 176, 177, 201, 202, 204, 216, 217, 218, 219, 220, 223, 224, 225, 226, 227, 229, 230, 231, 232, 233, 238, 239, 255, 256, 257, 269, 273, 275, 279, 289, 309, 310, 320, 327, 330, 331, 345, 355, 362.

Journalist, 30, 39, 100, 102, 110, 185, 186, 187, 190, 192, 210, 215, 216, 217, 218, 219, 220, 222, 223, 226, 227, 228, 229, 230, 231, 232, 233, 256, 278, 310, 317, 327, 337.

Judgement, 108, 123, 127, 128, 129, 150, 223, 324, 340, 341, 359.

K

Korea, 4, 256.

L

Language, 7, 16, 33, 45, 66, 74, 76, 140, 141, 146, 150, 152, 153, 157, 164, 165, 218, 219, 220, 223, 224, 232, 254, 260, 271, 299, 329, 357, 358, 359, 361, 362.

Law, 33, 35, 91, 97, 98, 107, 108, 109, 111, 113, 114, 115, 116, 118, 119, 121, 122, 125, 126, 128, 129, 131, 135, 138, 181, 215, 219, 222, 226, 259, 262, 270, 317, 320, 350, 358.

Layout, 5, 284, 312, 313, 314, 315, 316, 343.

London, 194, 257, 258, 303, 311, 346.

M

Magazine, 15, 56, 78, 100, 119, 132, 137, 139, 187, 188, 189, 190, 194, 204, 224, 226, 262, 273, 310.

Mass Communication, 6, 7, 8, 10, 11, 13, 14, 15,

17, 33, 44, 47, 49, 55, 56, 57, 58, 60, 81, 88, 92, 95, 144, 147, 154, 161, 163, 164, 201, 204.

Mass Media, 2, 3, 12, 22, 23, 25, 32, 41, 44, 46, 47, 48, 49, 54, 55, 56, 57, 59, 73, 74, 75, 81, 82, 83, 86, 92, 94, 95, 96, 147, 160, 161, 162, 167, 196, 198, 199, 200, 201, 202, 206, 352.

Media, 2, 3, 4, 5, 6, 8, 12, 13, 14, 15, 17, 20, 22, 23, 24, 25, 27, 30, 32, 40, 41, 43, 44, 46, 47, 48, 49, 50, 51, 52, 53, 54, 55, 56, 57, 58, 59, 71, 73, 74, 75, 76, 81, 82, 83, 86, 87, 88, 90, 91, 92, 93, 94, 95, 96, 100, 107, 111, 112, 118, 122, 144, 146, 147, 153, 160, 161, 162, 167, 170, 183, 184, 185, 186, 187, 188, 189, 190, 191, 192, 193, 195, 196, 197, 198, 199, 200, 201, 202, 203, 204, 205, 206, 207, 208, 209, 210, 211, 212, 213, 214, 223, 230, 331, 334, 352.

N

National, 1, 5, 10, 11, 19, 21, 28, 30, 32, 33, 39, 42, 45, 46, 47, 50, 51, 52, 53, 56, 77, 90, 110, 112, 147, 173, 176, 177, 186, 188, 189, 190, 193, 196, 198, 199, 206, 207, 210, 214, 216, 230, 232, 237, 240, 256, 259, 296, 300, 310, 318, 319, 320, 325, 335, 337, 338, 344, 348, 351, 353, 356.

Network, 46, 54, 279, 356.

News, 4, 8, 13, 17, 18, 20, 21, 25, 26, 27, 28, 29, 30, 31, 33, 34, 35. 37, 39, 40, 41, 42, 51, 58, 76, 77, 78, 79, 87, 95, 96, 106, 110, 115, 124, 137, 138, 139, 144, 145, 157, 191, 196, 199, 201, 205, 206, 215, 218, 220, 224, 225, 228, 235, 236, 237, 238, 239, 240, 242, 243, 244, 245, 246, 247, 249, 250, 251, 252, 253, 255, 256, 257, 262, 263, 264, 265, 266, 268, 271, 272, 273, 275, 276, 277, 278, 279, 280, 281, 282, 283, 284,

285, 286, 287, 288, 289, 307, 308, 309, 310, 311, 312, 313, 314, 315, 316, 321, 322, 325, 326, 327, 333, 334, 336, 337, 338, 339, 340, 341, 342, 343, 344, 345, 346, 347, 348, 350, 352, 353, 355, 356, 357, 359, 361, 362.

News Agency, 25, 26, 27, 28, 29, 30, 289, 340, 346, 362.

News Editor, 28, 41, 215, 245, 252, 266, 277, 278, 307, 325, 336, 337, 338, 339.

P

Page Layout, 312.

Pakistan, 79, 250.

Paris, 30, 251.

Parliament, 20, 21, 54, 73, 112, 115, 116, 125, 138, 151, 173, 175, 240, 250, 251, 259, 260, 271, 331, 360.

Patrika, 2, 311, 312, 318, 319.

Photograph, 131, 190, 225, 280, 281, 282, 284, 307, 308, 309.

Policy, 4, 39, 53, 60, 77, 109, 176, 249, 250, 274, 297, 300, 321, 323, 324, 328, 336, 342.

Political, 2, 10, 12, 21, 32, 33, 35, 46, 47, 48, 52, 54, 57, 59, 61, 73, 78, 81, 87, 92, 104, 146, 151, 156, 163, 202, 203, 207, 215, 224, 233, 252, 264, 269, 327, 329, 334, 350, 353.

Power, 4, 16, 33, 34, 37, 38, 40, 42, 44, 50, 54, 55, 75, 78, 92, 102, 104, 130, 132, 140, 167, 178, 202, 203, 204, 229, 237, 242, 265, 322, 323, 332, 340.

Press, 1, 2, 5, 6, 17, 18, 19, 26, 27, 28, 29, 30, 31, 32, 33, 37, 38, 39, 40, 41, 42, 44, 46, 50, 70, 75, 97, 99, 102, 103, 104, 106, 107, 109, 110, 111, 112, 113, 114, 115, 116, 118, 122, 123, 124, 125, 127, 129, 130, 131, 132, 133, 134, 135, 136, 137, 138, 139, 147, 151, 160, 161, 175,

177, 184, 185, 195, 196, 197, 200, 201, 202, 203, 204, 205, 208, 209, 213, 214, 216, 217, 222, 230, 249, 250, 251, 259, 271, 275, 276, 280, 285, 286, 289, 299, 314, 317, 318, 319, 320, 324, 333, 334, 335, 336, 346, 362.

Press Council, 5, 6, 19, 97, 99, 106, 112, 113, 115, 116, 123, 124, 125, 129, 134, 135, 136, 137, 139.

Press Trust of India, 27, 28, 346, 362.

Print Media, 4, 5, 17, 25, 75, 147.

Printing, 4, 5, 17, 18, 37, 40, 79, 198, 203, 216, 224, 237, 239, 279, 285, 286, 287, 289, 290, 296, 298, 303, 305, 306, 340, 341.

Production, 7, 47, 77, 172, 188, 198, 206, 291, 302, 303, 304, 322, 338, 339, 340, 349.

Professional, 5, 17, 27, 28, 48, 104, 109, 135, 137, 155, 158, 173, 177, 178, 179, 205, 206, 208, 215, 220, 225, 229, 230, 231, 257, 268, 276, 278, 297, 299, 300.

Programme, 13, 19, 20, 21, 22, 24, 25, 46, 51, 54, 57, 76, 169, 183, 186, 187, 192, 207, 209, 210, 212, 213, 214, 277, 354, 356.

Proof Reader, 286, 323.

PTI, 27, 28, 29, 30, 241, 249, 250, 345, 349, 351, 354.

Public Relations Society, 178, 181.

Publication, 15, 46, 98, 99, 103, 107, 108, 114, 117, 118, 119, 120, 121, 122, 123, 124, 127, 129, 130, 131, 132, 133, 138, 176, 188, 189, 190, 194, 256, 263, 271, 279, 285, 289, 290, 291, 293, 295, 297, 298, 301, 302, 335, 336, 339, 357.

Publisher, 37, 100, 108, 134, 176, 219, 317, 320.

Punjab Kesari, 311, 312.

Q

Qaumi Awaj, 110.

Quality of News, 251.

R

Radio, 2, 6, 7, 8, 12, 13, 15, 17, 19, 20, 21, 25, 26, 39, 41, 44, 45, 50, 51, 52, 55, 56, 57, 58, 70, 75, 76, 78, 79, 95, 140, 141, 145, 147, 154, 160, 161, 162, 164, 180, 187, 188, 189, 197, 198, 200, 201, 204, 205, 207, 224, 238, 310, 311.

Reader, 35, 38, 40, 140, 175, 227, 239, 240, 242, 244, 245, 251, 253, 272, 273, 274, 279, 286, 290, 302, 305, 309, 311, 314, 315, 316, 322, 323, 343, 346, 347, 353, 354, 357, 358, 361.

Religion, 33, 61, 62, 64, 73, 126, 225, 226, 238, 240.

Reporter, 9, 26, 28, 101, 138, 175, 215, 219, 224, 225, 226, 227, 237, 243, 244, 245, 248, 249, 250, 251, 255, 256, 257, 258, 259, 260, 261, 262, 263, 264, 265, 266, 267, 268, 269, 270, 271, 272, 273, 274, 275, 276, 277, 278, 279, 280, 281, 282, 285, 286, 287, 304, 305, 307, 308, 318, 335, 338, 342, 346, 353, 355.

Research, 10, 15, 25, 53, 85, 86, 88, 89, 90, 118, 146, 147, 164, 166, 185, 212, 243, 289, 291, 297, 298.

Rural, 20, 22, 23, 25, 33, 50, 55, 58, 73, 75, 161, 199.

Russian, 141, 219, 335.

S

Satellite, 3, 8, 20, 46, 60, 70, 78, 79, 150, 356.

Service, 19, 20, 23, 24, 25, 29, 38, 39, 53, 89, 90, 92, 101, 183, 184, 185, 186, 189, 192, 195, 201, 211, 246, 266, 289, 293, 337, 338, 348, 352, 353, 355, 356.

SITE, 20, 46, 51, 188, 265.

Society, 3, 9, 10, 11, 12, 13, 22, 32, 36, 43, 47, 49, 53, 55, 58, 59, 62, 69, 71, 72, 73, 74, 75, 76, 77, 80, 84, 91, 92, 96, 106, 114, 120, 148, 149, 156, 163, 171, 173, 176, 178, 181, 198, 199, 203, 205, 216, 223, 244, 263.

Sub-editor, 215, 220, 307, 309, 338, 339, 340, 341, 342, 343, 344.

T

Technology, 8, 11, 17, 51, 70, 73, 74, 75, 80, 96, 188, 211, 304.

Television, 3, 6, 8, 12, 13, 15, 19, 20, 26, 44, 45, 46, 50, 51, 52, 55, 56, 58, 60, 79, 87, 90, 91, 93, 95, 96, 111, 139, 140, 145, 147, 150, 154, 160, 161, 162, 165, 166, 180, 197, 198, 200, 201, 204, 205, 225, 311, 356.

The Hindu, 1, 109, 261, 318, 330.

The New York Times, 114, 120, 217, 253, 259, 274, 322, 324, 331, 334, 335.

The Statesman, 18, 107, 109, 110, 252, 333.

The Tribune, 109, 330.

Times of India, 99, 103, 104, 109, 247, 249, 312, 313, 317, 318.

Transistor, 7, 50.

Type Setting, 304, 305.

U

UK, 106, 113, 122, 135, 292, 296, 297, 298, 346.

UNESCO, 45, 46, 230.

UNI, 27, 28, 29, 30, 349, 350, 351, 352, 354.

USA, 45, 46, 80, 113, 121, 122, 289, 291, 293, 296, 298.

V

Video, 3, 10, 15, 78, 145, 161, 162, 198, 289, 293, 294, 301, 302, 304, 305, 306.

Voice, 5, 6, 42, 131, 144, 162, 175, 260, 262, 319, 329, 334, 335, 358, 359.

W

Washington, 42, 217, 250, 251, 259, 260, 277, 333, 356.

Western, 5, 45, 52, 62, 65, 66, 69, 74, 163, 165, 199, 201, 202, 203, 249, 256, 257, 275, 276, 337.

World War, 6, 18, 164, 204, 256, 257, 272, 273, 333.

Y

Yellow Pages, 196.

❑❑❑